T. W. Schultz
June 1974

Investment in Higher Education

Investment in Higher Education

Walter W. McMahon
University of Illinois

Lexington Books
D.C. Heath and Company
Lexington, Massachusetts
Toronto   London

Library of Congress Cataloging in Publication Data

McMahon, Walter W
    Investment in higher education.

    1. Education—Economic aspects—United States. 2. Univer-
sities and colleges—United States—Finance. 3. Human capital—United States. I. Title.
LC66.M32   338.4'3   73-18451
ISBN 0-669-91942-X

This work has developed under grants from the U.S. Office of Education,
Department of Health, Education, and Welfare and from the Spencer Foundation, John Hancock Center, Chicago, Illinois. However the content does
not necessarily reflect the position of either, and no official endorsement of
these materials should be inferred.

Published simultaneously in Canada.

Printed in the United States of America.

International Standard Book Number: 0-669-91942-x
Library of Congress Catalog Card Number: 73-18451

To the memory of my father

Contents

Preface

"Education" and "health" have become much more manageable for the economist in recent years because of breakthroughs in development of the theory of expenditures on them as *investment* in human capital. Educational capital, furthermore, while yielding both monetary and nonmonetary returns to individuals, is increasing in relation to physical capital, helping to explain patterns of international trade, and making an important contribution to economic growth. Although primary and secondary education are coming to be seen as a forces against inequality produced by inheritance and for greater equality of opportunity in coming generations, it is doubtful that higher education has as yet reached its full potential in this respect. With concepts of this significance, it is surprising that current expenditures on higher education have not as yet been studied as an important form of investment behavior, and most especially over time. A theoretical and empirical study of this type of investment decision is the purpose of this study.

The study is addressed to three types of readers. It is addressed to economists, some of whom have been preoccupied with the relation of investment in physical capital to growth and to economic fluctuations and have not yet come to realize the full significance of investment in human resources, especially education and health. Second, it is directed to interested policy makers, such as college and university administrators, members of state boards of higher education, or members of future study commissions on the financing of postsecondary education. Third, it is addressed to students and others in departments of economics and colleges of education who are interested in the economics of investment in human resources. Background in regression analysis is assumed, but apart from this the few special economic terms used are likely to be familiar, or to become familiar, to most readers.

This project has significantly benefited from the assistance and advice of many persons. I am especially grateful to H. T. James, who was instrumental in joining with my interest in this area at an early date. T. W. Schultz, G. Judge, M. D. Orwig, J. Maxey, E. Denison, R. Hartman, P. R. G. Layard, and G. Psacharopoulos have all had an important influence on the end result in various ways, although I would want to relieve all of them of any responsibility for the final product.

I wish to express my appreciation for the support that made this project possible. A grant from the Spencer Foundation covered computer costs, time released from teaching used for refinement of the basic model (Chapter 2), and research assistants. A grant from the U.S. Office of Education, Region V, was the primary source of time released from teaching, The

American College Testing Program and the National Institute of Education (DHEW) gave important assistance with the collection of the microeconomic data on individual families, part of which is used in analyses in Chapter 2 and described in Appendix D.

Alan Wagner has contributed important research assistance throughout, but most especially with Chapter 2 and Table 6-4. Virginia Klarquist assisted with Chapter 3, Peter Moore with the research underlying Chapter 4, and Jim Dyal with Appendix B. During a summer Willie Bailey gave useful assistance with parts of Chapter 5 and Bill Harris with the computer programming. The U.S. Office of Education grant supported Alicia Mullor for a summer while she helped in the preparation of Chapter 6 and Appendix C. A special personal debt of gratitude is due these graduate students, several of whom are now writing on related topics.

I would also like to express my appreciation to the University of Illinois for providing support for earlier work on primary and secondary education (1970), household saving and investment decisions (1971c), and public expenditure theory (1971a). The Brookings Institution generously aided me as a Guest Scholar in their Center for Advanced Study during the final months of manuscript preparation, and the London School of Economics as a Visiting Fellow during the period up through August 1973. I would like to thank Mrs. Charlotte Kaiser at Brookings and Mrs. Eileen Ellis at the London School of Economics for their excellent typing assistance. And last but not least, I am especially grateful to my wife, Carolyn, for her counsel and support throughout.

1

Introduction: Investment in Human Resources

Investment in Human Resources

The insight offered by viewing expenditures on higher education as an investment in human resources, with returns of various kinds expected at future dates, is leading to a basic revolution in the economics of higher education and has generated a disequilibrium in educational finance. This is partly due to capital and investment theory concepts having made education more amenable to economic analysis. It is partly due to investment in human resources being a concept easily understood by legislators, especially when it is interpreted broadly enough to include investment in education yielding a flow of future nonmonetary private consumption and social satisfactions. The impetus has also come in the United States from the series of educational financing crises that have raised the issues surrounding investment in higher education to a level of major national concern —crises that have contributed to similar types of fundamental questioning in northern European countries.

The financial distress and the new interest in its sources, which in turn raises more fundamental questions, have both come with the end of the golden age of expansion of higher education in the 1960s and a new plateau of slower growth.[1] Both the concern and interest have been stimulated by the decline in the fertility rate from the post war peak of 3.77 children per family in 1957, to 2.08 children per family in 1974. These demographic trends will continue to have implications for at least the next 18 years for both public and private institutions.

A second source of concern has been some weakening of job markets for college graduates. This coincided with a recession, followed by upward pressures from inflation on institutions' costs and with more general cuts in federal research funds. All served to aggrevate the financing crisis.

Third, the interest and concern has been evident in the work of the National Commission on the Financing of Postsecondary Education and in other provisions of the Education Amendments of 1972.[a] In this Act the

---

[a]The charge to the commission has been to study "the nature and causes of serious financial distress, . . . the level of existing state and local, endowment, private sector, and Federal support" and ". . . the impact of past, present, and anticipated private, local, State, and Federal support for post-secondary education," as a means of considering "alternative long range solutions." See U.S. Congress (1972, pp 49-50, 185).

1

Congress defined an important new departure in the form of "basic economic opportunity grants" designed to extend new educational opportunities to most children in low-income families for the first time, as well as to aid cooperating institutions.

Fourth, nationwide interest and concern has been widened by the extension of postsecondary education to over 40 percent of all 18-year-olds (12 percent in Britain) who now go on to college. This expansion of junior colleges, four-year colleges, and universities, which except for the junior colleges has had its counterpart in Britain, Germany, and elsewhere, means that there are very few families any more that are not involved in post-secondary educational decisions and interested in the issues.

In response to these concerns and to the opportunities offered by new developments in human capital theory, this book explores investment behavior over time by families and students, state and local governments, and the federal government. It offers a new focus on four important determinants of investment in higher education (and of investment in new knowledge created by research, a joint product) and considers a number of the implications.

The four main economic determinants considered are current income, expected returns, interest rates, and an index of desires for equity in educational opportunity. These influences are combined with the more commonly explored effects of demographic changes in the age composition of the population. Since educational capital is durable, and has a long production period, a model of investment in human capital with a flexible accelerator is employed. Investment in human resources therefore is viewed as an aspect of household saving and investment behavior.

Selection of the determinants tested is aided by development of the theory of family decisions to invest in higher education (Chapter 2) and of the theory of public investment decisions (Chapter 4) from which the analytical framework is drawn. Beyond this some evidence of sufficient variation in the explanatory variable over time, and some evidence of differential effects among individual decision-making units suggest the potential significance of each variable.

Current income (or wealth) is a theoretically acceptable determinant on the assumption, which is a reasonable one, that there are imperfect capital markets for financing educational capital so that larger family income lowers the financing costs. Income has been found to be significant in cross section data for individual household decisions by Brazer and David (1962), Feldman and Hoenack (1969), Bowles (1972, p. 234), as well as in Chapter 2. It also has been found to be significant in studies of enrollment demand by Campbell and Seigel (1967), Hoenack (1967), Miller (1971), and Bishop (1972), even though enrollment as the dependent variable leaves some of the investment that reflects quality and better learning in the tuition term, and leaves other components such as public investment or investment of foregone earnings even more unexplained. The capital markets for financing educational capital are apt to remain very imperfect in spite of improvements made by government guaranteed loans. This is because in addition to lender's risk (educational capital is less accessible to private lenders for use as collateral), there is also a large borrower's risk, since students, especially freshmen, are very uncertain of their abilities and of the future. There is an additional deterrent to borrowing in that it involves an important shift of educational costs within the family from the parents to the student.

The demographic determinant, the proportion of the population of college age (or of veteran status, in the case of federal investment), is given an economic role in the family investment decision model in Chapter 2. It can be logically expected to have an effect on each individual family's expected returns and hence on its investment decision, as well as on the political pressures parents bring on legislatures and on Congress that influence public expenditure. Those families without young adults of college age are not going to invest much; those with more children reaching college age in relation to the total number of persons in the family should tend to invest more. The presence of young adults of college age in the family investment decision model (as distinguished from the independent student model) offers a new investment opportunity to the decision unit since it creates a new possibility of future returns. This variable appears in most of the empirical studies already mentioned above in one form or another. Sometimes it is used to "deflate" the dependent variable by the number of eligibles, rather than as a separate explanatory variable. But even more important, in many higher education projections it has been given almost exclusive emphasis. This can be very misleading since it can result in too little emphasis being given to the other important economic determinants of investment demand considered here and hence of expenditure levels.

The third determinant considered is the effect of widespread desires for greater equality of access to postsecondary educational institutions. These are a subtle influence on levels of total expenditure affecting the level of total public investment. Desires for greater equality are related to desires for vertical equity among income groups, given some rather strong assumptions. In any event, the implicit income-distribution weights in the welfare function[2] can be regarded as having implications for the distribution of the net benefits of higher education among income groups.[b] Regarded as part

---

[b]Hansen and Weisbrod (1969) have pointed out the subsidy to students from high-income families at public institutions via low tuitions. Note, however, also the subsidy through grants to students from high-income families at private institutions revealed in Table 2-2.

of the literature on public expenditure development, such as in Musgrave (1969), the desire for greater equality is a potential determinant of the effective demands for public investment in higher education.

Equity considerations are probably also important in the way in which much endowment fund and gift income is spent. But the *level* of the endowment fund income of educational institutions is determined largely (but not entirely) by the size of inherited endowment funds and hence it will be regarded as predetermined in this study.

Finally, the last main determinants to be considered are the effect of expected returns and of interest costs on this type of investment behavior. The importance of pecuniary rates of return to student decisions about choice of fields is developed by Freeman (1971). There is the possibility that his findings for male students in the Boston area do not apply with equal force to freshmen or to those at less advanced levels. They may also be less appropriate to females, to other types of institutions, or where explicit consideration is given to expected nonmonetary returns. There is also the possibility that changes in rates of return have a less dominant effect than he suggests on the level of investment expenditure over time since estimates of private rates of return do not show substantial changes during the postwar period. Becker (1964, p. 128) has estimated them to be 9 percent in 1940, and 9 percent in 1950; Hines, Tweeten and Redfern (1970) have estimated them to be 9.7 percent in 1960.

There is the further possibility to be considered that investment in research creates new opportunities for investment in those types of education which lead to the embodiment of this new knowledge. This would shift the marginal efficiency of investment schedule outward, increasing investment demand and potentially raising observed rates of return. Research is a joint product, especially with graduate education, and can also create obsolescence in some kinds of educational capital. So given the interdependence especially of basic research with higher education, it is appropriate that this interdependence also should be considered.

Investment Decisions by Households, by State and Local Governments, and by the Federal Government

Although several different types of decision units must be considered in order to cover all the major investment decisions that result in expenditures on higher education and research, the investment process itself constitutes the unifying theme of this book.

A specific theory of investment behavior by individual families (and students) over the life cycle is set out in Chapter 2. In essence, investment in human capital occurs as families and students who are only partly independent of their parents produce additions to the student's (and hence to the family's) stock of human capital. They purchase formal education and books as derived demands for inputs, which then are combined with inputs of the student's time to produce a stock of "educational capital" for use later. The efficiency of this process is affected to some extent by the example set by the parents and the guidance utilized.

Demands for *current*, immediate, consumption satisfactions from college are included as part of the total demand for higher education but are not analyzed separately. A distinction is made between short-run investment demand, where all stocks are regarded as constant, and the longer run, where stocks of educational capital can grow, depreciate, and become obsolete with technical change and new knowledge.

There are other kinds of stocks beyond the decision unit's stock of educational capital, such as stocks of disembodied knowledge (e.g. libraries), psychological stocks of tastes and habits, and stocks of physical capital goods that appear in the analysis, so it is important to emphasize the distinction that will be made between stocks and flows. This distinction will also extend to the analysis of investment in research leading to the creation of new ideas, which adds to the stock of knowledge. The new knowledge also yields a flow into the future of monetary and nonmonetary returns to individuals and to the society.

Families, state and local governments, and the federal government are basically different types of decision units. Their investment decisions therefore are considered separately, using four structural models, each of which is drawn from its appropriate theoretical framework and adapted for use with aggregate data over time. These models are presented, respectively, in:

Chapter 3—Investment by Families in Higher Education

Chapter 4—State and Local Investment in Higher Education

Chapter 5—Federal Investment in Higher Education

Chapter 6—Federal Investment in Reasearch at Institutions of Higher Education

Family and student investment at public and at private institutions is analyzed separately. This permits some limited estimates of the effect over time of relative changes in private and public tuition levels, although it is the common objective of the production of educational capital, rather than the competition between types of institutions, that is the primary focus of this analysis. Investment made by families and students through their expenditures on tuition and fees, room and board, and foregone consumption are analyzed in separate regressions. The reason for doing this is that excess foregone earnings (over maintence expenditures) are an investment largely made by the student in his own education, whereas room and board expenses are an investment from the point of view of the parents (assuming they help a son or daughter who would otherwise have taken employment), and are subject to a monetary budget constraint. If there are imperfect capital markets, and short or uncertain private investment horizons, the family budget constraint will be more relevant to these out-of-pocket outlays.

Investment by state and local governments in higher education is considered in Chapter 4. It consists of support going to public universities, public four-year colleges, public two-year junior colleges, and private four and two-year colleges and universities, each of which is analyzed separately. The data has been extended and refined to permit analysis by these categories throughout the entire postwar period. State and local investment in higher education includes state and local investment in research performed at universities. In contrast to federally supported research, most state-supported research is not done on a contract basis and cannot be separated from teaching on a nationwide basis in U.S. data, given the current state of the art.

Federal investment in higher education, as distinguished from research, is considered in Chapter 5. Federal investment in higher education dates back to the Morrill Land Grant Act of 1862; it is made primarily at public institutions. Federal support is analyzed separately for public universities, four-year, and two-year institutions, as well as for private universities, four-year and two-year colleges. However, federal support of investment in education at private institutions has been small.

Over 50 percent of the federal support for research, however, goes to private universities. This investment in research is considered in Chapter 6, again separating universities, four-year, and two-year institutions, and public from private. A considerable amount of attention has been given to the development of a new annual series on federal investment in research at institutions of higher education that has not been available previously. The detailed breakdown by type of institution for the postwar period, and for public and private institutions extending back to 1929, is presented in Appendix C. The analysis of investment in research is conducted separately from the analysis of investment in education. This is because it is expected that these two different types of investment demands may respond to somewhat different factors.

The Data and Methods of Analysis

Economic theory is employed to develop hypotheses about family and student investment decisions in Chapter 2. These hypotheses then are tested using, in part, microeconomic data for individual student families, but also as a means to the analysis in Chapter 3 of data for all U.S. households in the postwar period. Similarly, a development of the theory relevant to public expenditure decisions and brief references to the pertinent literature are to be found at the beginning of Chapter 4.

The microeconomic data appearing in Chapter 2 was collected from 2,578 1972-73 freshmen and 2,766 1972-73 sophomore, junior, and senior students and their families. The questionnaires sent to the students, and the Family Financial Statements filled out by the parents that yielded these numbers of usable responses are reproduced in Appendix D. The survey was designed to collect extensive financial information on investment expenditure for the academic year, parents' income and assets (from parents), detailed sources of student income, test scores, and the monetary and nonmonetary returns expected from higher education. The numbers of usable responses above represent 74 percent and 78.2 percent response rates, respectively, and cover students at all types of instiutions. The survey is described in W. McMahon and A. Wagner, *A Study of the College Investment Decision* (1973) in more detail. It is shown there that the income distribution of the respondents is almost identical to the income distribution for all families covered in the *Current Population Reports*. There is no attempt to fully analyze this microeconomic data in this book, but it is drawn upon to consider effects explored in the time series analyses.

Data used in Chapters 3 through 6 for the United States are for 1929 through the present. They are drawn primarily from the U.S. Office of Education's *Biennial Survey of Education* (1962) and *Financial Statistics of Institutions of Higher Education* (1973), the U.S. Department of Commerce *National Income and Product Accounts* (1973) issues of the *Survey of Current Business,* the U.S. Bureau of the Census *Current Population Reports,* (1972) and the National Science Foundation *Federal Funds for Research, Development, and Other Scientific Activities* (1973). Mr. George Lind of the National Center for Educational Statistics was very kind in supplying unpublished data that helped to reduce somewhat the 2 to 3 year lag before published financial statistics on institutions of higher education are available. Annual estimates of the stocks of educational capital for 1928-72 (measured at original cost) also have been developed and are reported together with the sources of the underlying data in Appendix B.

The primary statistical method used for testing the hypotheses suggested by the theory is regression analysis, together with tests of the significance of individual regression coefficients. There are some descriptive tables, charts, and frequency distributions dealing with how postsecondary education is financed in the U.S. But the main focus is on testing hypotheses by means of least squares multiple regression, which is more appropriate than factor analysis or other methods for this purpose. Restricted three-stage least squares simultaneous equation estimation is used for some analyses of family decisions.[c] Simultaneous equation estimates also are prepared in Chapter 6 when estimating joint investment demands for higher education and research. The objective, however, is not to improve estimation theory, so the use of simultaneous equation estimation is appropriate only where the reasons are substantive economic ones.

Autocorrelation is removed from the residuals if the Durbin-Watson statistic is not within an acceptable range by use of a first-order autoregressive transformation estimated by use of a Cochrane-Orcutt iterative technique. Where a missing variable can be found that can logically replace this autoregressive term, or if the missing influence can be assumed to be represented adequately by this first-order autoregressive process, then the regression coefficients have been estimated free of bias.

Specification errors also can arise in other ways, such as when key explanatory variables are omitted, or when redundant or interacting variables are included. To avoid this, other potential determinants are tested and even if they are not significant the results are shown. Variables of little significance in and of themselves are sometimes a useful finding. When multicollinearity is found to be above .8 the specification has been changed, usually by eliminating one of the variables on the grounds that both essentially measure the same thing. If the internal correlation is below .8, and hopefully far below, the multicollinearity is regarded as within acceptable limits. Variables whose coefficients exceed these standard errors and whose signs are theoretically correct are kept, given the objective of testing hypotheses under *ceteris paribus* conditions in so far as these can be enforced statistically. This procedure is also tantamount to minimizing the estimated variance of the predictions.

The predictions that are made for state and local investment in postsecondary education to 1980 are dynamic conditional predictions. They use the autoregression coefficient and the first differences in the residuals to obtain predictions for each successive year beyond the sample period. They are conditional upon the tuition policies specified and on predictions of real income to 1980 made by the Eckstein-Fromm D.R.I. econometric model. They also use demographic projections available in the U.S. Bureau of the Census *Current Population Reports,* but the number of young adults reaching college age on into the 1990s is firmly based on the number of children already born. In the years after that, demographic projections

---

[c]This method is used for example, for some estimates of enrollment demand where a supply side must be specified as it must be in any effort to obtain coefficients for the price term that are free of simultaneous bias. The choice between specifying a supply side that has to do with production costs in different kinds of educational institutions, or with the supply-of-funds, depends upon the theoretical context within which the rest of the model is specified. In most cases the net present value formulation, rather than the private internal rate of return version, is used both in Chapters 2 and 3 to keep production costs explicit.

depend heavily upon the assumption made about whether or not the current 2.08 children per family replacement level fertility rate is going to continue.[d]

Implications for Efficiency, Growth, and Equity

There are important implications for national economic policy, as well as for investment decisions made by individual families, institutions, and state governments, arising from viewing expenditure on higher education as an investment in human capital—implications having a bearing on the continuing financial crisis. The most important have to do with insights gained about the effects of new methods of financing higher education on rates of economic growth, on employment and price stability, and on the intergenerational transmission of income inequality.

With respect to growth, investing more where the rates of return are highest is its very essence, not only for growth within individual decision units but also for growth in the nation. A better understanding of the actual investment behavior of families can aid the design of financing arrangements that would improve the efficiency with which all investment decisions are made. And these improvements are not always in conflict with commonly held notions of equity. For example, steps toward providing greater equality of opportunity by providing grants to students from low income families tend to increase the elasticities of and reduce the differences among the supply of funds curves faced by individuals. This not only reduces the inequality in earnings later, but also generally improves the allocation of the total investment in human capital by reducing the inequality in marginal rates of return, thereby increasing efficiency.

There are other aspects of efficiency that lie beyond the scope of this study. For example, manpower studies can help to isolate surpluses and shortages, such as the much debated surplus of primary school teachers and critical shortage of doctors and paramedics trained in preventive medicine which illustrate waste and allocative inefficiency that also retard growth. Similarly, improvements in managerial decisions within educational institutions can both improve quality and increase efficiency. More generally, studies of the investment behavior of families, students, institutions, governments, and of changes in the ultimate demands for the services of human capital can enable all types of decision units to develop more efficient policies as each knows better how the others can be expected to behave.

---

[d]When an allowance is added for immigration, the result is slightly above 2.11, which is replacement level fertility.

The implications for employment and price stability of changes in the levels of investment in postsecondary education seem to have been given even less attention in the literature. If full weight is given to the fact that foregone earnings are lower in recessions, the resulting higher rates of return to investment in these periods could be built into federal financing arrangements so that postsecondary education becomes a stabilizing force.[e] If young adults were encouraged to lengthen their training in recessions, and shorten it during periods when they could help to ease inflationary pressures by entering the labor force, it would contribute both to employment and price stability. In contrast a student loan program without the proper safeguards could follow the common pattern of heavier household borrowing during periods of prosperity, aggravating both unemployment and inflation.

With respect to equity, there has been increasing concern about the net benefits of higher education going primarily to young adults from high-income and high-asset families, thereby tending to transmit inequality in the distribution of income to the next generation. To cite one important example, there is a strong interdependence between equity in higher education and the pressing problems of inequality among school districts and among states affecting primary and secondary school finance.[f] Equity questions are partially outside the scope of analytical economics because they require ethical judgments. Given a public desire, however, to reduce regressivity, studies such as those of the investment behavior response of disadvantaged families to basic economic opportunity grant and student loan programs have important implications for the design of the programs needed to accomplish the desired results.

These and other implications for policy decisions influencing growth, stability, and equity dramatize the need for study of the basic influences on investment in higher education and research. Some influences such as those related to the Vietnam war demonstrations or to the 1971-72 recession were more transitory, and hence should be separated from those influences that are more lasting. Others are similar to those producing roughly comparable developments in Britain, Germany, and other parts of Europe. The results can be incorporated in structural models useful in

---

[e]This is one implication of the increasing recognition of the value of time in economics, e.g., Becker (1965) or (1972). It assumes that the nation follows fiscal and monetary policies that, designed to maintain full employment, avoid surpluses in this and other major labor markets in the long run, but that operate with lags and other sources of short-run errors.

[f]For tests of the dependence of primary and secondary school expenditures on income and wealth within states see James, Thomas, and Dyck (1963), and between states see McMahon (1970). The policy problem posed by the resulting inequality is discussed by Reischauer and Hartman (1973).

improving upon the simple demographic extrapolations often used for projections.

To do this, it is necessary to go more deeply into the fundamental economic questions brought to the fore by the current financing crisis. It is in the best interest of society that these more basic questions about current decisions be faced. Many questions about investment decisions and many policy dilemmas will remain unresolved. But some progress at a more basic level offers the best promise for eventually increasing society's well-being by improving the efficiency and equity with which resources are allocated.

2 The Economic Theory of Decisions to Invest in Higher Education

Most decisions to invest in higher education are made while giving consideration to the return flows of income and nonmonetary satisfactions expected in future periods. This multiperiod orientation to the future makes them similar to other types of investment decisions that are made by households (including investment in durable goods and houses), by businesses, and by governmental units.

The logical place to start is with an analysis of decisions to invest in human educational capital by private households. This is because a large part of the total investment in the society is financed by families and students out of their own resources. Even that portion which is public investment reflects in part an amalgamation of individual family desires. A portion of the expenditure is current consumption, rather than investment, but this will be included as dependent on current income in the basic model used below. It is on better knowledge of private investment and consumption decisions that public policies wishing to be effective in improving allocative efficiency and equity must build.

In this chapter, the economic theory of choice is developed and applied to the problem of analyzing family and student decisions to invest in higher education. The next chapter will consider how the aggregation of individual household decisions can yield an investment function useful in explaining total investment in higher education by households over time.

I. The Basic Dynamic Model

The basic model assumes that the decision unit looks forward to the returns from education it expects to receive in the current and future periods, and then adjusts its actual stock of educational capital toward the longer-run desired level that this implies. The short-term dynamic adjustment process shown in Eq. 2.1 and the desired stock of educational capital determined by Eq. 2.2 together summarize the basic dynamic model. Each part touched on in this summary in Part I will be derived in more detail later in Part III of this chapter. The model will be seen to be consistent with the alternative rate of return formulation, e.g., Becker (1967), while offering new

13

perspectives on short run investment behavior, on family decisions, as well as on a number of other points. The stock adjustment process is:

$$I_t = \theta_t[S_{Et}^* - (1 - \delta)S_{Et-1}] \tag{2.1}$$

where I_t = real investment in higher education,

S_{Et}^* = equilibrium educational capital stocks, measured in constant dollars,

S_{Et-1} = actual stocks, measured in constant dollars, at original cost,

δ = a rate of depreciation and obsolescence, and

θ_t = the dynamic adjustment coefficient.

The partial adjustment of actual depreciated stocks, $(1 - \delta)S_{Et-1}$, toward desired levels, S_{Et}^*, is important because the production of educational capital involves a process of learning that takes considerable time. Attainment of a bachelor's degree, for example, takes about four years, and therefore the adjustment coefficient governing the investment made in any one year toward this objective can be expected to be less than one. In addition to this technological constraint, there are restrictions placed on the speed of adjustment by the aversion to borrowing due to borrowers' uncertainties about their future capacities, limits on the extent to which families wish to shift costs away from parents to students through use of student loans, and lenders' risks; all limit annual investment toward what can be financed out of current income and assets.

The new investment portion of this flexible accelerator, i.e., $\theta_t(S_{Et}^* - S_{Et-1})$, in effect transforms desired capital changes that are determined by long-run considerations into actual investment expenditures. Since θ_t is a speed of adjustment to be determined by utility maximization (below), the model defines a disequilibrium path, i.e., a path of stock disequilibrium which is also a flow equilibrium with respect to the velocity with which stock equilibrium is approached. If θ_t were constant, the new investment in the flexible accelerator would amount to a geometric distributed lag. The second part, $\theta_t(\delta S_{Et-1})$, provides for replacement investment. It is the lagged adjustment process with different adjustment speeds that is the rationale for this being a dynamic model by which gross investment (I_t) is explained.

For the individual, the depreciation rate (δ) reflects forgetting as well as the obsolescence created by the gradual encroachment of new knowledge. For the family, or for all families taken as an aggregate, this depreciation of the educational capital stock must also be interpreted to reflect losses through retirement and death. For the society taken as a whole, replacement investment is an important part of the total.

Studies of investment in physical capital employ a variety of theories for specifying desired capital. But the validity of this flexible accelerator mechanism for analysis of situations where there is both a capital stock adjustment process and a long gestation period is one thing on which the alternative theories do agree.[1] And the gestation period for human educational capital is the longest of all.

The equilibrium stock of educational capital is determined by longer-run considerations drawn from a life-cycle theory of household saving and investment decisions. The resulting stock of educational capital desired by students and their families at the stage where the son or daughter reaches age 18 is hypothesized in Eq. 2.2 to depend upon the present value of the expected additional earnings made possible by college (Y_{Bt}^e), the non-monetary returns expected (X_{Bt}^e), which are especially important for females planning marriage, a psychological stock of parental education tastes and habits (S_{Pt-1}), and disturbances, (U_t):

$$S_{Et}^* = f(Y_{Bt}^e, X_{Bt}^e, S_{Pt-1}, u_t) \tag{2.2}$$

The determinants of desired educational capital stock (measured in dollar units) in this reduced-form equation are derived from a structural demand for real educational capital and from its marginal costs of household production, illustrated in Fig. 2-1. The hypotheses are, simply, that the demand for educational capital (measured in knowledge units, and for a given set of tastes and habits), as shown in Fig. 2-1, is increased by increases in the monetary or in the nonmonetary returns expected from a college education. The increased demand for knowledge results in increases in desired educational capital stocks (S_{Et}^*), measured in dollar units. This follows because the latter are the product of the increased quantity demanded and of a supply price (P_{et}), given by a marginal cost curve that is assumed throughout to be upward sloping.

The size and direction of the effect of the price (P_{et}) of educational capital (S_{et}, measured in knowledge units) on the longer-run desired stock measured in value terms (S_{Et}) depends on the elasticity of demand. If it is assumed that the elasticity with respect to price is near unity, the effect of this price on total investment outlays will be negligible, and it should be left among the disturbances (2.2). In the short run there are increases in P_{et} that together with constraints or borrowing and income can act to curtail the amount of investment. But with the elasticity unknown, the longer-run price will be left among the disturbances (2.2) for the time being.

The longer-run desired stock of education is that which is desired by the decision unit as it looks forward over the remainder of its life cycle from its current age at time T. So Fig. 2-1 applies to a given age, or to a family with a son or daughter of age 18 where the family is regarded as the decision unit. The demand for educational capital and hence investment opportunities shift downward with advancing age, of course, because less time remains to collect the returns. But in Fig. 2-1, the decision unit has anticipated this, with the anticipated returns underlying demand DD being only those that begin after the date of graduation. The anticipation of advancing age as human capital is produced also affects the shape of the long-run marginal cost curve. LRMC rises largely because with a growing stock, foregone earnings are expected to rise faster than the marginal product of time used in producing more educational capital. Differences in age (or the presence or absence of children of college age) therefore are important sources of differences both in demand and in costs among families. These differences affect net returns. Hence the number of children of college age in the family can be expected to affect the amount of investment in higher education by each decision unit.

Substituting the longer-run determinants given by Eq. 2.2 into Eq. 2.1 for S_{Et}^* changes nothing but simplifies the two-equation basic dynamic model into a single equation:

$$I_t = \theta_t [\, f(Y_{Bt}^e,\, X_{Bt}^e,\, S_{Pt-1},\, u_t) - (1 - \delta)S_{Et-1}] \tag{2.3}$$

The short run aspects can be made more specific. In summary of points that are developed later in Part III:

1. Financing constraints as measured both by parents' disposable income, (Y_{Dt}), and by borrowers' risk as measured by μ limit the amount of investment undertaken in any one year. But in addition to Y_{Dt} and μ there are technological and time constraints implicit in θ_t, and the hypotheses as stated apply to families with students of given ability.

2. The expected nonmonetary contributions of higher education in later life (X_{Bt}^e) are the result of the expected contribution of education to the production of utility service flows (Becker's "commodities"). The expected contributions in turn depend on S_{Pt-1}. But a suitable direct measure of expected nonmonetary contributions is not available in time series data.

3. A linear function is assumed to be a reasonable first approximation, as when using the first part of a Taylor expansion.

A result incorporating these three considerations is

$$I_t = \beta_1 Y_{Dt} + \beta_2 Y_{Bt}^e + \beta_3 S_{Pt-1} + \beta_4 \mu + \beta_5 (1 - \delta)S_{Et-1} + \epsilon_t \tag{2.4}$$

This is the basic equation to be estimated.[2] The new disturbance term ϵ_t can

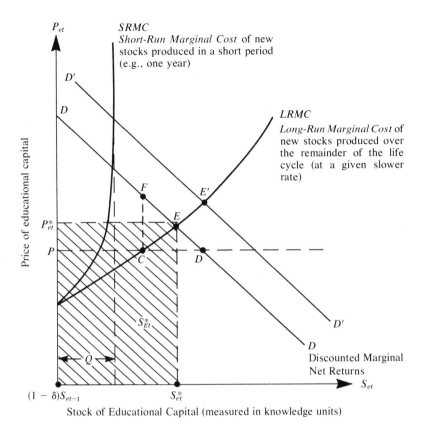

Figure 2-1 Demand for and Cost of Household Production of Educational Capital, Long and Short Run

be extended later to incorporate interest rate effects (Chapter 3) and equity effects (Chapter 4).

In summary, increases in expected returns from higher education cause the demand curve for the total knowledge to be acquired to shift to the right as illustrated in Fig. 2-1. The variables used to measure these expected returns as they affect demand appear (together with those affecting LRMC) in the reduced-form equation (2.2) when the discounted marginal returns are set equal to costs. The larger equilibrium stock of educational capital that this implies increases the investment by the student and his family, initially to something greater than zero. But the long gestation period and related technological constraints, as well as the borrowers' risk which tends to limit investment toward what can be financed out of current income, imply a partial, short-term dynamic adjustment mechanism (equivalent to a distributed lag) that is given by Eq. 2.1.

Eq. 2.4 is a simplified yet applicable version of this basic dynamic model designed to convey the main thrust of the argument. It summarizes the determinants of investment in higher education, most of which are given direct attention later. They include current income, expected returns (dependent in part on age), tastes for further education, an uncertainty discount reflecting borrowers risk, the deterrent effect of accumulating educational capital stocks, interest rates, and in the case of public investment, desires for vertical equity. These determinants are drawn from a model developed later in this chapter that is designed for the analysis of actual investment behavior, as distinguished from merely assuming optimal accumulation, or ceteris paribus responses to private marginal rates of return.

II. Investment by Families and Students in the United States

Because college students are at a stage where they are gradually severing their dependence on the family unit, it is necessary to consider who comprises the relevant decision unit for the purpose of making college investment decisions. It will also put the matter in better perspective if a few basic facts are presented about the size, composition, and sources of the private investment being made in higher education.

Family or Student Decisions?

Is the decision to invest in educational capital a decision made primarily by the family including the prospective student or is it one made independently by the student? If it is usually a family decision, then a model of household saving and investment decisions is most appropriate. Such a model would start out with households maximizing a multiperiod utility function, similar to the traditional economic theory of household investment in durable capital goods or in a home, and subject to appropriate family multiperiod budget and time constraints. It could develop the interdependence with the family's investment in health, with installment credit and mortgage financing, and with parents' saving over their life cycle as they plan toward retirement. If, on the other hand, the decision is made independently by the student as he contemplates his own future, especially now that the voting age has been lowered to 18, an independent student model is more appropriate. In this event, the parents' income and assets have a different significance and more attention is likely to be given to student borrowing.

Unfortunately, neither the family saving and investment decision model nor the independent student model will suffice for all purposes, and a simple choice is not possible. Decisions at the lower-school level are basically parental decisions. Choices at the graduate level are essentially made by independent students, and those at the undergraduate level are likely to involve individual variation and be somewhere in between. Following this line of reasoning, the choice made by the prospective freshman to enter and to finance a college education is more likely to be a family decision, and the selection later of a major field is more likely to be independent.

Since primary attention in this study will be directed to the private investment made in undergraduate education, most attention will be devoted to developing and applying a model of family investment decisions; nevertheless the choice among occupational fields, graduate study, and other uses of the independent student model are related and will not be ignored. Another reason for this course of action is that more attention has been given heretofore in the human capital literature to development of the independent student model. Freeman's (1971) interesting analysis of the choice among occupational fields using microeconomic data centering on advanced male undergraduate students in the Boston area is an example of this. But there are other important elements in the literature basic to the analysis of household decisions. Becker's (1965) important article, for example, on the "Theory of the Allocation of Time" is concerned with the production of utilities by households. Schultz (1971) has long been inclined to look at households, and the two *JPE Supplements* dealing with family investment in children and with "Marriage, Family Human Capital, and Fertility" (see T. W. Schultz, ed., 1974) have further advanced this view. It is also true as suggested above that traditional economic theory has normally assumed that households maximize a utility function, thereby regarding households as the basic decision unit.

There are several possible assumptions in a family saving and investment decision model with respect to the degree of homogeneity within the household. It may not be too bad an approximation to assume that the tastes of the parents' and the student are homogeneous, especially where the latter is a prospective freshman, and that the family budget constraint is relevant. A good part of the psychological stock of tastes and habits (S_{Pt-1}) held by the younger family members are likely to be acquired from within the home environment over many years. An alternative possibility is to assume that the utility function is that possessed by the head of the household who has previously taken the tastes of the prospective student and other family members into account. In either event, the parents' aspirations for the son or daughter are relevant, and the family budget constraint which includes the income and assets of the prospective student applies.[3]

Parental and Student Contributions by Income Level at
Each Type of Institution

A brief look at the investment in higher education made by the typical
family will help to make clear the scope and nature of the private investment to be analyzed. It will also offer additional perspective on the choice
of assumptions about when the family and when the independent student is
the appropriate investment decision-making unit.

Table 2-1 indicates the average direct investment in higher education
made by families in each income quartile with students at each type of
institution. Table 2-2 shows the sources of these investment funds. As
indicated previously, the data are from a nationwide survey of 1972-73
nonfreshmen undergraduates conducted by the author. The incomes of the
respondents, all of whom were applicants for financial aid, are distributed
by nationwide income quartiles that correspond to those for all U.S.
families as given by the U.S. Bureau of the Census *Current Population
Reports*.[4] These quartile breaking points are slightly lower than those for all
families with children in college.

The average direct private investment expenditure at public universities ranges from $1,856 per year for families in the lowest-income quartile
to $2,361 for those in the highest. This $2,361 is more than the $1,620 spent
by the high-income families at private universities. This is a surprising
observation, in view of the attention that has been called by Hansen and
Weisbrod (1969) to the subsidy provided through low tuitions at public
institutions to high-income families. Grants provide a larger subsidy to
students from high-income families at private institutions than they do at
public institutions, as a may be seen in Table 2-2.

The direct private investment in higher education by families with
children in college, which includes parental support of room, board, and
other living expenses (on the assumption that the student would otherwise
have become self-supporting after high school) averages about $2,000 per
year. This is more than the average family's direct investment in health
through expenditures on medical care, averaging $788 in the same year, or
more than the average of $1,587 invested in durables. Including foregone
consumption (i.e., excess foregone earnings) doubles the total annual
private investment. The annual total investment in human capital made by
families with children in college in fact comes to considerably more than the
average annual total family investment in physical consumer capital goods
and houses.[a]

---

[a]Some of the expenditure on room and board must be regarded as an expenditure for the current
consumption satisfactions enjoyed by students, somewhat the same as durables that are consumed
in the current year. Investment in consumer capital goods includes in addition to durables an annual
average investment of $1,000-2,000 in the acquistion of owner-occupied houses, but does not

Tuition and fees are a relatively small fraction of total private investment. Net of grants, tuition and fees come to only about 1 to 17 percent of total out-of-pocket expenditure,[b] and an even smaller fraction of total private investment. Even when including the institution's full costs to compute total social investment by adding state support, endowment fund income, federal aid, and other such sources, it is important to note that the largest fraction of total social investment costs still are borne by families and students.

Table 2-2 reveals the sources of the total direct investment expenditure by households. Direct expenditure does not include consumption foregone, which is equal to "excess" foregone earnings. For the third, or next to highest, family disposable income quartile, 16 percent of total expenditure (before grants are deducted) comes from grants. Grants and student borrowing are both somewhat more important to students from lower-income families, accounting for 47 percent of total resources of students from families in the lowest-income quartile and about 33 percent of the total for students from families in the top half of the income distribution. This difference is far smaller than might be expected in view of the fact that these are the primary sources of efforts to provide greater access to able students from poor families. Also, at private four-year institutions, student borrowing is larger for students from higher-income families.

The parents' actual contribution increases both absolutely and in relative importance as a source of support at higher family disposable personal income levels. It is significant that this happens at public as well as at private institutions, as may be seen in Table 2-2. Past student savings increase in importance as a source of funds as family income increases, but only for students at public institutions (see Column 2). This use of savings is offset by students from high-income families at private four-year institutions by borrowing and by larger parental contributions (see Column 5).

Other interesting relationships can be observed by further study of Tables 2-1 and 2-2. But these comments should serve to illustrate the composition and sources of the private family and student investment in educational capital to be analyzed. The remainder of this chapter will deal with the economic theory basic to the derivation of the model presented above. Non-economists may wish to omit some of the technical aspects and proceed to the empirical analysis beginning in Part IV of investment in higher education by individual families, followed by the analysis of total investment over time in Chapter 3.

---

include the purchase of financial assets, some of which finance new business investment in physical capital goods.

[b]These percentages are not weighted for the underrepresentation in the sample of students from private institutions. The statement, however, refers to tuition net of grants, which are smaller relative to gross tuitions at private institutions.

Table 2-1

Investment in Higher Education by Families and Students (Means for 2,342 full-time students)

Family disposable income quartiles	Public			Private		All institutions	
	Univ.	4-year	2-year	Univ.[a]	4-year	Mean of sample	% dir. pvt. exp.[b]
I. Lowest to $6,002							
Tuition and fees	590	433	419		1,112	578	1[b]
Room and board	935	781	759		789	824	46
Other expenditures	928	851	1,051		812	938	53
Total direct pvt. exp.[b]	1,856	1,577	1,674		1,972	1,777	100
Foregone consumption[c]	2,699	2,930	2,752		2,961	2,800	
II. $6,003-$9,000							
Tuition and fees	624	508	372		1,217	649	6[b]
Room and board	952	832	760		827	856	45
Other expenditures	913	891	994		846	930	49
Total direct pvt. exp.[b]	2,006	1,741	1,746		2,143	1,910	100
Foregone consumption[c]	2,697	2,839	2,808		2,889	2,776	
III. $9,001-$12,184							
Tuition and fees	555	524	361	748	1,296	645	11[b]
Room and board	909	907	796	711	834	868	43
Other expenditures	931	986	1,043	564	905	940	46
Total direct pvt. exp.[b]	2,038	2,059	1,878	1,323	2,386	2,047	100
Foregone consumption[c]	2,722	2,669	2,723	3,287	2,823	2,754	

IV. $12,185 and Over							
Tuition and fees	657	513	418	735	1,377	718	17[b]
Room and board	954	928	818	799	866	898	38
Other expenditures	1,014	1,146	1,564	691	861	1,059	45
Total direct pvt. exp.[b]	2,361	2,327	2,651	1,620	2,588	2,366	100
Foregone consumption[c]	2,594	2,488	2,180	2,273	2,835	2,605	

Source: Nationwide survey conducted by the author in 1972—3 with the help of the National Institute of Education (U.S. Health, Education, and Welfare) and the American College Testing Program. See Appendix D for the survey instruments, and McMahon and Wagner (1973) for a further description. Family disposable income is computed from income reported by the parent on the Family Financial Statement Block W (from Federal Form 1040). The income distribution in this sample corresponds very closely to the income distribution for all families in the 1971 *CPR*.

Specific Sources: Gross tuition and fees = Question 13AI, Appendix D; room (13CI) + board (13DI); other expenditures = books (13BI) + medical (13EI) + durables purchased (13FI) + travel (13HI) + clothing (131.1I) + entertainment (131.2I) + laundry (131.3I) + personal care (131.4I) + beverages (131.5I) + all other (131.6I) adjusted to an academic-year basis.

[a] There is an insufficient number of students in each cell in the two or three lowest-income quartiles in this column for the means to be meaningful.

[b] Total direct *private* expenditures by those in each income quartile is the sum of the three components shown net of grants (from Table 2-2), which are first subtracted from the gross tuition and fees shown here. Percentages refer to the unweighted sample.

[c] Foregone consumption equals total opportunity costs less the "room and board" and "other" expenditures shown above. Opportunity costs are assumed here to be $4,562 for all students, the same as that given by *Current Population Reports*, Series P 60, no. 85 (1972), earnings for white high school graduates, net of property income, after taxes, and extrapolated backward from age 30 to age 22 using the appropriate age-earnings profile from Hanoch (1967).

Table 2-2
Sources of Investment by Families and Students in Higher Education (Means for 2,342 full-time students)

Family disposable income quartiles	Public Univ.	Public 4-year	2-year	Private Univ.[a]	Private 4-year	All institutions Mean of sample	% of dir. exp.[b]
I. Lowest to $6,002							100
Grants	597	488	555		741	563	24
Student borrowing	648	516	362		555	547	23
Parents' contribution	544	459	338		547	487	21
Student job	258	282	503		332	342	15
Spouse's job, other	192	114	263		155	181	8
From savings[c]	214	206	208		383	220	9
II. $6,003–$9,000							100
Grants	483	490	380		747	525	22
Student borrowing	638	655	380		525	584	24
Parents' contribution	460	505	489		943	544	22
Student job	310	305	530		345	358	15
Spouse's job, other	208	111	134		97	153	6
From savings[c]	390	165	213		233	271	11
III. $9,001–$12,184							100
Grants	357	358	322	700	649	406	16
Student borrowing	546	590	443	115	688	548	22
Parents' contribution	639	613	504	775	888	658	27
Student job	362	438	499	312	422	413	17
Spouse's job, other	99	78	74	85	94	91	4
From savings[c]	392	340	358	36	294	337	14

IV. $12,185 and Over							
							100
Grants	264	260	149	605	516	309	11
Student borrowing	504	414	416	170	662	472	18
Parents' contribution	972	872	519	900	1,063	904	34
Student job	392	395	625	221	396	418	16
Spouse's job, other	153	166	202	20	68	139	5
From savings[c]	340	480	889	309	399	433	16

Source: See Table 2-1 Source note.

Specific Sources: Grants above are defined in Question 14BI, Appendix D. Student borrowing = 14CI + 14EI; parents' contribution = 14AI; student job = 14DI; spouse's income and other = 14HI + 14GI.

[a] There are not enough students in the two or three lowest-income quartiles in this column for the means to be very meaningful.

[b] Computed as a percent of total direct investment expenditure (Table 2-1) before grants are deducted.

[c] Computed as total direct investment expenditure (Table 2-1) before grants are deducted less all sources of funds as shown above.

III. The Economic Theory of Investment by Families in Higher Education

Derivation of the family's short-term investment demand for higher education (i.e., of the basic model in Eq. 2.1 and 2.2) involves:

1. Maximizing lifetime utility flows subject to a multiperiod budget constraint to obtain the total demand for educational capital for the remainder of the life cycle shown as *DD* in Fig. 2-1.
2. The costs of producing the stock of educational capital, shown as LRMC, that together with the demand will yield the total optimal monetary and nonmonetary flows.
3. Additional short-term constraints on derived demands for educational inputs that limit the amount of investment expenditure undertaken in any one year, such as those imposed by the technology of production of learned skills, the limits on borrowing, and the constraint of current income.

Some of the elements, especially in step 2, have been developed previously by Ben-Porath (1967) in his "Production of Human Capital and the Life Cycle of Earnings." Two important extensions, however, will be made:

1. First, expected nonmonetary private returns from higher education will be included in an additional demand (i.e., distance *CF* in Fig. 2-1). These are widely recognized (e.g., Becker (1967, p. 8), Michael (1972)). But including them here extends the partial solution based only on expected monetary returns developed by Ben-Porath. The latter partial solution is illustrated by demand price *PP* with the solution at point *C* in Fig. 2-1.

2. Second, the constraints on investment in the short run, such as family income and wealth, technological-type learning constraints, tastes, and borrowers' risk will be permitted to affect actual investment decisions.

Introducing expected nonmonetary returns both includes consumption time and incorporates the returns expected from liberal arts programs. These returns range from the nonmonetary and child-rearing benefits associated with the education of those women who do not plan to enter the labor force full time, to greater access to social and cultural leisure time opportunities. This step partially explains the continuing strong private demand for undergraduate liberal arts training as part, at least, of most students' total postsecondary education.[c]

The short-run constraints, on the other hand, are important in generat-

---

[c]This does not include nonmonetary social benefits (i.e., externalities), but only those private returns relevant to the theory of private investment decisions. The treatment, however, of private nonmonetary returns may be a useful first step toward accommodating social benefits.

ing what could be interpreted as a disequilibrium path, in the sense that long-run educational capital stock equilibrium is never attained. But this is consistent with a flow equilibrium that gives a more central role to influences on actual investment from the family's income and wealth.

Flows of Expected Satisfactions

To derive the family's total nonmoney and money-income-related investment demands for educational capital, its multiperiod ordinal utility function may be stated simply, but generally, as follows:

(2.5) $$U_T = U(x_{1t}, \ldots, x_{nt}) \qquad t = T, \ldots, L \qquad (2.5)$$

where $x_1, \ldots, x_n =$ consumption service flows from all consumer capital stocks and from other goods,

$U_T =$ utility as of the current period T, a present value expressed as dependent on current and expected future service flows since $t = T, \ldots, L$. The function U includes therefore an implicit rate of discounting, μ_t, of expected future utilities, and

$L =$ the last period in the family's life cycle, defined here as the expected date of death of the student.

Since the family will be the basic unit of analysis, its last period will include the discounted future satisfactions of any remaining children as of that date.

The implicit rate of discounting of all future utilities can reasonably be assumed to be positive, with $\mu_t > 0$ for all t. If events in the more distant future are more uncertain with more widely dispersed probabilistic values, and if families are risk averse, then using dispersion as a measure of risk implies heavier positive discounting of those utilities that lie in the more distant future. If in addition to this, students are unsure about their abilities, their future income necessary to purchase these future utilities is also uncertain. The classical Fisherian conditions are not appropriate in this case, for it is likely that expected future income is discounted by even more than the family's real marginal time preference under conditions of uncertainty.

The Production of Flows of Satisfactions

The service flows appearing in the utility function as $x_{1t}, \ldots, x_{nt}$ are produced within the household using market-produced goods and the household's own time. These flows which Becker (1965) has referred to as "commodities" can be thought of as generated by a technological relation in which the q_{it} are quantities of nondurable market goods purchased, and t_{ct} is the leisure time spent in consumption.

$$x_{it} = \alpha_0 q_{it}^{\alpha_{it}} t_{ict}^{\alpha_i} \qquad i = 1, \ldots, n; t = T, \ldots, L \qquad (2.6)$$

These inputs are subject to a time constraint on total consumption time t_{ct} and a budget constraint on the market goods. The time constraint is:

$$\sum_i t_{ict} + t_{wt} + t_{et} = t \qquad (2.7)$$

$\sum t_{ict}$ = total time spend in consumption,

t_{wt} = time spent at work, and

t_{et} = time spent producing educational capital.

This time constraint will be subdivided later to accommodate the individual family members, and be substituted into the multiperiod budget constraint 2-10 below, in the process of obtaining the derived demand for market goods.

But it is now possible to let α_i in the i production functions be a function of the stock of education S_{et-1} and of past consumption experiences x_{it-j}:

$$\alpha_i = \phi_i(S_{et-1}, x_{it-j}) \qquad i = 0, 1, \ldots, n; t = T; j = 0, \ldots, \infty \quad (2.8)$$

The amount of satisfaction yielded by each market good depends upon the contribution of education to the "efficiency" of consumption, in Michael's (1972) terms.[d] Education may increase the satisfaction yielded by a book read during leisure time for example, but decrease the interest in a stock car race. In this sense the α_{it} may be interpreted also as a set of taste parameters.[e]

With this extension, the derivative of the production function 2.6, $\partial x_{it}/\partial S_e$, is the consumption service flow from good i added by one unit of educational capital. The total value of the nonmonetary contribution of one unit of educational capital to consumption satisfactions is $\sum_{it} (\partial x_{it}/\partial S_e) p_{it} x_{it} D_t$ where p_i are the shadow prices of the service flows and D_t is a discount factor. This contribution of education to future nonmonetary returns is, in addition to the contribution made by educational capital to

---

[d]Michael's treatment differs slightly in that he treats education as a Hicks-neutral environmental variable like α_0.

[e]The production technologies (or tastes) held in the present are assumed to prevail in the future for the purpose of appraising expected future service-flow utilities.

money earnings, to be considered below. An advantage of the i different relations of educational capital to consumption service flows is that one homogeneous stock of educational capital can have a different effect on the production of each service flow, eliminating the need to introduce heterogeneous educational capital stocks.

Multiperiod Utility in Terms of Market Quantities

The utility function now may be rewritten in terms of market quantities to be consistent with the purchase quantities that are in the budget constraint. This can be accomplished by merely substituting the i production functions (2.6) into the utility function (2.5) for the x_{it} service flows, to obtain:

$$U_T = U(q_{1t}, \ldots, q_{nt}, t_{ct}; \alpha_0, \ldots, \alpha_n) \qquad t = T, \ldots, L \qquad (2.9)$$

Present utility looking forward over the life cycle is now a function of the quantities of market goods, the amount of consumption time, and a set of production technology (or taste) parameters dependent on educational capital stocks and past consumption experiences.

When utility is maximized subject to the budget constraint, the parameters $\alpha_0, \ldots, \alpha_n$ enter as "shift" parameters in all of the demand functions.[5] But although this effect of past learning on the individual demand functions has far-reaching implications for resource allocation, it is one particular demand function, the family's investment demand for higher education, in which we are particularly interested.

The investment demand for higher education will be shifted upward by larger expected nonmonetary satisfactions due to the contribution of higher education to the greater efficiency of production of consumption utilities. It is only reasonable to assume that these are positive overall, since if education increases efficiency during work time, it should have a similar effect during consumption time. That is, the algebraic sum of all positive and negative nonmonetary satisfactions $\sum_{it} (\partial x_{it}/\partial S_e)p_{it}x_{it}D_t$ would increase the demand price a distance like CF in Fig. 2-1. Note that larger money earnings[f] make it possible to purchase more goods ($q_1, \ldots, q_n$), which in turn yield utility flows, so that in the last analysis *all* final returns from higher education are nonmonetary.

Measurement of the Parameter α_i

The technological coefficients $\alpha_1, \ldots, \alpha_n$ that effect the efficiency of production of consumption services are learned partly through schooling,

---

[f]Education used during work time to produce monetary returns is considered in a later section of this chapter.

(e.g., cognition), and partly through past consumption, (stimulus-response-reinforcement). To recognize the importance of the latter, the α_i's, which are explicitly also a function of the past service flows from the corresponding ith good,[g] are a broader kind of education capital to be called psychological stocks S_{Pt-1}. They depend on education and also on past experience with the type of service flow in question.[h]

When considering the demand for higher education q_{1t}, both the contribution of education to consumption utilities and the past experience or habit effect are best measured in terms of the family's past experience with education. In particular, if tastes for further education are relatively homogeneous within the family, the hypothesis is that the educational attainment of the head is an appropriate measure of S_{Pt-1}—i.e., of α_1 in the production function (2-6). Two points suggest that this is important, and reasonable. First, Brazer and David (1962) early found the educational attainment of the father to be one of the more important determinants of college enrollment in a multivariate analysis using cross-section data.[i] Second, the son or daughter is likely to learn consumption technologies from his parents through shared consumption experiences over a long period of time. It is reasonable to expect that he would form some of his expectations about future returns from education based on them.

As the student's experiences at college and outside the home begin, however, to diverge from those of his parents, he is apt to acquire expectations about the returns from education that differ from theirs. To take this increasing degree of independence into account, the hypothesis for the measurement of S_{Pt-1} will be modified so that the student's educational attainment will displace that of his parents as soon as his own educational attainment exceeds theirs.

This measure of the psychological stock of production technologies may be assumed to change only slowly, although there may be occasional disturbances to them such as from campus demonstrations, and wars. In the short run, all stocks may be taken as given and fixed for any single family for purposes of analysis of purely economic effects on investment.[j]

---

[g]The permanent income hypothesis based on a distributed lag on past incomes is mathematically equivalent to using lagged consumption by use of a Koyck transformation. However, the expected future income aspect of the permanent income hypothesis must resort to a learning process of this type in the last analysis, if it is to explain how income comes to be viewed as "normal" or "permanent" via inelastic expectations.

[h]The interpretation of parameters in the utility function as psychological stocks learned through past experience has a strong tradition in economic theory. See the work by Houthakker and Taylor (1970), Pollak (1970), von Weizsacker (1970), Gorman (1969), Duesenberry (1952, III), Davis (1952), and Brown (1952).

[i]For graduate enrollment, however, a 1973 study of the background of college faculty by the American Council of Education has found the educational attainment of their parents to have an average not far beyond 8th grade.

[j]This does not preclude cross-sectional differences among families, which may be viewed as longer-run differences, however.

The Multiperiod Budget Constraint

The household's total (i.e., long-run) desired investment in higher education may be derived by maximizing this multiperiod utility function subject
to three constraints. The constraints are on the income available over the
life cycle for expenditure on market goods, on time, and on the production
of educational capital. Each of these will be considered in turn.

The Budget Constraint. The multiperiod budget constraint extending forward over the remainder of the life cycle says simply that the sum of the
family's current income (Y_{DT}), expected income (Y_{Dt}^e), and initial resalable
assets, ($\sum_j p_{jT-1} S_{jT-1}$) must equal the sum of all expenditures on market
goods, ($\sum_j p_{it} q_{it}$) and planned bequests ($\sum_j p_{jL} S_{jL}$). Expected future values
are all discounted back to their present values at the expected rate of return
on assets. This budget constraint, which is not yet a total resource constraint since it does not include the value of consumption time, is as
follows:

$$Y_{DT} + \sum_{t=T+1}^{L} \frac{Y_{Dt}^e}{(1+r)^{t-T}} + \sum_{j=1}^{n} p_{jT-1} S_{jT-1}$$

$$= \sum_{t=T}^{L} \sum_{i=0}^{N} \frac{p_{it} q_{it}}{(1+r)^{t-T}} + \sum_{j=1}^{n} \frac{p_{jL} S_{jL}}{(1+r)^{L-T}} \qquad (2.10)$$

where Y_{DT} = current real disposable income of the family, consisting of
income from labor and from property,

Y_{DT}^e = expected real disposable income of the family, including
the student's expected earnings after college, for periods t
$= T + 1, \ldots, L$, and

S_{jT-1} = initial resalable assets,

S_{jL} = terminal assets. (To distinguish stocks from flows of current income, assets are not regarded as the discounted
present value of property income including amortization
of the capital value, but are assumed to be held by the
family with interest income in each period included in
disposable income.)

p_{it} = current and expected future prices, $i = 1, \ldots, n; t = T,$
$\ldots, L$. One particular price, p_{T+F}, is the net tuition and
fee price of purchased formal educational inputs.

q_{it} = quantities of all goods, one of which is formal higher
education.

r = a cumulative mean of expected rates of return on assets.

Maximizing the utility function, shown in Eq. 2.9, subject to this budget constraint permits a solution for the quantities of market goods demanded in each period, but not for leisure (i.e., time spent in consumption t_c), until the constraint on the total amount of time available in each period is substituted into this budget constraint. The substitution converts it into a constraint on total resources, a constraint that includes the value of all time, rather than just the value of work time.

The thrust of much of the research on investment in human capital in recent years has been to show that expected future money income, Y_{Dt} in the budget constraint, is not given but is determined largely by investment in formal education.[k] So, in the process of determining the optimum as between real income and leisure, not only the time constraints but also the constraints on production of educational capital that are necessary to obtain future money income must be taken into account.

Time and Earnings. Educational capital is imbedded in individual persons, not homogeneously in all members of the family group, with differential effects on earnings. In particular, the value of work time for the parent is likely to be higher than that for the student. So to take this into account, it is first necessary to rewrite the household time constraint (2.7) in hours available to each member of the family. The constraint on the total time in hours available to the entire family is the simple sum of these individual constraints:

Adult: $t_c' = t_{ct}' + t_{wt}'$

Adult: $t_t'' = t_{ct}'' + t_{wt}''$ (2.11)

Student: $t_t = t_{ct} + (1 - s)t_{wt} + st_{wt}$

where s = the proportion of work time devoted to the production of educational capital and $(1 - s)$ = the proportion of work time devoted to work. To simplify the exposition, it will be assumed that the adult members of the family are sufficiently advanced in age so that for them it is not to their advantage to invest further time in their own education. Hence for them $s = 0$, which is a likely case. Consider a graph like Fig. 2-1 with increments to the family head's—and not the student's—educational stock, (S_{et}'), measured on the horizontal axis. The corresponding demand curve DD is apt to be low, because there are fewer years remaining in which the family can expect to receive returns, and the marginal cost of investing is higher. Accumulating human capital, S_{et}', is likely to raise the price of time proportionately more than it raises the marginal product of time in the production of new human capital. With no excess of demand over costs in

---

[k] Future earnings are also affected by investment in health, on-the-job training, and mobility, of which all similarly are investment in human capital.

the positive quadrant, there will be no new investment in the parent's education. If sufficient returns were to be expected, however, there could be some use of refresher courses to maintain or update the parent's educational capital stock in spite of the effect of the more advanced age.[l]

Next, these definitions can be used to write an earnings function.[m] In it, the family's disposable income for each current and future year depends upon the family head's education (S'_{et}) and time at work (t_{wt}), the student's education (S_{et}) and time (later) at work, and the family's property income, all net of taxes:

$$Y_{Dt} = wS'_{et}t'_{wt} + wS_{et}(1 - s)t_{wt} + r\sum_{j=1}^{n} p_{jt-1}S_{jt-1}, \quad t=T, \ldots, L \quad (2.12)$$

The rental price, or wage (w) per unit of human capital and the rate of return on assets (r) are taken as parameters, since a single family can be assumed to have little effect on market rates by the supply of either educational or financial capital it offers on the market. However, some families may have no net assets, but only debt, and face higher borrowing rates in imperfect markets that put them on a lower multiperiod budget constraint. This would operate to restrain investment by these families.

This earnings function (2.12) and the time constraints (2.11) can now be substituted into the multiperiod budget constraint (2.10) for current and expected income (Y_{Dt}, for $t = T, \ldots, L$). The earnings function serves to reexpress earnings in terms of the value of the time involved. Since t'_{wt} and $(1 - s)t'_{wt}$ now appear, the time constraints (2.11) can then also be substituted into the multiperiod budget constraint for them. This broadens the income constraint on purchases into a total resource constraint. It says that the sum of the value of all the family's work time, consumption time, and receipts from property over the life cycle equals the sum of the value of all purchases, consumption time, and terminal assets.

The Production of Educational Capital. To arrive at the stock of educational capital that will optimize monetary and nonmonetary returns over the remainder of the life cycle, the family would need to maximize the present value of the current and expected market and nonmarket satisfactions to be derived from the student's stock of higher educational capital. The resulting long-run desired stock illustrated at S^*_{et} in Fig. 2-1, assumes the length of period t to be more than ample (e.g., 10 years) to produce the desired increment to the existing stock Q_{et}. The student's high school education is shown as S_{et-1} at the origin; it is the initial endowment as of the

---

[l]Question 30 in Appendix D-1 illustrates some of the kinds of postgraduate educational experiences on which data was collected from student's parents in the College Investment Decision survey.

[m]Earnings functions found in a large literature generated by current research usually include ability as a determinant, which is taken here as given, and exclude property income.

end of the preceding period. The desired increment is obtained by setting the discounted marginal net returns attributable to college, shown as DD in Fig. 2-1, equal to the long-run marginal cost of producing this increment. The next step, therefore, must be to derive this long-run marginal cost curve.[6]

Let additions to the stock of educational capital (Q_{et}), measured in knowledge units (via skill performance and written tests), be produced by means of the following household production function:

$$Q_{et} = \beta_0(s_t t_{wt})^{\beta_1} q_t^{\beta_2} \tag{2.13}$$

The variable inputs are:

$s_t t_{wt}$ = the students time, where s_t is the fraction of potential work time available within a long period chosen to be spent in the production of higher educational capital, and

q_t = quantities of formal education (or enrollment). It includes the services of teachers and classrooms purchased through tuition.

β_0, β_1, and β_2 are parameters. β_0 is an "environmental variable"[7] which affects the student's opportunities and the efficiency with which educational capital is produced by the household. It is assumed to depend upon the parents' education (S'_{et-1}). β_2 relates to the effectiveness with which the student can utilize formal schooling. It depends on his own educational capital (S_{et-1}), which, in turn, reflects the quality of his past schooling and his ability. β_1 refers to the efficiency with which the student can use his own time, and is assumed to depend upon his ability to concentrate, reflecting his motivation, habits, and ability. It is assumed that $\beta_1 + \beta_2 < 1$, although β_1, could be expected to be positively correlated with β_2 and the sum of the two would be larger for the best educated, able, students.

The Cobb-Douglas form is a reasonable first approximation for the more general form $Q_{et} = Q(s_t t_{wt}, q_t)$ and helps to keep the discussion clear. But beyond this it will not be defended on theoretical grounds. The fraction of work time spent in formal education (s_t) is a variable to be determined that remains below one so long as the period chosen for the analysis is long. If, for example, t is 10 years, if Q_{et} is the knowledge equivalent of a four year bachelor's degree of given quality, and if the student attends college 9 months a year, $s_t = 0.3$.

The following costs to the household constrain its production of educational capital:

$$P_{et}Q_{et} = p_{T+F}q_t + p_{R+B}q_t + (ws t_w S_{et-1} - p_{R+B}q_t) \tag{2.14}$$

That is, the total cost of investing in higher educational capital in dollars (which has been designated S_{Et} in Fig. 2-1) is composed of outlays on tuition and fees, on room, board, and other living expenses, and foregone consumption, the latter in parentheses. It is the short-run outlays on these that appear in Table 2-1, and they are a primary focus of the analysis in this book. Throughout:

p_{T+F} = the net tuition and fee "price," after grants, of one academic year of formal education,

p_{R+B} = a price index for room, board, and a standard market basket of basic student necessities,

(wst_wS_{et-1}) = foregone earnings; the amount the student could have earned if he had stopped after completing his high school education (S_{et-1}) and used the time spent in college (st_w) in gainful employment.

The room, board, and other out-of-pocket expenditure is an investment by the family, as indicated previously, only because of the assumption that the student would have become self-supporting after high school if he had not gone to college. It is time invested by the independent student, but it also represents some consumption that is not foregone in favor of the future. Lower room and board costs may be a significant factor in lowering out-of-pocket investment costs to low-income parents, contributing to the expansion of urban campuses and junior colleges. They will be analyzed separately in Chapter 3.

Foregone consumption, the remainder of the total investment cost which appears in Eq. 2.14, is a large and important component of total investment costs both to the individual and to the society, as was seen in the data in Table 2-1. It is a residue from the opportunity costs represented by earnings foregone. It will sometimes be referred to as "excess foregone earnings" in Chapter 3 even though foregone consumption is more accurate. It can be small or even negative for those students who are poorly equipped to get alternative employment in periods when unemployment rates are high. The result is that in these periods the costs of investing in educational capital are lowest.[n]

The long-run marginal cost function can now be derived by maximizing output as given by the production function for educational capital (2.13) subject to this total outlay constraint (2.14). It amounts to exactly the same

---

[n]Another example of low foregone consumption is to be found where an unskilled student is supported luxuriously by wealthy parents. But in this case, the parental investment costs are higher.

thing to minimize cost (2.14) at each level of output (2.13). The inputs of enrollment (q_t) and of time in college ($s_t t_{wt}$) are treated as variables, and the long-run demands for each of these can be derived.[a] They are:

Enrollment: $\qquad q_t = \dfrac{\beta_2}{\beta_1 + \beta_2} \dfrac{1}{p_{T+F}} P_{et} Q_{et}$ $\qquad\qquad$ (2.15)

Time Spent: $\qquad s_t t_{wt} = \dfrac{\beta_1}{\beta_1 + \beta_2} \dfrac{1}{w S_{et-1}} P_{et} Q_{et}$ $\qquad\qquad$ (2.16)

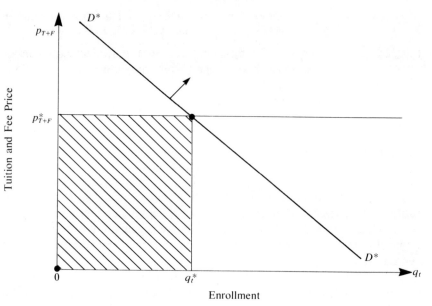

Figure 2-2 Long-Run Enrollment Demand

---

[a]Form the Lagrangian, take the partials for $s_t t_{ct}$, q, and λ:

$$Q_t = \beta_0 (s_t t_{ct})^{\beta_1} q_t^{\beta_2} + \lambda (PQ_t - w(s_t t_{ct}) S_{et-1} - p_t q_t) \qquad (a)$$

$$\partial Q_t / \partial s_t t_{ct} = \beta_1 \beta_0 (s_t t_{ct})^{\beta_1 - 1} q_t^{\beta_2} - \lambda w S_{et-1} = 0 \qquad (b)$$

$$\partial Q_t / \partial q_t = \beta_2 \beta_0 (s_t t_{ct})^{\beta_1} q_t^{\beta_2 - 1} - \lambda p_t = 0 \qquad (c)$$

$$\partial Q_t / \partial \lambda = PQ_t - w(s_t t_{ct}) S_{et-1} - p_t q_t = 0 \qquad (d)$$

To solve for q_t and $s_t t_{ct}$, divide (b) by (c) to get (e):

$$w(s_t t_{ct}) S_{et-1} = (\beta_1/\beta_2) p_t q_t \qquad (e)$$

which may be substituted into (d) to obtain:

$$PQ_t = \left(\frac{\beta_1}{\beta_2} + \frac{\beta_2}{\beta_2} \right) p_t q_t$$

$$\qquad\qquad\qquad\qquad\qquad (f)$$

which when solved for q_t gives Eq. 2.15.

Then Eq. 2.16 may be obtained by symmetry.

Notice that these demands for enrollment and for years spent in college are downward sloping in relation to tuition and market-wages. But they are constantly shifting outward in response to a larger total desired outlay on educational capital ($P_{et}Q_{et} = S_{Et}^*$).

The long-run total cost function for educational capital can now be derived by substituting these demands for inputs back into the production function,[p] and by solving for $P_{et}Q_{et}$. Long-run marginal cost then can be obtained by taking the partial derivative of the total cost function with respect to Q_{et} to get:

$$ P_{et} = \left[\frac{1}{\beta_0} \left(\frac{wS_{et-1}}{\beta_1} \right)^{\beta_1} \left(\frac{p}{\beta_2} \right)^{\beta_2} \right]^{\frac{1}{(\beta_1+\beta_2)}} Q_{et}^{\frac{1}{(\beta_1+\beta_2)} - 1} \qquad (2.17) $$

This is the long-run marginal cost function, as illustrated in Fig. 2-1. It slopes upward because $(\beta_1 + \beta_2) < 1$, and because as wS_{et-1} in Eq. 2.17 increases with age, the long-run marginal cost curve in Fig. 2-1 would slope upward more steeply in response to the increasing opportunity costs of time. In addition, it will slope upward even more steeply for the less well-educated or poorly motivated student ($\beta_1 + \beta_2$ smaller). Students lacking starting advantages will secure a smaller amount of advanced education, since even with given demand, the intersection with higher costs on Fig. 2-1 defining their equilibrium investment in educational capital would be further to the left, and S_{Et}^* would be smaller.

The Solution for the Equilibrium Stock (S_{Et}^*). The solution for the equilibrium time path for educational capital stock (S_{Et}), measured in dollars, now may be summarized in four steps:

1. Decisions are made that allocate the time of each individual family member between work time and consumption time in each period in hours. The result appears in the time constraints in Eq. 2.11, and is taken as given.

For costs to be minimized in producing the satisfaction flows (x_{it}), the ratio of the marginal product of market goods (q_{it}) and leisure time (t_{cit}) would have had to be equal to the ratio of the price of the good (p_{it}) to the wage (e.g., wS_{et-1}') obtainable on the market by each family member.[q] If the

---

[p]This gives

$$ Q_{et} = \beta_0 \left(\frac{\beta_1}{\beta_1 + \beta_2} \frac{1}{wS_{et-1}} P_{et}Q_{et} \right)^{\beta_1} \left(\frac{\beta_2}{\beta_1 + \beta_2} \frac{1}{p_{T+F}} P_{et}Q_{et} \right)^{\beta_2} $$

and

$$ P_{et}Q_{et} = (\beta_1 + \beta_2) \left[\frac{1}{\beta_0} \left(\frac{wS_{et-1}}{\beta_1} \right)^{\beta_1} \left(\frac{p_{T+F}}{\beta_2} \right)^{\beta_2} \right]^{\frac{1}{(\beta_1+\beta_2)}} Q_{et}^{\frac{1}{(\beta_1+\beta_2)}} $$

[q]Extensive attention has recently been given to this allocation of time between leisure and work by Ghez and Becker (1972). They find that as educational capital increases, the increasing value of

wage of family members differs, they may choose different amounts of work time.[r]

2. Work time is allocated between the production of educational capital and gainful employment.

This implies minimizing the costs of producing any given amount of educational capital (i.e., obtaining LRMC via Eq. 2.13 and Eq. 2.14). It also implies maximizing the present value of the stream of future earnings in Eq. 2.12 plus expected nonmonetary returns from higher education given by $\sum_{it} (\partial x_{it}/\partial S'_{et-1}) p_x x_{it} Q_{et} D_t$, all net of total investment costs $(P_{et} Q_{et})$. This is the equivalent to finding the intersection of the total discounted marginal net returns given by the demand curve in Fig. 2-1 and the long-run marginal cost curve to obtain the equilibrium solution S^*_{et}.

The downward slope of the demand for educational capital is likely. First, there is likely to be declining marginal productivity of education in producing total service flow utilities. Second, there is the possibility of declining marginal utility of all service flows, or of real income. This insures a solution with marginal costs, which in turn are due to productivity in producing additional educational capital that rises more slowly than the opportunity cost of the time needed.

3. Given the desired total investment in education (S^*_{Et}) and hence the family's income over its life cycle, the family decides upon the timing of its consumption. This desired, optimal investment is not independent of consumption decisions, however, because borrowing to finance investment also helps to distribute consumption over time. The typical family borrows earlier in its life cycle, including some borrowing to finance investment in education, then saves and lends later.[8] But if it is investing in educational capital while facing high borrowing rates in imperfect capital markets, its investment in educational capital and its lifetime income are likely to be curtailed.

The second and third steps taken together are equivalent insofar as the investment in educational capital is concerned to calculating the internal rate of return (including nonmonetary returns) and financing the investment by borrowing so long as this rate of return exceeds the market rate of interest.

4. Finally, the longer-run desired stock of educational capital (S^*_{Et}) has been derived. It can be expressed as a function of things that shift the demand function, such as expected monetary returns (Y^e_{Bt}) and expected nonmonetary returns (X^e_{Bt})—that therefore also appear in the basic model.

---

work time and increasing opportunity cost of leisure lead to a larger percent of total time spent at work.

[r] An optimal combination of commodities is implied by the commodity equilibrium conditions in addition to these cost minimizing conditions.

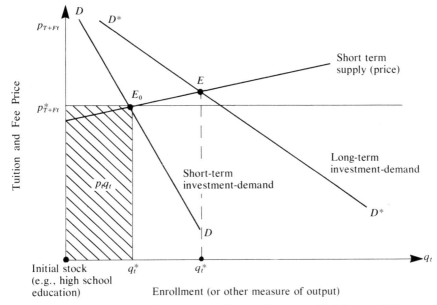

Figure 2-3   Short-Term Investment Expenditure on Tuition and Fees

But when the period chosen is shorter, and capital markets are imperfect, investment is limited by production technologies and by family income. This results in a partial attainment of equilibrium stocks (S_{Et}^*) via a flow equilibrium considered in the next section.

Short-Term Investment Demand

Lifetime investment in educational capital cannot be achieved in any one year. Due to the time constraint in the short run (with $s = 1$ and $s_t t_{wt}$ fixed), the shadow price of educational capital (P_{et}) rises sharply. This serves to limit short-term investment to Q as shown in Fig. 2-1. That is, SRMC becomes vertical at some point, defining an absolute limit to the amount of educational capital that can be produced in any given short-term period irrespective of how much money and effort is invested.

But in addition to this, *the short-run shadow cost $P_{et}Q_{et}$*, which is the *total outlay* required to secure this amount of educational capital, also is large. The family may be prepared to spend this amount over a four year period, for example, but not in a single year. It is constrained by its current income, accompanied by constraints on borrowing, and this becomes part of the flow equilibrium relevant to the derived demand for inputs shown by *DD* in Fig. 2-3. The short-run derived demand limits investment expenditure on tuition and fees (there are comparable effective demands not illustrated for room, board, and excess foregone earnings) to to $p_t q_t$ in Fig. 2-3.

The short-run supply curve in Fig. 2-3 would be horizontal since the demand is from one individual family except for the fact that tuition net of grants is somewhat higher for those families that have larger family income. Higher demand can be expected with higher income, so that the supply price rises with it as need analysis procedures are applied.

The actual time path is merely a series of these short-run expenditure flows. At the end of each period, the family may be assumed to reevaluate the whole situation, deciding on a new equilibrium stock (or re-deciding on the old one), and to follow this with an additional investment which also constitutes a further partial stock adjustment. It is an iterative procedure, but the equilibrium stock of educational capital is a shifting target and may never be attained.[s]

The long run marginal cost curve in Fig. 2-1 is generated under conditions where all factor inputs are variable, including time. That is, within the longer period of given length there is assumed to be ample time to produce the amount of educational capital necessary to attain the desired level, and hence an optimal production period is implied by the solution for s, the fraction of total work time to be used. In the short period the amount of time available however, is not only fixed, but it is also too small to produce the entire desired stock of educational capital. So time, and current income, which in the long run are not effective limiting factors in this same sense, both do become effective constraints in the short run that govern the flow equilibrium under which the educational capital in fact is produced. Even with no shifts in S_{et}^*, it would be possible for the short term flow equilibrium to significantly under or over-shoot the long-run optimum defined in the absence of these short term financing constraints.

The constraint on borrowing arises both because of lender's risk, which will be designated by the rate γ_1, and borrower's risk, which is related to the "fog of uncertainty" and measured by an average uncertainty discount rate μ. From the point of view of the lender, financial institutions are hesitant to approve loans on the security of human capital alone. This is because human capital cannot serve as resalable collateral to secure the principal, and because lenders are uncertain about the future earning capacities of the student, I will assume that they are willing to lend a fraction of the student's expected future income that is dependent on the rate of discount (γ_1) for lender's risk.

---

[s]For the long run, stock equilibrium suggests full adjustment of actual stocks, with $S^* = S$. Therefore θ may be substituted into the utility function and budget constraint (similarly for health, for consumer durables and owner-occupied houses), and adjustment costs added to the constraint to get a solution for the optimal speed of adjustment.

With respect to borrower's risk, students are reluctant to borrow because they are uncertain about the future possibilities in fields they wish to enter, are uncertain about their own abilities to succeed in the academic program and later in the field as the means of earning funds for repayment, and also because they are likely to have shorter time horizons.[t] Translating expected future income into a certainty equivalent by adding an average discount rate μ for borrower's risk, the entire discount factor used for reducing expected future income to its present value as well as for discounting it both for lender's and for borrower's risk is $(1 + r + \gamma_1 + \mu)^{t-T}$. As t increases, the more distant returns expected from education are discounted more heavily. This limited access to expected future income through borrowing will be expressed as a fraction of current assets as follows:[u]

$$\sum_{t=T+1} \frac{Y_{Bt}^e}{(1 + r + \gamma_1 + \mu)^{t-T}} = \gamma_2 p_{jT-1} S_{jT-1} \tag{2.18}$$

The budget constraint, *as it applies to the investment expenditures that can be made in the current period T* (including analagous treatment of parental borrowing) is:

$$Y_{Dt} + (1 + \gamma_2 + \gamma_3) p_{jT-1} S_{jT-1} = \sum_{i=1}^{n} p_{iT} q_{iT} + p_{jT} S_{jT} \tag{2.19}$$

This additional constraint must be included in the optimization as a special constraint on any expenditures made during the current period, which is the period in which we are primarily interested. As indicated above, in each new period, the family resets $t=T=0$, re-evaluates the future, and decides on current expenditure, leaving a path of actual expenditures representing successive short-run flow equilibria through time. In effect, this determines θ_T, the speed with which the desired investment in educational capital is implemented in the current period.

The θ_T in Eq. 2.1 therefore depends upon the family's current disposable income (Y_{Dt}), the rate of interest (r), the rate of lender's risk (γ_1), and the rate reflecting borrower's risk (μ).[v] The dependent variable in Eq. 2.1 is total investment by families resulting from *derived* demands as was illustrated in Fig. 2-3 (or Eq. 2.15 and 2.16) for investment via tuition and fees,

---

[t] See Hartman (1972) and Thurow (1969). Schultz (1970) suggests that "the fog of uncertainty is everywhere concealing the more distant value of education" (pp. 148-49), and ". . . if student sovereignty has an Achilles' heel, it is in the domain of information . . ." (p. 182).

[u] Since student borrowing acts in part to shift costs from parents income (Y_{Dt}) to students expected income (Y_{Bt}), this could be an important additional deterrent to student borrowing. Preliminary regressions with the 1972-73 McMahon and Wagner (1973) microeconomic data reveal that student borrowing is a negative determinant of actual parental support in a multiple regression equation.

[v] The returns from education can be more easily captured through the tax system, and the lender's risk is reduced.

for investment in room, board, and related living expenses, and for investment of time via excess foregone earnings, all of which are inputs in the production of educational capital.

The derivation of the final investment demand equation for each of these investment components generates the hypotheses that relate to the logic of the appearance of each explanatory variable and the direction of its effect as these appear in Eq. 2.4, repeated as Eq. 2.20 below. In summary, the family's multiperiod utility function (Eq. 2.9) is maximized, taking period t to be a short period such as one year, and including in the utility function the household production of nonmonetary returns (or "commodities") using educational capital stocks. The maximization is subject to a total resource constraint composed of the multiperiod budget constraint (2.10), the additional short-term budget constraint on expenditures within period T (2.19), the short-term time constraints applicable to each family member (2.11), the earnings function (2.12), and the constraints on the short-run production of educational capital (Eqs. 2.13 and 2.14). Optimization implies the satisfaction of the monetary and nonmonetary return maximizing and cost minimizing conditions subject to the constraints. The investment demand equations are obtained from the first-order conditions for the quantities q_{iT} to be purchased at given prices. These demand functions include the following ones, expressed in linear form, for each input mentioned above used in the production of educational capital:

$$I_{it} = p_{it}q_{it}$$

$$= \beta_1 Y_{DT} + \beta_2 Y_{BT}^e + \beta_3 S_{PT-1} + \beta_4 \mu + \beta_5(1 - \delta)S_{ET-1} + \epsilon_t \qquad (2.20)$$

This is the investment demand function of the basic model containing the hypotheses discussed above. Some key hypotheses will be tested next using cross section data, and all will be considered further in Chapter 3 using time series data.

IV. Some Empirical Tests Using Microeconomic Data

This Eq. 2.20 has been estimated using two sets of microeconomic data for individual families with college-age children, with the results presented in Tables 2-3 and 2-4 and Eq. 2.21.

The first set is the Bureau of Labor Statistics Consumer Expenditure Survey data, from which all 1,424 families have been selected that have children of college age. This selection eliminates the effect of family age structure as an index to potential returns from college because all of these families are presented with the investment opportunity implicit in having children of the appropriate age. The shifting of the demand curve, however, with age caused by changes in the number of children ages 18-22 in the household (or population, all measured as C_{18-22}), will have an important role in Chapter 3. C_{18-22} is one index of Y_{Bt}^e because the time series data includes families who are at other stages in their life cycle. There are no measures of μ and of S_{Et-1} in this BLS data.

Current family disposable income *is* a highly significant determinant of investment in tuition and fees (the only component of family investment in higher education that can be separated out in this BLS data) for all families, as well as for white and black families taken separately. In fact, Table 2-3 constitutes very strong evidence on the significance of family disposable income as a determinant of investment at the microeconomic individual family level.

Table 2-3 also reveals that S_{Pt-1} from the basic model (Eq. 2.20) is a highly significant positive influence on investment expenditure by all families, as may be seen in lines one through three of Table 2-3. Families then have been partitioned by income quartile in the attempt to hold constant, in part at least, the strong effect of current income and bring out the separate effects of S_{Pt-1}. It can be seen when this is done that S_{Pt-1} remains significant in all cases except for black families in the two middle-income quartiles. This measure of the contribution of education within the family to the production of nonmonetary returns from education is significant between families. As an index to the formation of tastes within the family for higher education, it is possible that the heads of very few middle-income black families in this BLS urban sample have been to college.

Table 2-4 reports *net* interfamily income elasticities found for the BLS cross-section data. The net income elasticities are positive, highly significant, and just over unity (i.e., 1.15) for all families. They are higher for nonwhites (1.53) than for whites (1.07), especially in the lower income groups. Gross income elasticities over time normally are higher, often estimated to be in a range between 2.5 and 3.0. The net intertemporal elasticities will be considered in the next chapter, but all of the net elasticities do suggest that as income per family in the United States continues to grow, family investment expenditures on higher education also can be expected to grow.

Finally, an ex ante private monetary rate of return has been calculated for each of the 2,766 non-freshman student respondents in the 1972-73 College Investment Decision Survey that was described under Tables 2-1 and 2-2 above. It is a pure internal rate of return based on differences in

Table 2-3
Investment in Tuition and Fees by Individual Households with College-Age Children, 1960-61 BLS Data
(*t*-statistic in parentheses below coefficients, coefficient significant at .05 level underlined.)

Truncated Eq. 2.20	Dependent variable	Current income Y_{DT}	(Years of educ. of head) S_{PT-1}	Race ($W=1$ $N-W=0$)	Constant term	R	n
All families	$p_T + Fq_T$	.017 (9.49)	20.0 (8.09)	−28.6 (−1.07)	−158 (−5.23)	.39	1424
By race	$p_T + Fq_T$ (Nonwhite)	.017 (3.45)	13.1 (3.09)		−104 (−2.66)	.39	185
	$p_T + Fq_T$ (White)	.017 (8.72)	21.4 (7.63)		−200 (−7.03)	.39	1239

45

Income quartile I (Low)	$p_{T+F}q_T$ (Nonwhite)	.012 (.94)	8.1 (2.04)	−54.8 (−1.13)	.24	97
	$p_{T+F}q_T$ (White)	.012 (1.70)	8.0 (3.27)	−67.2 (−2.09)	.24	265
Income quartile II	$p_{T+F}q_T$ (Nonwhite)	.061 (1.10)	−.12 (−.01)	−287 (−.87)	.19	37
	$p_{T+F}q_T$ (White)	.011 (.62)	6.4 (1.70)	−38.5 (−.34)	.11	324
Income quartile III	$p_{T+F}q_T$ (Nonwhite)	.0003 (.01)	−1.6 (−.26)	107 (.29)	.06	23
	$p_{T+F}q_T$ (White)	.038 (1.96)	14.7 (3.28)	−360 (−2.05)	.22	330
Income quartile IV (High)	$p_{T+F}q_T$ (Nonwhite)	−.012 (.31)	51.4 (2.44)	−83.4 (−.13)	.46	28
	$p_{T+F}q_T$ (White)	.007 (1.58)	46.0 (5.38)	−303 (−2.64)	.32	320

Source: Bureau of Labor Statistics, Consumer Expenditures Survey Data, 1960-61

Table 2-4
Elasticities
Investment in Tuition and Fees by Individual Households with College-Age Children, 1960-61 BLS Data
(t-statistic in parentheses below coefficients, coefficient significant at .05 level underlined.)

Truncated Eq. 2.20	Dependent variable	Current income Y_{DT}	(Years of educ. of head) S_{PT-1}	Race ($W=1$ $N-W=0$)	Constant term	R	n
All families	p_T+rq_T	1.15 (10.00)	.90 (7.43)	−.04 (−1.34)	−4.43 (−10.39)	.37	1424
By race	p_T+rq_T (Nonwhite)	1.53 (5.77)	.40 (1.81)		−5.30 (−5.60)	.45	185
	p_T+rq_T (White)	1.07 (8.48)	1.05 (7.47)		−4.27 (−9.14)	.36	1239

Income quartile I (Low)	$p_{T+F}q_T$ (Nonwhite)	.42 (.93)	.40 (1.71)	-1.49 (-.96)	.21	97
	$p_{T+F}q_T$ (White)	-.10 (-.53)	.53 (2.96)	.273 (.41)	.18	265
Income quartile II	$p_{T+F}q_T$ (Nonwhite)	3.99 (.95)	-.07 (-.13)	-14.4 (-.91)	.16	37
	$p_{T+F}q_T$ (White)	.23 (.18)	.59 (2.01)	-.739 (-.15)	.12	324
Income quartile III	$p_{T+F}q_T$ (Nonwhite)	-1.12 (-.16)	-.59 (-.81)	6.06 (.22)	.12	23
	$p_{T+F}q_T$ (White)	6.04 (3.70)	.95 (3.17)	-23.9 (-3.72)	.27	330
Income quartile IV (High)	$p_{T+F}q_T$ (Nonwhite)	-1.91 (-.54)	2.00 (2.09)	7.48 (.50)	.44	28
	$p_{T+F}q_T$ (White)	.80 (1.59)	1.94 (5.50)	-3.84 (-1.87)	.32	320

Source: Bureau of Labor Statistics, Consumer Expenditures Survey Data, 1960-61

student responses to questions about what they expect to earn upon graduation and what they expect to be earning 25 years later (in real terms) as revealed by questions 20 and 21 in Appendix D. No expected nonmonetary returns are included, although an estimate of these which was calculated based on the responses to questions 5 and 6 was found to average between 5 and 10 percent in McMahon (1974), only slightly below expected monetary returns. The monetary rates of return are calculated by fitting Hanoch's (1967) age-earnings profiles to the two point estimates of expected returns given by the student, subtracting the earnings attributable to a high school education at each age as given by census data, multiplying the difference by an α coefficient of .66 in the attempt to remove increments to earnings not attributable to the college training, and solving iteratively for the rate of return when these expected returns are set equal to actual compounded college costs. The latter are based on answers given to questions 4 and 13 in Appendix D together with an estimate of foregone consumption. The resulting monetary rate of return, r_M^e, may be interpreted as a measure of differences in the investment demand curve (shifts in the MEI) among students. It can be compared directly to factors affecting the supply of funds, such as the rate of interest at which funds can be borrowed, and to the availability of funds from parents. The latter is measured by including the parents disposable income, Y_{DT}, in the regression, which was obtained directly from the parents by use of the Family Financial Statement shown in its entirety in Appendix D. The dependent variable is annual total investment by the family, including the parents actual contribution (the student's contribution taken alone is even more responsibe to differences in rates of return), a form that reflects the type of institution chosen. These ex ante rates of return should be clearly distinguished from ex post rates, calculated from age earnings profiles for persons of the same race, sex, and occupation choice as given by census data. The unadjusted results (given some simultaneous bias) for shifts in the MEI among families are:

$$I_{HT} = \quad 166 r_{MT}^e + \quad .036\ Y_{DT} + \quad .0001 p_{jT-1} S_{jT-1} + 4347 \qquad R = 0.20 \quad (2.21)$$
$$\quad (44) \qquad (.004) \qquad (.001)$$

The standard errors (rather than the t-statistics) are shown below each coefficient in parentheses. It may be seen that the monetary rate of return expected by the student from his planned college investment *is* a highly significant determinant of total family private direct investment in higher education.

3

Investment by Families in Higher Education

The major sources of fluctuations and growth of investment in higher education by families over time will be the focus of this chapter. The analysis will make use of the logic of individual family investment decisions over the family's life cycle that was developed in the preceding chapter. But the version used of the basic dynamic model will require adaptations that make it appropriate for use with aggregate economic data.

A search for more basic sources of fluctuations and growth in investment has several important implications. The crisis, alluded to in Chapter 1, in the financing of higher education has variously been attributed to an overinvestment in people (causing job-market gluts), to Viet Nam demmonstrations, to inefficient management, to demographic causes of declining enrollment, and to the effect of inflation on costs. In fact, the urgency of the crisis, and the confusion about its causes, has had the result that a basic charge to the National Commission on the Financing of Postsecondary Education was to investigate "the nature and causes of serious financial distress facing institutions of postsecondary education."[1] The Commission has made proposals for federal aid to institutions, cost measurement and reporting, and student grants and loans that all depend in part on the positive analysis of the causes of the distress, as well as on the effect of financing constraints on investment by families and by state and local governments.[2]

There are other implications of investigating the sources of growth of investment in education. They include implications for the growth of real income per family and for increasing equality in the distribution of income, not to speak of the possibilities for improving the quality of human life.[3] In view, of their importance, it is surprising that there has been so little economic analysis of the determinants of investment in higher education by families over time. Much of the intertemporal analysis of expenditures, or of enrollment, has tended to merely extrapolate trends using high school graduation rates without analyzing family investment decisions.[4] A related approach, which is limited, but useful for some purposes, has been to emphasize demographic statistics alone. Other parts of the literature consider manpower requirements while limiting the focus to differences in demands among job markets.

To study investment in higher education by households over time in a way that permits simultaneous consideration of several of the explanatory variables requires the use of aggregates. Longitudinal data on individual families that contain measures of these determinants, and that have been collected often enough over a long enough period of time, simply do not exist. Cross section tests are useful, but generalization of results to behavior over time requires verification.

So aggregates do reveal unique information about intertemporal behavior. But from the point of view of testing hypotheses about individual family investment decisions, the use of aggregates produces results that must be viewed as only exploratory. Where useful hypotheses about individual decisions are thereby identified, they can often be tested further in microeconomic data. Furthermore, aggregates contribute insights into effects that are strong enough not to be netted out by decisions made by other micro-units, or by cross-effects from other variables, and this is useful information in its own right.

Parts I and II adapt the basic dynamic model to the analysis of investment in higher education by all families over time and consider measurement of each variable. Part III presents regression results for investment in tuition and fees, room and board, and total investment, considering public and private institutions separately. The appendix to this chapter presents an enrollment model that considers the tuition issue.

I. The Basic Dynamic Model for Time Series Analysis

The basic model presented in Chapter 2 as Eq. 2.1, 2.2, and 2.4 will be repeated here with the modifications necessary to the analysis of time series data for all families. Such data include families that are at all different stages in their life cycles. The three equation model, followed by discussion about how each variable will be measured, is:

$$I_{Ht} = \theta_t \left[S_{Et}^* - (1 - \delta) S_{Et-1} \right] \tag{3.1}$$

$$S_{Et}^* = f(Y_{Bt}^e, X_{Bt}^e, S_{Pt-1}, u_t) \tag{3.2}$$

Moreover, after substituting 3.2 into 3.1 for S_{Et}^*, applying the current income borrowing constraint, and substituting C_{18-22} as one estimate of the potential for future returns:

$$I_{Ht} = B_1 Y_{Dt} + B_2 C_{18-22} + B_3 S_{Pt-1} + B_4 r_t + B_5 (1 - \delta) S_{Et-1} + \epsilon_t \tag{3.3}$$

where Y_{Dt} = aggregate real disposable income,

$C_{18-22} =$ the number of children of college age as a percent of the population,

$Y_{Bt}^e =$ expected per capita earnings attributable to college,

$S_{Pt-1} =$ the parents' education,

$r_t =$ a long-term rate of interest,

$S_{Et-1} =$ higher educational capital stocks as of the end of the preceding year, measured in dollars at original cost,

$S_{Et}^* =$ desired stocks

$\delta =$ a rate of depreciation and obsolescence of educational capital,

$\theta_t =$ the short-term dynamic adjustment coefficient, serving to emphasize the partial adjustment in any one year of actual stocks toward desired levels, and

$\epsilon_t =$ a disturbance term representing the after-effects of the campus demonstrations, wars, and other disturbances.

Total investment by households in 1958 dollars, I_{Ht}, which includes foregone consumption, is also broken down into its components in the regressions of net investment in tuition and fees, and parental investment in room and board, all three first at public and then at private institutions.

II. Hypotheses and Measurement of Variables

Macroeconomic hypotheses concerning the *significance* of each variable and the *direction* of its effect on investment in Eq. 3.3 do not follow except by analogy from the signs of the corresponding partial derivatives in the microeconomic reduced-form effective demand functions discussed in Chapter 2. Nevertheless, the most interesting explanatory variables are those that have a logical causal relation to investment decisions at the microeconomic level. The hypotheses about the direction of the effect of each explanatory variable on the level of investment will be the same as the hypotheses about the sign of the corresponding effect for individual families.

Current income (Y_{Dt}) is expected to have a positive effect on all components of investment in higher education, assuming that educational capital is a normal good. The effect is expected to be significant as indicated in Chapter 2 because borrowing against expected income is inhibited by lender's risk (in the absence of collateral) and, but more especially, by borrower's risk and shortsightedness (based largely on the uncertainty of students about their capacities). Parents therefore, rather than students, bear most of the out-of-pocket costs. The income elasticity of investment demand over time is expected to be high because of the presence of a modified accelerator or capital stock adjustment effect, absorbing some transitory income, similar to that which operates with consumer durable goods.

Young adults aged 18-22 as a percent of the population (C_{18-22}) and *income expected from training* (Y_{Bt}) are both expected to have a positive and significant effect on investment by families. C_{18-26} is a variable introduced by aggregating families, rather than by looking only at families who have children of college age—as was done in Part IV of Chapter 2. Families are at all different stages in their life cycles, with each family's demand curve illustrated as *DD* in Fig. 2-1 shifting downward with age. The presence of eligible young college-age adults shifts *DD* outward since it indicates new investment opportunities due to significant expected future returns. And for all families in the U.S. taken as a whole, the high postwar fertility rates of 3.77 children per family at the peak in 1957 led to a higher proportion of the population[a] reaching college age in the 1963-72 period, and hence to larger expected returns.[b] The age range is extended to 26 to accommodate the potential for graduate study, delayed entry into college, and other forms of postsecondary training.

Apart from the number of potential students, the monetary returns that could reasonably be expected by each student from college training (Y_{Bt}^e) can be hypothesized to have an independent positive effect on the amount of investment undertaken.[5] This variable is measured as the mean annual earnings of persons who have completed four years of college or more, less the mean annual earnings of high school graduates, expressed as are all other nondemographic variables in constant (1958) dollars.[c] To obtain the *fastest* growth in output, families must invest their resources where *relative* rates of return are highest. But there are no adequate measures of private monetary rates of return over time to investment in higher education in the U.S. Those that do exist for ten-year intervals

---

[a] Strictly speaking, this should be the population of *families*, or of *households* (which includes unattached individuals), rather than the total number of persons. But definitions of households—based on place of residence—used by the census are not appropriate, because students living away from home are regarded in our analysis as part of the family. The annual estimates of population were chosen as more accurate for this purpose.

[b] Campbell and Siegel assume C_{18-24} to be significant by using it to deflate enrollment data in their time series regressions; see Campbell and Siegel (1967). The Hoenack (1968) and Massachusetts Board of Higher Education (1969) studies use the same procedure in analyzing enrollment in cross-section data, but without relating it to the returns expected by individual families.

[c] These earnings are not reduced by application of the constant .66 α coefficient often used to eliminate wages and salaries not attributable to the increment in education since it wouldn't affect the significance of the regression coefficients. The measure also uses the common assumption that ex ante returns reflect expectations based on current earnings differentials.

suggest that those rates of return have not changed significantly, at least up to 1960.[6] This is in spite of the influx of GI Bill graduates in the labor force from 1950 to 1960; the rates also reflect the continuing growth of aggregate demand for human-capital-intensive goods and services. Yet even if rates of return diminish, a positive *absolute* difference in expected income, net of investment costs, would continue to act as an inducement to invest.

Psychological stocks (S_{PT-1}) relating to higher education are hypothesized to have a significant positive effect on further investment. The effect is from the expected contribution of further education to the household production of future nonmonetary satisfactions, and from a taste-habit effect based on the family's past experience with higher education.[d] The best measure of S_{PT-1} available for all families is the number of adults aged 35 to 64 who have completed four or more years of college.

There is an interdependence in expected nonmonetary returns and in tastes between parents and their children contained in this hypothesis that can be a potentially important "pull" factor generating investment demand. It is not just that going to college is the "thing to do," or the product of unthinking habits, but instead that it is related to the best estimate the family is able to make based on the education and tastes that it has of what the future nonmonetary returns for the son or daughter will be.

The rate of interest (r_t) on new first mortgages will be used to measure the primary rate at which students and their families have been able to borrow to finance college and to adjust family consumption over time toward optimum levels (see Hirshleifer [1958] Fig. 1). Increases in the rate of interest shift investment demands in Fig. 2-1 above to the left.

The uncertainty discount (μ) used in Chapter 2 to measure differences in borrower's uncertainty and lender's risk (γ_1) will not be used in any of the aggregate regressions. There is no satisfactory measure of the extent to which risk has changed over time.[e] It could be hoped, however, that the leadership of the new Federal student loan program ("SALLY MAE") will study further the incidence of borrowers' uncertainty and means of reducing it.

Stocks of higher education capital (S_{Et-1}) can be expected to have a negative effect on gross new investment as desired (equilibrium) capital stock levels are approached. This satiation effect on additional families can be expected to operate also for the entire economy. In the longer run, however, this is weakened by the "depreciation" of the existing stock caused by retirement and death and by obsolescence.

---

[d] See the discussion of household production of consumption utilities in Eq. 2-7, and the addition of a taste-habit effect to the measurement of α_i following Eq. 2-8.

[e] Tests are being made of its effects using the microeconomic data for individual families described in Appendix D and in McMahon and Wagner (1973).

The measure of the stock of educational capital in the economy created by higher education, (S_{Et-1}) is based on the original cost to the society of the resources used in getting it produced, less losses as a result of deaths, and is valued in constant (1958) dollars. The procedures used in preparing the estimates are those pioneered by T. W. Schultz (1971, p. 129) for estimates of the total stock, including that created by primary and secondary education, and are described in detail in Appendix B.

There are two problems with these measures when it comes to using them in the basic dynamic model. The first is that the stock of higher educational capital possessed by all households in the society (1.8) S_{Et-1} includes that which is imbedded in the parents S_{Pt-1}. This part of the stock does not deter new investment in young adults via a stock adjustment effect.

The second problem, and one requiring some further consideration, is that the measure of S_{Et-1} explained in Appendix B does not include the effect that the new knowledge has in creating obsolescence of the existing stock of higher educational capital. The effect of new ideas on the obsolescence of existing scientific knowledge has been studied by S. Rosen (1970), and he suggests that it is substantial. We therefore must consider it further.

New knowledge created by research, at rate ρ (partly replacing δ), has two effects. It causes existing stocks of higher educational capital to become partially obsolete, therefore reducing the deterrent effect of S_{Et-1} on new investment. But it also creates new opportunities for investment in human capital since the stocks embodying the new knowledge can earn a greater return in the marketplace, increasing S_{Et}^*. Put another way, new knowledge does incur social costs, especially among older people who no longer find it feasible to invest, since their investment demands have shifted downward with age. It simultaneously offsets diminishing returns to new educational capital by making existing stocks obsolete. But more positively, the kinds of new opportunities for investment in educational capital that are open through institutions of higher education are largely those created by new basic research done at universities.[f] Therefore ρ can and later will be made endogenous (see the exploration of the determinants of expenditures on university-based research, Chapter 6).

The doctors not aware of modern medical techniques, the economists and politicians not aware of modern economic stabilization methods, and the people in all fields not able to use modern computers where they can be useful offer illustrations of obsolescence of educational capital and of opportunities for new investment. For purposes of measurement, and only as a first approximation, the effects of a slow steady accretion of knowledge on the difference between actual and desired stocks will be represented by

---

[f]Once the new technology is imbedded in new machine designs, much of the new learning probably occurs on-the-job. See Arrow (1962).

a first-order autoregression coefficient (ρ) extrated from the residuals. The first-order autoregressive transformation is of the form:

$$\epsilon_t = \rho\epsilon_{t-1} = u_t$$

Each equation is re-estimated many times to get new regression coefficients and new residuals until a convergence of ρ indicates that all first-order autoregression has been extracted from the residuals. The ρ's finally obtained are shown below in Tables 3-1 through 3-5. They have been estimated from data for 1930-68 or 1946-68 as indicated there, and can be used in dynamic predictions. Expenditures on research will be explored in Chapter 6 as an alternative index to increments to knowledge.

Own-price and cross-price effects $(p_{it}$ and $p_{jt})$ in Tables 3-1 through 3-6 are tried instead of being left among the disturbances because separate regressions are estimated for investment at public and at private institutions. The subscript i refers to the component of expenditure indicated in Table 3-1 (e.g. tuition and fees) at the ith type of institution (e.g. public, or private). However the dependent variable is investment (e.g. $p_{T+F}q_{Pub}$ in line (3)), not enrollment of constant quality, so the price effects on expenditure can be either positive or negative depending in part on the elasticity of these derived demands for inputs. However the signs of the own-price terms should be compared to the corresponding ones in this chapter's appendix, where enrollment is a jointly dependent variable in a simultaneous equation model.

III. Empirical Results: Investment in Higher Education

The basic investment function for household investment in higher education given by Eq. 3.3 has been estimated with all variables included as shown in Table 3-1. The net-regression coefficients and t statistics therefore offer one simultaneous test of all hypotheses discussed for the 1946-68 period.

Then in Table 3-2 all equations were re-estimated after the variables infrequently reaching the .05 level of significance and having high multicollinearity with other significant variables are dropped from all equations. These reduced equations in turn are re-estimated again for the entire 1929-68 period (omitting the war years), with the results shown in Tables 3-3 and 3-4 to check the stability of parameters and to observe the elasticities.

Investment in Higher Education by Families

Total investment by families over time at *public* institutions is shown in

Table 3-1
Investment by Families in Higher Education, 1946-68
(t-statistic in parentheses below coefficient: coefficients significant at .05 level are underlined.)

Investment (dependent variable)	Current income Y_{Dt}	Expected returns Y_{Bt}	College-age pop. C_{18-26}	Interest rates r_t	Parents tastes S_{Pt-1}	Stock of HE capital S_{Et-1}	Price at pvt. (pub.) P_{Jt}	Own-price P_{it}	(New knowledge) ρ
(1) Total investment, public	.043	.793	49,343	17.73	-.473	12.05	2.810	-8.063	-.34
	(6.54)	(1.88)	(4.68)	(.08)	(-.72)	(1.98)	(1.32)	(-2.16)	
$R^2 = .998$									
D.W. = 2.29									
(2) Total investment, private	.018	.948	-7,021	-696.33	-1.00	1.88	-8.180	9,470	-.35
	(4.83)	(4.04)	(-1.19)	(-5.70)	(-2.73)	(.55)	(-3.92)	(7.96)	
$R^2 = .997$									
D.W. = 2.34									
(3) Tuition, fees, public	.004	-.026	5,366	78.30	.003	-.531	1,494	-2.022	-.71
	(14.52)	(-1.91)	(16.88)	(6.28)	(.07)	(-1.37)	(6.06)	(-6.75)	
$R^2 = .999$									
D.W. = 2.21									

(4) *Tuition, fees, private* R² = .997 D.W. = 2.17	.003 (2.81)	.035 (.69)	4.825 (4.47)	−64.22 (−1.68)	−.106 (−.82)	.244 (.19)	−903 (−.97)	2.131 (2.67)	−.13
(5) *Room and board, public* R² = .996 D.W. = 2.32	.004 (2.05)	−.116 (−.92)	22.352 (13.2)	186.46 (3.27)	.307 (1.58)	2.55 (1.07)	88.53 (.06)	1.439 (.72)	−.03
(6) *Room and board, private* R² = .986 D.W. = 1.73	−.001 (−1.08)	.028 (.29)	7.221 (5.65)	7.71 (.18)	.251 (1.85)	−.554 (−.33)	−3,158 (−2.24)	5,216 (4.69)	.07

Table 3-2

Investment by Families in Higher Education 1946-68

(*t*-statistic in parentheses below coefficient: significant coefficients are underlined.)

Investment (dependent variable)	Current income Y_{Dt}	College-age pop. C_{18-26}	Interest rates r_t	Own-price p_{it}	Constant term	(New Knowledge) ρ
(7) Total investment, public	.045	66,829	469.8	−70.07	−20,228	−.11
	(12.95)	(10.57)	(3.29)	(−.03)	(−9.60)	
R² = .997						
D.W. = 1.84						
(8) Total investment, private	.003	19,592	−187.5	6,597	−5,370	−.04
	(1.71)	(8.95)	(−1.94)	(8.04)	(−8.61)	
R² = .995						
D.W. = 1.84						
(9) Tuition, fees, public	.004	5,800	45.84	−182	−1,858	−.29
	(16.52)	(20.86)	(2.94)	(−1.58)	(−21.32)	
R² = .997						
D.W. = 2.13						

(10) Tuition fees, private R² = .997 D.W. = 2.24	$\dfrac{.003}{(4.51)}$	$\dfrac{5,817}{(11.02)}$	$\dfrac{-55.8}{(-2.19)}$	$\dfrac{1,247}{(7.73)}$	$\dfrac{-1,643}{(-9.10)}$	−.07
(11) Room and board, public R² = .995 D.W. = 1.65	$\dfrac{.009}{(9.37)}$	$\dfrac{19,373}{(14.50)}$	$\dfrac{152.6}{(3.05)}$	$\dfrac{2,536}{(2.84)}$	$\dfrac{-7,262}{(-10.29)}$	−.07
(12) Room and board, private R² = .982 D.W. = 1.42	$\dfrac{.0003}{(-.41)}$	$\dfrac{6,458}{(7.10)}$	$\dfrac{13.5}{(.36)}$	$\dfrac{4,103}{(6.99)}$	$\dfrac{-3,866}{(-8.77)}$	.02

Table 3-1 by Eq. 1. It is determined primarily by current disposable personal income (Y_{Dt}) the number of college-age young adults as a percent of the population (C_{18-26}), and an index of the average price of tuition, fees, room, and board per student at public institutions (p_{it}). Other explanatory variables are not significant at the .05 level.

Total investment at *private* institutions, Eq. 2, is also positively influenced by current income (Y_{Dt}^e) as hypothesized. But beyond this, it has been more significantly influenced by the absolute real returns expected from a bachelor's degree (Y_{Bt}) than by changes in the size of the college-age population. This may be the result of restrictions on admission at private institutions in this period. Real interest rates (r_t) appear to significantly deter total investment in education at private but not at public institutions (see Eqs. 2, 3, and 5). The positive relation to all components of investment at *public* institutions suggests in fact that higher interest rates have not significantly deterred current out-of-pocket expenditures there, perhaps because borrowing is a less important source of student finance at public institutions.

The results for the components of total investment labeled tuition and fees, and room and board in Eq. 3 through of 6 Table 3-1 are consistent with the results just discussed for total investment, whether at public or private institutions with respect to the significance and sign of each coefficient. Foregone consumption is not analyzed separately, although it is a part of total investment in Eqs. 1 and 2.[g]

The own-price effect is negative at public institutions for total investment (Eq. 1) and for investment via expenditure on tuition and fees (Eq. 3). In Eqs. 3 and 4 the p_{it} is an index of tuition and fees *per student* first at public and then at private institutions, respectively, in constant dollars. There is a positive own-price effect at private institutions in Table 3-1, Eqs. 2, 4, and 6 and in Table 3-2, Eqs. 8, 10, 12. (There is however, a rather strange negative cross-price effect, measured as the price of the corresponding component of household investment at the other type of institution).[h] The positive own-price effect at private institutions suggests an inelastic supply curve at those institutions, so that prices rose more sharply there with growing demand. This situation is illustrated in Fig. 3-1b in the appendix to this chapter where it will be investigated further.

---

[g]Foregone consumption is measured here as manufacturing wage rates times college enrollments (adjusted for unemployment and for the length of the school year) and net of room and board costs. It constitutes about one-third of the total investment by households.

[h]Another cross-price effect from market wage rates viewed as an inducement by strong labor markets to school leaving—discussed as a factor shifting marginal cost in Chapter 2 (i.e., wS_{et-1} in Part III)—was tried by re-estimating all equations in Table 3-1. In no case was it significant, perhaps because it is correlated with Y_{Bt}^e. For a significant effect at the primary and secondary level, however, see Popp (1972, Table 5).

In Table 3-2 estimates are presented for total investment, tuition and fee, and room and board equations after the variables that have been found to be least significant overall are dropped from all equations. Those dropped include the parents' education (S_{Pt-1}), measured by using the *number* of parents who have completed a college education, and the household stock of higher education measured at original cost (S_{Et-1}). These are highly correlated with one another ($r = .994$) as expected, as well as with current income ($r = .989$ and .993, respectively). Expected increments to earnings per graduate (Y_{Bt}^e) is generally less significant in Table 3-1 than is current real disposable income (Y_{Dt}), with which it is positively and highly correlated ($r = .91$). So even though Y_{Bt}^e can be expected to represent a somewhat different effect for private institutions than C_{18-26}, because of this correlation with Y_{Dt} it is omitted for now from Table 3-2 through 3-5, leaving C_{18-26} as a partial measure of the society's expected returns.

The results in Tables 3-2 and 3-3 reveal that current income (Y_{Dt}) and college-age young adults as a percent of the population (C_{18-26}) are both consistently positive and significant both in the postwar period and in the entire 1929-68 period as hypothesized. One possible exception is the equation in each table dealing with room and board expenditures at private institutions. The parameters obtained for the 1946-68 years in Table 3-2 for those variables have signs that are quite stable and are of the same order of magnitude as those obtained for the entire 1928-68 period including the prewar years in Table 3-3. High interest rates over the entire 1929-68 period taken as a whole in Table 3-3 have not been a significant deterrent to investment in this form of human capital. But they do have in Table 3-2 a negative coefficient that suggests that they could have been a significant deterrent to investment at private institutions and to investment there through tuition and fees in the postwar years (see Eqs. 3.8 and 3.10).

The use of a first-order autoregressive transformation of the residuals (via ρ) frees the resulting regression coefficients of any bias due to autocorrelation of a first-order type found in the residuals. The interpretation of ρ in Table 3-1, however, is clouded by the use of a stock term, S_{Et-1}; which has not been adjusted for obsolescence. However, ρ is re-estimated in Tables 3-2 and 3-3 without S_{Et-1}. It is small and insignificant in the postwar period taken alone (Table 3-2), with the possible exception of Eqs. 7 and 9. Yet, for the entire 1929-68 period, as shown in Table 3-3, it is large and positive for all investment at private institutions. This could be interpreted as a proxy for δS_{Et-1} and through it a stimulus provided by the accumulation of new knowledge through research to investment in human capital formation at private colleges and universities.

Multicollinearity among all the remaining explanatory variables is low, as shown in Table 3-4, except for that between Y_{Dt} and own-price p_{it}. These two are more highly intercorrelated in the postwar years than they are for

Table 3-3
Investment by Families in Higher Education, 1929-40, 1946-68
(*t*-statistic in parentheses below coefficient: significant coefficients are underlined.)

Investment (dependent variable)	Current income Y_{Dt}	College-age pop. C_{18-26}	Interest rates r_t	Own-price p_{it}	Constant term	(New knowledge) ρ
(13) Total investment,						
public	.048	56,324	375.18	-1,510	-17,821	-.005
	(30.21)	(13.27)	(6.88)	(-1.59)	(-2.53)	
R² = .995						
D.W. = 2.02						
(14) Total investment						
private	.015	5,051	-23.3	1,602	-3,227	.67
	(6.05)	(.90)	(-.34)	(1.55)	(-3.83)	
R² = .993						
D.W. = 1.59						
(15) Tuition, fees,						
public	.004	5,694	39.33	-6.10	-1,854	-.13
	(32.30)	(17.30)	(11.25)	(-.12)	(-37.4)	
R² = .994						
D.W. = 2.05						

(16) Tuition, fees, private	$\dfrac{.003}{(4.40)}$	$\dfrac{4,802}{(3.95)}$	$\dfrac{13.35}{(.88)}$	$\dfrac{1,023}{(4.74)}$	$\dfrac{-1,903}{(-9.54)}$	.60
$R^2 = .995$					
D.W. = 1.98					
(17) Room and board, public	$\dfrac{.011}{(23.28)}$	$\dfrac{15,304}{(10.18)}$	$\dfrac{81.51}{(4.75)}$	$\dfrac{261}{(.63)}$	$\dfrac{-4,882}{(-16.18)}$	.18
$R^2 = .992$					
D.W. = 1.91					
(18) Room and board, private	$\dfrac{.002}{(2.37)}$	$\dfrac{1,567}{(.55)}$	$\dfrac{-9.48}{(-.48)}$	$\dfrac{230}{(.77)}$	$\dfrac{533}{(.96)}$	.96
$R^2 = .984$					
D.W. = 1.32					

Table 3-5

Elasticities of Investment by Families in Higher Education; 1946-68 and 1929-40, 1946-68

(Data in natural logs; t-statistic in parentheses; significant coefficients are underlined.)

Investment (dependent variable)	Current income Y_{Dt}	College-age pop. C_{18-26}	Interest rate r_t	Own-price p_{it}	(New knowledge) ρ	$R^2_{u_t}$ ($\rho=0$) SE_{u_t}	$R^2_{e_t}$ (after ρ) SE_{e_t}
For 1946-68 Only:							
(19) *Total investment,*							
public	2.91	.72	.92	-.73	.23	.966	.985
D.W. = 1.05	(6.27)	(2.20)	(2.28)	(-.85)		.112	.075
(20) *Total investment*							
private	.01	.42	-.20	2.00	.04	.950	.995
D.W. = 1.93	(.06)	(6.02)	(-1.35)	(9.17)		.086	.026
(21) *Tuition, fees,*							
public	1.76	.30	-.13	1.85	-.03	.989	.997
D.W. = 1.71	(7.00)	(2.72)	(-.50)	(5.72)		.082	.044
(22) *Tuition and fees,*							
private	.44	.07	-.26	1.82	.31	.987	.998
D.W. = 2.23	(1.88)	(.64)	(-1.44)	(9.10)		.072	.028

For The Entire 1929-68 Period:

(23) *Total investment,*									
public	$\dfrac{2.39}{(10.35)}$	.34 (1.12)	.16 (.55)	$\dfrac{.27}{(.68)}$	.45	.988	.993		
D.W. = 1.81						.108	.085		
(24) *Total investment,*									
private	$\dfrac{.98}{(4.33)}$	−.05 (−.24)	$\dfrac{-.66}{(-2.76)}$	$\dfrac{.80}{(2.73)}$	.53	.992	.994		
D.W. = 1.64						.066	.056		
(25) *Tuition and fees,*									
public	$\dfrac{1.33}{(4.10)}$	−.19 (−.48)	−.08 (−.20)	$\dfrac{2.22}{(5.16)}$	.65	.984	.990		
D.W. = 1.64						.109	.085		
(26) *Tuition, fees,*									
private	.34 (1.52)	−.28 (−1.30)	−.22 (−1.08)	$\dfrac{1.91}{(9.49)}$	.62	.979	.995		
D.W. = 1.60						.102	.048		

Table 3-4

Zero-Order Correlation Matrix: Independent Variables Used in Tables 3-2, 3-3, and 3-5

	Y_{Dt}	C_{18-26}	r_t
1946-68:			
(Table 3-2)			
C_{18-26}	−.12		
r_t	.15	−.34	
p_{it}	.96 to .98	−.33 to −.17	.20 to .27
1929-68:			
(Table 3-3)			
C_{18-26}	−.73		
r_t	−.78	.78	
p_{it}	−.19 to .87	−.47 to .48	−.40 to .72
1946-68:			
(Table 3-5)	$\ln Y_{Dt}$	$\ln C_{18-26}$	$\ln r_t$
$\ln C_{18-26}$	−.22		
$\ln r_t$	.18	−.35	
$\ln p_{it}$	.97 to .98	−.37 to −.23	.20 to .28

the entire 1929-68 period. The price index for tuition and fees per student at private institutions goes up when real disposable income goes up; these are the most highly intercorrelated at private institutions.[i]

The net income elasticities over time for real investment expenditures are shown in Table 3-5, first for the postwar period taken alone and then for the entire 1929-68 period. The three most striking facts about these results are as follows:

1. All the income elasticities of real investment expenditure are much higher at public than at private institutions.

2. These differences between income elasticities are similar in the postwar period to what they are when the prewar period is also considered.

3. The *net* income elasticity for student and family investment expenditure at public institutions is well over unity, ranging between 1.3 and 2.9!

The high income elasticities at public institutions suggest an accelerator effect on investment in human capital following increases or decreases in real income.

But as for the smaller income elasticities of investment at private institutions, this can be explained as indicated above in terms of tuition-price rises that go with and depend on the growth in income. The significant

---

[i]See the further analysis of this situation below, which is also consistent with the price effects observable in the simultaneous equation estimates appearing in the appendix to this chapter.

67

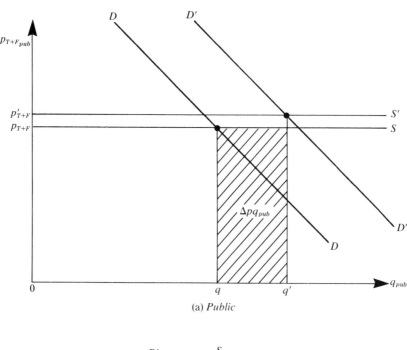

(a) *Public*

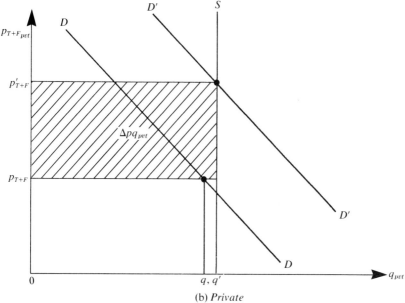

(b) *Private*

Figure 3-1   The Effect of Increased Income on Demand and on Investment

positive relation of tuition to investment at private institutions has been observed in all of the tables. This situation is illustrated above in Fig. 3-1(b), with admissions policies at private institutions restricting expansion and leading to a more inelastic supply of places at private institutions. Demand shifts outward at both types of institutions due to growth in income. Prices at private institutions are flexible upward to p'_{T+F} in Fig. 3-1(b), but less so at public institutions in Fig. 3-1(a). The result is that real investment at public institutions increases by amount Δpq_{pub}, and at private institutions by amount Δpq_{pvt}. The latter is correlated with, and in response to, tuition-price increases that would have been impossible without the induced increases in demand.[j]

It is not suggested that tuition has not risen at all at public institutions over time, only that it has risen more slowly than at private institutions. For the 1929-1968 period in fact, the index of tuition-price at public institutions rose from 69 to 130 (1958 = 100), while at private institutions it rose from 52 to 152. This is a doubling of public institution tuitions, compared to a tripling of private tuition rates.

The explanation offered in Fig. 3-1 is consistent with the higher-income elasticities of expenditure at public institutions. It also explains the lower-income elasticities in cross-section data. It is consistent with the high correlation between tuition-price at private institutions and income, and with the positive relation of this tuition-price to student and family invest-ment expenditures at private institutions.

IV. Conclusions: Sources of Fluctuations and Growth

The major sources of fluctuations and growth of investment in higher education by students and their families may be summarized as follows:

1. Y_{Dt}, real disposable income reflecting the growing, but fluctuating, ability of families to finance investment in human capital, is a highly significant determinant of investment in human capital in almost all cases, either directly or indirectly. This is consistent with the basic short-term dynamic model which has postulated borrower's risk as a constraint on borrowing, and therefore current income becomes an effective constraint on annual investment expenditure. The strength of this income effect was also consistent with the findings using two different sets of microeconomic data in Chapter 2.

---

[j]Net income elasticities of expenditure on tuition and fees were found to be positive and greater than unity in microeconomic data in Chapter 2, Part IV, as well. But the cross-section elasticities are lower than those in Table 3-5, Eqs. (21) and (25). Need-analysis procedures used in cross-section data raise the effective price to higher-income families based on their greater ability to pay.

Table 3-6
Enrollments in Higher Education: Actual 1970, and Projected 1980-2000 (in thousands)

Year	Total no. of persons[a]	Percent change	Under-graduate[a]	Percent change	Graduate students[a]	Percent change
1970	8,649		7,443		1,206	
1980	11,446	32.2	9,720	30.6	1,726	43.1
1990	10,555	− 7.8	8,882	− 8.6	1,673	− 3.1
2000	13,209	25.1	11,221	26.3	1,988	18.8

[a]These are opening fall enrollments in all cases, not adjusted to an FTE basis or assuming an unusually rapid expansion of enrollments of part-time or nondegree students.

Source: Carnegie Commission on Higher Education (1973), *Final Report.*

2. C_{18-26}, young adults as a percent of the population, are a major source of new investment opportunities and significantly related to investment, especially at public institutions. Y_{Bt}^e, reflecting variation in expected monetary returns per student, is less important, though it may be more important to investment at private institutions.

3. r_t, interest rates, appear to be more of a deterrent to investment at private than at public institutions. Student borrowing, which is positively correlated with parental borrowing (and negatively correlated with the actual parental contribution!) was seen in Table 2-2 to be more important as a source of student financing at private than at public institutions.

4. S_{Et-1}, increasing stocks of higher educational capital in the society, do not appear to be a significant deterrent to the continuing growth of investment.[k] There is the counterbalancing effect of the income-induced growth of demand for human-capital-intensive goods and services. There is also the effect of new knowledge created by research, as measured by ρ as it makes some existing higher educational capital obsolete and acts as a stimulus to additional new investment. This point will be investigated further in Chapter 6.

A crisis in the financing of higher education has been precipitated by the fact the the percent of young adults in the population (C_{18-26}) rose from 10.9 percent in 1960 to 15.8 percent in 1972, after which it flattened out. This leveling off coincided with the ending of both the war and the draft, which were artificial stimuli to enrollments, and with the 1971-72 recession, during which the growth of real disposable income ceased and unemployment grew. The combination of those factors curtailed investment and placed a strain on public and private institutions alike.

_____

[k]However S_{Pt-1} does not appear to be a strong stimulus either, in spite of its significance in cross-section data in Part IV of Chapter 2.

With the resumption of growth of real income and Federal policies to maintain full employment, this strain eases somewhat. However, inflation continues to raise costs, and the decline in fertility rates from 1955 through the present eliminates C_{18-26} as a continuing source of growth of real investment demand. But it would be a mistake to overlook the effects from the continuing growth of real income, the continuing growth of demand for human-capital-intensive services, and the effect of new knowledge in creating new investment opportunities. All of these latter are economic influences whose net effects, when combined with the effect of pessimistic demographic trends, suggest a slower but continuing growth of real investment in higher education by students and their families.

Appendix: Enrollment Demands and the Tuition Issue

The effects of the decline in fertility rates from the peak of 3.77 children per family in 1957 to 2.08 children per family in 1974, as well as the decline in the number of white males enrolled in the 1972-74 period, has led to dire concern throughout the higher education community about continuing declines in enrollment. The Carnegie Commission on Higher Education's (1973) projections in its final report,[7] for example, are as shown in Table 3-6. They indicate absolute declines in enrollment from 1980 to 1990 of 8.6 percent for undergraduate and 3.1 percent for graduate enrollment. The effects of the ending of the draft and of the 1971-72 recession to the side, the demographic factors do suggest some slackening of the rate of growth of enrollment demand.

To bring the kind of effects on investment discussed in this chapter to bear on enrollment through their effects on enrollment demand and costs separately, the simultaneous demand and supply model shown in Table 3-7 was estimated. Enrollment is not a homogeneous commodity, but by estimating the model separately for public and private institutions, the q term becomes more homogeneous, and the price effects as between those two sectors can be considered.

The model was estimated by using restricted three-stage least-squares simultaneous-equation estimating methods. The restriction is imposed on the price term on the cost side because the net tuition and fee price is the relevant price in a demand for higher education expressed by students and their families. Yet it falls short of the full cost price that must be covered by institutions, and hence must appear on the supply side since it is what is relevant to institutional economic behavior. So the full unit costs (p) are expressed as a function of the number enrolled (q) and an index of wage and salary rates paid by institutions (w_t) in real terms. Then the subsidy is subtracted from both sides of each supply equation. The state and local tax subsidy per student is p_{S+L}; the Federal nonresearch subsidy per student is p_F; and the endowment fund income, gift, and grant subsidy per student is p_G. The total of these as illustrated in Eqs. 3.4 and 3.5 is first subtracted from the left in Table 3-7, Eqs. 28 and 30, and then subtracted from the right.

$$p_{pub} - 1.00(p_{S+L} + p_F + p_G)_{pub} = p_{T+F(pub)} \qquad (3.4)$$

$$p_{pvt} - 1.00(p_{S+L} + p_F + p_G)_{pvt} = p_{T+F(pvt)} \qquad (3.5)$$

The coefficient in the regression equation of the term in parentheses in Eqs. 28 and 30 must be restricted to -1.00. Then $p_{T+F(pub)}$ and $p_{T+F(pvt)}$ are jointly dependent in each model.

The results reveal significant effects from income, young adults as a percent of the population, and the education (and tastes) of parents on enrollment demand. Increases in faculty and other wage rates (w_t) shift the

Table 3-7
Demand by Families and Supply by Institutions of Higher Education, 1946-68
Restricted Three-Stage Least Squares Estimates of Structural Enrollment Model
(t-statistic in parentheses below coefficients; significant coefficients are underlined)

Endogenous variables   Public institutions

Demand:

(27) $q_{pub} = .0124\ Y_{Dt} + 21982\ C_{18-26} + .471\ S_{Pt-1} - 6.64\ p_{T+F(pub)} - 5526.9$
      (2.66)   (4.83)   (2.48)   (−1.28)   (−11.65)

Supply:

(28) $p_{T+F(pub)} = -.0802\ q_{pub} + 8.99\ w_t - 1.00\ (p_{S+L} + p_F + p_G)_{pub} + 226.0$
      (−2.50)   (4.31)   (−4.40)   (2.43)

Endogenous variables   Private institutions

Demand:

(29) $q_{pvt} = 9697\ C_{18-26} + .605\ S_{Pt-1} - 6.59\ S_{Et-1} + .248\ p_{T+F(pvt)} - 1378.6$
      (7.13)   (4.22)   (−3.24)   (.371)   (−4.05)

Supply

(30) $p_{T+F(pvt)} = .2912\ q_{pvt} + 7.70\ w_t - 1.00\ (p_{S+L} + p_F + p_G)_{pvt} - 256.6$
      (3.05)   (8.36)   (−3.51)   (−4.93)

cost functions significantly upward at both types of institutions as would be expected.[l] The supply schedule at public institutions after adjusting for these shifts, however, would appear to be almost perfectly elastic or even show some slight economies of scale (external economies) in (3-4) taking the public sector as a whole. This is the situation that was pictured in Fig. 3-1(a). At public institutions, the price term has the normal negative relation to demand. At private institutions, the tuition-price term has a positive relation to enrollment demand, and a steeper positive slope on the supply side, as was suggested in symbolic form in Fig. 3-1(b). The positive price effect on the demand side is probably because of the closer correspondence of increases in $p_{T+F(pvt)}$ with those factors that shift demand outward, as was illustrated schematically in Fig. 3-1(b).

Finally, it is clear that maintaining low-tuition policies at public institutions makes higher education available to a larger fraction of the population as incomes rise and demands increase, Fig. 3-1(a). They are also a competitive check on tuition increases at private institutions. In a period of slack demand, however, the implications for total enrollment of large dramatic jumps in tuition, such as have been proposed by the Committee for Economic Development[m] or the full cost pricing model, are more serious.

---

[l]This source of upward shifts in real costs per student has been emphasized by the Committee for Economic Development in its policy statement on the *Management and Financing of Colleges* (1973). This has affected both public and private colleges (Table 7, and ibid., p. 10). The problem with basing policy on this is in use of enrollment, rather than increments to the stock of educational capital measured in knowledge units, as the measure of output. The relevant production function in this case has a great deal to do with improvements in educational psychology, technqiues of meeting differentiated learning problems, and increases in both the quantity and quality of learning by each student.

[m]See the 50 percent increases proposed by the CED (ibid., p. 25). The statement made above depends, of course, on the size of the compensating increases in BEOG and other grant funds, a point to be considered in the next two chapters.

4 State and Local Investment in Higher Education

Public support for higher education has come primarily from state and local governments. It was encouraged at an early date by the Morrill Land Grant Act of 1862 which provided a basis for the establishment of state institutions. Basically the role of state support is one of supplemental assistance to the production of educational capital by households. But its size and relative importance continues to be second only to the investment in human resources made by individual families themselves through their expenditures on tuition, fees, room, board, and their investment of additional foregone earnings.

The main thrust of this state and local supplemental support has been toward extending higher education to a larger proportion of the population, while broadening its scope to develop basic arts and science applied to agriculture, engineering, business, and more recently, in urban social services. Although other very important scientific and cultural developments have also been supported, a major state and local emphasis continues to be on the development of vocational skills. Even Christopher Jencks (1972), who stresses the limitations to the effectiveness of formal education, regards job competence as important to lifetime income. So there surely has been an effect in the direction of extending higher education to the middle classes, and extending the fruits of economic growth more widely in the population than might otherwise have been the case. Following the Land Grant Act whole new fields and new curricula were created in fields like agriculture. Now as postsecondary education is gradually extended to the poor through junior colleges and BEOG's, there is an important need again for the creative development of workable new curricula, this time curricula that is meaningful to the urban poor if the experiment is to be successful.

The objective of this chapter is to test for and attempt to isolate the three or four most important determinants of state and local support. The potential significance of the income inelasticity of state and local tax revenues for example, is much debated. A public expenditure theory framework is needed to screen out those variables that do not have a logical relation to public expenditure levels and to help resolve the familiar dilemmas arising out of multicollinearity. After a description of patterns of state support, a public expenditure theory framework is provided in Part I. After this, the effects on investment by states and localities that it suggests are tested in Part II. Finally, in Part III, those parameters that appear to be relatively stable are used in some condition predictions extending to 1980.

State and local investment at publically and privately controlled institutions is analyzed separately, parallel to the similar separation in Chapter 3 of investment by families. In addition to these totals, however, current expenditures at universities, four-year institutions, and two-year junior colleges are also considered separately. Universities and four-year institutions receive public support primarily from state governments, whereas public junior colleges, which have expanded so rapidly in recent years, draw a significant portion of their support from localities.

A few words of caution about two points are needed. First, the data aggregate expenditures by all state and local tax and expenditure deicision-making units, even though expenditures are disaggregated by type of educational institutions. The results, therefore, must be interpreted with care since they must be viewed as exploratory from the point of view of testing hypotheses about influences on the behavior of individual state government decision-making units. Second, predictive results should not be confused with those obtained from a normative model. One important aspect of cost-benefit models is the implicit assumption of continuation of *existing tax rates* in order to consider what changes in rates would be necessary to meet normative objectives. The objective here, however, will be to project expenditures *based on past* expenditure *propensities*, which reflect in part the propensities to change tax rates. This type of predictive public expenditure theory is useful to the formulation of policy within educational insitutions and state boards of higher education. Federal aid policies to be effective also need to be able to predict state and local patterns in the absence of newly contemplated Federal action.

I. Predictive Public Expenditure Theory

A brief look at trends in private and public support for higher education may help to put the analysis of influences on the level of state and local support that follows in perspective.

Household, State and Local, and Federal Investment

The third column in Table 4-1 indicates that state and local investment in higher education at public institutions is about one-third the total investment made at these institutions by families. It is about equal to the out-of-pocket room and board expenditures there by families. These patterns were roughly the same in 1946 and in 1929. When expenditure at private institutions is included, total state and local investment is about one-fourth of total investment in educational capital by households.

Table 4-1
Family, State and Local, and Federal Support of Higher Education, Selected Years

Sources of total investment in educational capital	(1) 1929 millions current $	(2) 1946 millions current $	(3) 1968 millions current $	(4) Real average annual growth rate, 1946-68 (in constant dollars)[a]
Public Institutions				
1. *Family*	352.3	1,210.5	16,258.4	9.9%
2. Tuition and fees	27.3	69.0	1,399.0	12.0%
3. Room and board	153.5	425.1	4,323.7	8.5%
4. Excess foregone earnings (beyond room and board)	171.5	716.4	10,535.7	10.4%
5. *State and local*	125.9	307.2	5,421.1	11.3%
6. *Federal aid* (to education)	14.7	135.9	552.1	4.1%
7. *Gifts and endowment income*	5.9	22.0	270.3	9.5%
Private institutions				
8. *Family*	456.3	1,319.2	8,193.8	6.1%
9. Tuition and fees	110.0	190.4	2,431.0	9.7%
10. Room and board	210.7	503.6	1,913.5	3.8%
11. Excess foregone earnings	135.6	625.2	3,849.3	6.1%
12. *State and local*	7.3	16.3	130.3	7.3%
13. *Federal aid* (to education)	1.1	133.7	204.5	−.3%
14. *Gifts and endowment income*	69.6	150.7	1,061.5	6.7%

Sources: Lines 2, 5-7, 9, 12-14, U.S. Office of Education, *Financial Statistics for Institutions of Higher Education,* (1968) Table 3, pp. 12-13, and corresponding tables in earlier *Biennial Surveys;* lines 3 and 10 multiply enrollment from the same source by average room and board charges at public and at private institutions from West, Farrell, and Blakeslee (1964) and National Center for Educational Statistics (1970). Lines 4 and 11 multiply these enrollments by the product of average hourly earnings in manufacturing excluding overtime, the average weekly hours of work (both from the *Statistical Abstract*), 25 weeks of work foregone by the student, and the employment rate in the civilian labor force from the Council of Economic Advisors (1974).

[a] 1946 and 1968 figures are first deflated by the Personal Consumption Expenditures deflator, 1958 = 100.

At private institutions, however, state and local government support is replaced by gift and endowment income, which provides a similar subsidy to families with children in college. But the much lower postwar annual growth rate of gift and endowment income has diminished its relative size to only about 20 percent of the state and local aid provided to public institutions. This has operated to force the private institutions toward the smaller, higher family income segment of the college market. As the Federal Basic Economic Opportunity Grants providing aid to families based on need are more completely funded, private institutions are at a less serious competitive disadvantage in attracting significant numbers of students from lower-income families.

State and local investment has been about ten times the size of Federal investment in human capital formation at public institutions. Federal investment in higher education at private institutions has been small, but relatively more important than that of the states. (See Appendix C for the development of data separating Federal aid to education at higher educational institutions from contract research. The allocation of joint costs is somewhat arbitrary, of necessity, but it is consistent over time.) It is revealing to see how slowly Federal support of education at both public and private institutions has grown—more slowly than any other source of support at either place. To the extent that Federal support increases following the Education Amendments and appropriations for the new grants by the Congress it will affect this growth rate, but it nevertheless will still leave Federal support smaller than that from states and localities.

Overall, and in summary, support by families through tuition and fees, and support by state and local governments, in that order may be seen in Table 4-1 to have grown more rapidly in real terms than any other sources of support at either public or private institutions in the postwar years. Total state and local support, as indicated by the $5,551 million total in Table 4-1, goes overwhelmingly to the publicly controlled institutions. It is second in size only to the support coming directly from families, and is many times Federal aid. The following sections seek to explain key influences determining the level of this important state and local supplementary support.

Public Preferences and the State's Budget Constraint

The model to be developed briefly in this section seeks to capture the essence, but not all of the detail, of the expenditure level determination process, and to find stable relations in the political-economic decision process. In essence the state will be regarded as a quasi-independent economic decision-making unit, influenced by the tastes of the electorate (and by members of the electorate who are organized into pressure groups) as well as by autonomous elements unique to the tastes of key public officials. These tastes are all assumed to be represented by a "democratic state preference function," which in turn is constrained by the total economic resources available to the state and the tax handles available at any given time. The resulting solution is a joint solution of tax and expenditure sides and leads to testable hypotheses.

The philosophy underlying the joint solution goes back at least to the Magna Carta and to the evolution of legislative control over expenditure categories that evolved throughout the Gladstone ministry. The relation of expenditure to the underlying resource base has been discussed by Musgrave (1969, chap. 3), Buchanan (1968), Burkhead and Miner (1972) and by a rich public expenditure theory literature extending backward through history (e.g., Musgrave and Peacock (1958)). The continuing evolution of budgeting and tests of specific public expenditure models have been considered by Schultze (1968), Gramlick (1969), McMahon (1971), and others cited there.

State Preferences. A "democratic state preference function" will be assumed to exist that has the character of a well-ordered utility function possessed by representative key elected officials such as the governor and/or key legislators. They act in making decisions on expenditure levels as agents for the electorate, or groups within the electorate, while simultaneously acting with a degree of autonomy.

This social preference function which in one sense is a descendent of the "social indifference curves" discussed within a welfare context by Samuelson (1956) may be assumed to reflect the perceptions by the public official of the tastes of the electorate, since if it seriously fails to do so the elected official is likely to being replaced at election time. In this event there would be a discrete shift in the ruling democratic state preference function. The tastes of the electorate for particular public goods (and separately the disutility of particular taxes) are revealed but imperfectly to the public official through the mail, opinion polls, lobbyists, past experience with voting patterns, demonstrations, newspaper editorials, hearing testimony, and other forms of communication.

For these communications from citizens to be effective it is an important and necessary condition that there be viable alternative candidates available to the electorate at regularly scheduled elections. In the case of expenditures on higher education, candidates for office would normally tend to match current policies with those in power when there is widespread agreement in the electorate, and to develop alternative expenditure policies if there is not. If it is assumed that the state governments are financed by use of a predetermined set of tax handles (such as the sales tax), the net incidence of the expected benefits and tax costs of an increment to expenditures on higher education would be known in an approximate way by legislators and key policy makers concerned with levels of funding. Although it is unlikely to be a purely economic calculation, some groups in the electorate normally can be expected to favor more and some less expenditure on higher education. Therefore a realistic opportunity exists for the opposition if the discrepancy between current expenditures and the preferences of most of the electorate becomes large. They can develop the issue and enhance their chance of election.

This model of public expenditure decisions made by governmental units under conditions of representative democracy is more appropriate for analysis of the determinants of expenditure on higher education than are the two extreme polar cases of authoritarian dictatorship or of individualistic pure voting, about which so much has been said in the public expenditure theory literature. Authoritarian state preference functions maintained with the aid of military power used to control the electoral process may be common in other parts of the world, but they are not accurate prototypes of U.S. state or Federal governments or of most other governments in the Western democracies. Similarly, individualized voting "for and against" earmarked tax-expenditure packages is an idealized model advanced by Buchanan (1968) and others which deals with a type of direct voting by citizens on expenditure levels. This does not offer an empirically relevant model of the way expenditures on higher education are determined. Citizens instead vote for candidates, candidates who, after election and in anticipation of future elections, decide on appropriations and taxes separately, by operating under general-fund budgeting procedures.

Specific objectives for public investment in higher education can best be reconciled within the context of broader social goals (and later, of economic constraints) as they apply to that program. Therefore the democratic state preference function is first expressed in the most general, and simplest possible, terms as a means toward identifying the problem before relating this modified welfare function to subsidiary objectives:

$$W_T = W(\sum_{k=1}^{m} g_{kt} Y_{kt}) \qquad t = T, \ldots, L \qquad (4.1)$$

where Y_{kt} = real personal income of the kth family before taxes,

g_{kt} = weights attached to the income of the kth family (or kth income class in the income distribution),

T = the current period, and

L = the end of the elected official's planning horizon (so there are implicit rates of discount attaching to real incomes expected in future periods).

The responsible elected official is free to attach whatever weights he chooses to the real income and hence to the utility of the k individual families or income clases. A solution in welfare theory for the bliss point, of course, would require that these weights be assigned by an independent and omniscient ethical observer. But in practical political economy is it is reasonable to assume that the weights are sufficient to retain the support of those groups on which the public official primarily depends for reelection.

But in addition to this, it is reasonable to assume that weights assigned by both parties will be in the direction of favoring a more egalitarian income distribution than that which would appear if every *dollar of income* were given equal weight. For although votes are not distributed on a strictly one-man-one-vote basis, they are distributed more equally than are income dollars. It is not suggested that final public expenditure outcomes are egalitarian, only that they are *more* egalitarian than if there were only dollar votes.

This source of a bipartisan incentive to extend the benefits of post-secondary education farther down in the income distribution than it would otherwise be extended has had an important impact on the size and character of public support. The Land Grant Act and related low tuition at public institutions have led to the extension of postsecondary education to the sons of middle-income farmers and to the urban middle class. The support of junior colleges lowers effective room, board, and transportation costs and extends it further. And the provisions of the Education Amendments of 1972 which lower the cost of student loans and of tuition to families based on financial need operate in the same direction.

Before maximizing the function given by (4.1) subject to the society's total resource constraint, then minimizing the disutility given by (4.1) subject to tax handle constraints to obtain a logical specification of potential determinants of expenditure on higher education, a comment is needed about the relation of the general objectives given by (4.1) to the specific objectives of higher education. The Rivlin Report (1969) sets out objectives of Federal support typical of those often stated by leaders in higher education. They are (ibid, pp. 3-4):

1. Increasing the number and proportion of educated people,
2. Increasing equality of opportunity for higher education,
3. Improving the quality of higher education,
4. Preserving diversity in higher education and advancing autonomy and academic freedom,
5. Strengthening graduate education and institutional research and the public service capabilities of higher educational institutions, and
6. Encouraging the efficient use of resources in higher education.

Objectives 1-5 can be regarded as means to the attainment of the more ultimate end of larger and more more equitably distributed current and future real family income that is given by (4.1), broadly interpreted to include nonmonetary real income. They are stated as unconstrained goals, (as in Eq. 4.1), whereas objective 6 reasonably suggests that the maximum real return from higher education arising from pursuit of 1-5 is to be attained subject to cost minimizing constraints.

Resource and Tax-Handle Constraints. In the first stage of the public expenditure decision process, when appropriations for higher education are being considered, current and expected future utilities arising from higher education, other public goods, and private goods as given by the total "welfare" function (4.1) are constrained by the total resources available to the society. This total resource constraint is

$$Y_T + \sum_{t=T+1}^{L} \frac{Y_t^e}{(1 + r)^{t-T}}$$

$$= \sum_{t=T}^{L} [p_{S+Lt}q_t + (p_{T+F} + p_G + p_F)_t q_t + \sum_{i=1}^{n} p_{it}q_{it}] \qquad (4.2)$$

It would be expanded to include the value of leisure time, but this aspect has been developed in Chapter 2, and will not be repeated here. The terms are defined as follows:

Y_T = aggregate real personal income in period T, before taxes,

Y_t^e = expected future aggregate real personal income, before taxes,

q_t = enrollment in higher educational institutions,

p_{S+Lt} = state and local subsidy per student (a shadow price to the state),

$(p_{T+F} + p_G + p_F)_t$ = tuition and fee, gift and endowment income, and average Federal subsidy per student, taken here as predetermined,

q_{it} = the quantity, and

p_{it} = the price (or shadow price) of all other public ($i=1$, . . ., h) and private ($i=h+1$, . . ., n) goods.

This says that current and expected future personal income up to the end of the state's planning horizon must equal all public and private expenditure in current and future periods. Initial assets are assumed equal to the discounted present value of terminal assets at the end of the planning horizon and subtracted from both sides to simplify the constraint.

Tax handles and limits on borrowing constrain further the resources available to the state government for higher education. Borrowing by the state and its localities against future income, Y_t^e above, is limited by most state constitutions. They now regard net new investment in human capital formation in legal terms as current expenditure rather than as part of the state's capital budget. The tax-handle and borrowing constraint is

$$p_{S+Lt}q_t + \sum_{i=1}^{h} p_{it}q_{it} = t_1 \sum_{i=h+1}^{n} p_{it}q_{it} + t_2 Y_t + F_t + B_t + R_t \qquad (4.3)$$

where $p_{S+Lt}q_t$ = state (and local) expenditure for post secondary education (subsidy per student times enrollment),

$p_{it}q_{it}$ = all other state (and local) expenditures (where $i = 1, \ldots h$),

t_1 = a sales tax rate, a parameter, but only in the short run,

t_2 = an average income tax rate, a parameter, but only in the short run,

F_t = federal grants-in-aid to the state government, including Federal grants to higher educational institutions,

B_t = the effective state (and local) borrowing limit, a pre-determined parameter, and

R_t = all other revenue.

This says that total expenditure by the state government and its localities must equal total tax revenue plus Federal grants-in-aid plus borrowing. When Federal aid is accompanied by formulas or mandates of various types, it has additional net incentive effects on particular expenditures that augment the dollar-for-dollar revenue replacement effect on the tax side shown above.

State and Local Investment-Demand. The effective demand by the state for investment in higher education now can be derived.

To simplify the derivation, the production functions that use higher education to produce future income and utility flows in the preference function similar to those used in Chapter 2 can be used[a] to re-write the state preference function in terms of quantities of inputs as follows:

$$W_T = W(q_{it}, \alpha_{it}, g_{kt}) \qquad t = T, \ldots, L; \quad i = 1, \ldots, m \qquad (4.4)$$

The q's refer to quantities of formal higher education and of other public and private goods. The α's are taste parameters, dependent on the stock of education and on past consumption experiences. (The educational stocks contribute to the efficiency with which nonmonetary satisfactions are produced.) The g's are the implicit income-distribution-type weights discussed above that are assigned by elected public officials to families in each real income quintile.

Investment demand is derived by maximizing the state preference function (4.4) subject to the resource and tax-handle constraints (4.2) and (4.3). That is, differentiating (4.4) with respect to q_{it} subject to (4.2) and (4.3), and remembering that enrollment demand is a derived demand, derived from the demand for educational capital, the eventual result is a set of first-order conditions that may be solved for total enrollment demand for the current period. This total society-wide demand is illustrated as DD in

---

[a]See the use of education and time in the production of utility flows within households in the discussion surrounding Eqs. 2-6 through 2-9 and 2-11 through 2-12.

Figure 4-1. Given the full cost price as given by the average costs, and given the Federal aid (p_F), endowment fund subsidy (p_G), and household per-student contribution (p_{T+F}), the state and local investment $p_{S+L} q_{pub\ T}$ necessary to accomplish the objective can be determined.

This investment is illustrated by the shaded area in Fig. 4-1. It implies a simultaneous solution for the most pertinent tax rate (e.g., t_1) under assumptions that other revenues in the tax function (4.3) have been predetermined[b], and that expenditures on higher education and tax policy are decided on under general-fund budgeting procedures. It is the distance between the two demand curves that is the state effective demand for higher education and for more equal educational opportunity.

Short-Term Dynamic Stock Adjustment Effects. Fig. 4-1 illustrates the derived demand for formal education used as an input in the production of higher educational capital (S_{Et}). The resulting gross additions to society's depreciated stocks of higher educational capital are not likely to attain their equilibrium (in the sense of political optimum) levels immediately following changes in income, the numbers of young adults as one measure of expected returns, or the other determinants of state decisions appearing above. Slow production and slow adjustment of large stocks to new stock equilibrium levels are likely.

The first part of Eq. 4.5 brings out the fact that enrollment demand is a derived demand. It makes the implicit production function for the production of educational capital by households explicit by assuming for this purpose that it is of Cobb-Douglas form. The part of Eq. 4.5 that is in parentheses allows for the possibility of a partial adjustment of society's total stocks in any one year.

$$q_{pub} = \frac{\beta_2}{\beta_1 + \beta_2} \frac{1}{p_{S+Lt}^\gamma} \{\theta'_{S+L}[S^*_{Et} - (1-\delta)S_{Et-1}]\} \qquad t = T \qquad (4.5)$$

This is rearranged to obtain the state and local investment demand function shown as Eq. 4.6 below. First, multiply 4.5 on both sides by p_{S+L}; second introduce the short term budget constraint (and limits on state and local borrowing) that were discussed in Chapter 2 and that limit investment to a partial adjustment to desired levels but in equilibrium with current

---

[b]Joseph A. Pechman's (1972) "Distribution of Federal and State Income Taxes by Income Class" offers further evidence on the tax side of public sector egalitarian tendencies that also could be interpreted as deriving from the g_k income-class weights in our democratic state preference function (4.4). To derive tax decisions, disutility from the preference function (4.4) would be minimized by trying alternative tax packages using the tax definition (4.3) at given expenditure levels.

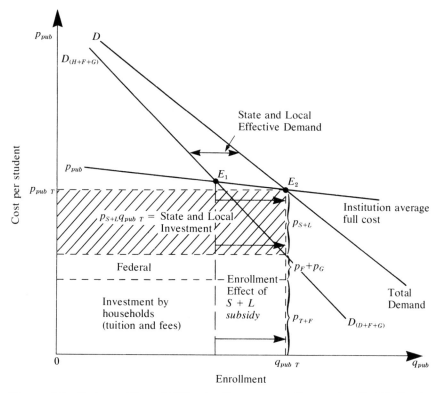

Figure 4-1 State and Local Effective Investment-Demand at Public Institutions: Derived Demands For Formal Postsecondary Education Used in the Production of Stocks of Human Capital.

income flows,[c] and then replace S_{Et}^*. This leads to the investment demand function to be estimated empirically:

$$I_{S+Lt} = p_{S+L}q_{pub} = f[Y_t, Y_{Bt}^e, C_t, g_{kt}, p_{S+Lt}, \rho, (\delta - 1)S_{Et-1}] \quad (4.6)$$

The effect of increases in real current personal income before taxes (Y_t), used as a measure of the state's total resource base, on state (and local) investment is expected to be positive assuming that higher education is a normal good. Under similar conditions, the sign of the coefficient of the

---

[c] See Eqs 2.6 through 2.9 and 2.12 through 2.21 for further discussion of the production of educational capital and of short-term limits on the adjustment toward S_{Et}. "Equilibrium" is interpreted there in ways appropriate to that context.

expected monetary return per student (Y_{Bt}) is also expected to be positive, assuming that the state preference function reflects an expectation that higher education will contribute positively to the economic growth of the state. C_t, a measure of the number of young adults as a percent of the population, is the other dimension of potential expected returns shown separately in Eq. 4.6.[d] Larger percentages of young adults mean more children in the eligible age-range whose parents want the state to assist in opening up educational opportunities. This shifts total state and local demand in Fig. 4-1 outward, which at any given-full-cost price will increase state and local expenditure. The Gini coefficient of income inequality (g_{kt}) viewed as a measure of the gap from desired greater equality derives from a taste parameter in the democratic state preference function that comes directly into the derived investment demand equation (Basman (1956)). The egalitarian influences on public expenditure is measured only imperfectly by this Gini coefficient. But the sign of its coefficient could be expected to be positive if larger state effort to reduce inequality is significantly stimulated by larger inequality.

A larger cost to the state per student (p_{S+L}) can be expected to restrict state *enrollment* demand as suggested by the term $1/p_{S+L}^{\gamma}$ in (4.5), (with $\gamma \geq 0$ by the Slutsky theorem). Nevertheless, how total *expenditure* is affected depends upon the elasticity of both state and private investment-demand. If $\gamma < 1$, which is likely, then the effect of increases in unit cost to the state on state investment expenditure can be expected to be positive.

A stimulus to net *new* investment in postsecondary educational capital can be expected from the new investment opportunities created by new knowledge and new basic research. Expected returns from vintages of human capital embodying new developments are hypothesized later to be shifted in proportion to the trend in the real resources devoted to basic research. If the existence of such a stimulus to investment leaves a positive trend in the residuals, then ρ could be expected to be large enough to be significant and positive.

Finally, larger existing stocks of higher educational capital (S_{Et-1}) can be expected to act as a deterrent to further state and local investment in higher education, but only after other influences on gross investment have been fully taken into account. The obsolescence rate, for example, stimulates replacement investment (δS_{Et-1}), and if not captured by ρ, weakens the deterrent effect of existing stocks.[e] S. Rosen (1971) suggests that obsolescence rates of scientific knowledge are high (p. 28) but less than unity. If $-(1 - \delta) < 1$, it is a reasonable hypothesis that large existing stocks,

---

[d] Parents and state officials are assumed to respond to the expectation that the young adults will be, or could be, graduating from high school.

[e] Most "depreciation" arises as a result of retirement and death, which the measurement of S_{Et-1} has already attempted to take into account. See Appendix B.

certeris paribus, act to deter further state and local investment in higher education.

II. Regression Results for Investment by State and Local Governments

The model developed above for a single state government is applied by analogy to the analysis of aggregate investment by all state governments, as shown in Table 4-2. Each investment function contains exploratory tests of all hypotheses discussed above. The tests are for investment in human resources by states at all public and at all private institutions (in Eqs. 4 and 8), at public and private universities (in Eqs. 1 and 5), at public and private four-year colleges (in Eqs. 2 and 6), and for both state and local investment at two-year junior colleges (in Eqs. 3 and 7).

The results for 1946-68 are compared in Table 4-3 to results for 1929-68 to appraise the stability of the parameters. The latter, then, are used in Table 4-4 for further tests and conditional predictions to 1980. Appendix A gives the sources of data for all variables.

Major Determinants of State and Local Investment in Higher Education

When the major effects suggested by the preceding analytical framework are tried simultaneously in Table 4-2, all variables that are significant at or near the .05 level in all equations have signs consistent with the hypotheses. The attempt made through multivariate analysis to hold the other variables constant statistically at their means provides a test that is more rigorous than simpler one- or two-variable analyses of the effect of each variable on each type of investment. The degree of consistency with the hypotheses is remarkable and encouraging.

One consistently important determinant of state and local real current expenditure on postsecondary education is current real personal income (Y_t). Its effect is always positive and significant at the .05 level. The marginal propensity to invest is 0.6 percent at public institutions, but considerably less than that at private institutions.

A second important determinant is the size of the potential college population (C_t). This is not too surprising since the fact that parents want educational opportunities for their children is frequently taken explicitly into account in state planning. The variable C_t is defined in this chapter, assuming that there is some advance state planning, as the proportion of the population age 16-22 in the four-year college equations, and age 16-20 in the two-year junior college equations. The highly significant and positive coefficients are consistent with the hypothesis in all cases except for junior colleges. There the strongest effect of the numbers of young adults on expenditure levels may have come only in the more recent years.

Table 4-2
Investment by State and Local Governments in Higher Education, 1946-68
(*t*-statistic in parentheses below coefficient; significant coefficients are underlined.)

Investment (Dependent variable)	Pretax personal income Y_t	College age pop.[a] C_t	Inequality (Gini coefficient) g_{kt}	Actual growth rate of GNP[b] g	Own (shadow) price p_{S+L}	Stock of HE capital[k] S_{ET-1}	Constant term	ρ	R^2 (after ρ) SE_ϵ
(1) *Public universities* ($R_u^2 = .952$, $SE_u = 115$) D.W. = 1.93	.0029 (3.79)	13,706. (5.52)	1,346 (1.37)	-20.2 (-2.79)	.619 (3.10)	.036 (1.57)	-3,627. (-5.65)	.53	.997 30.4
(2) *Public 4-yr colleges* ($R_u^2 = .919$, $SE_u = 75.5$) D.W. = 1.80	.0018 (2.69)	13,396. (7.00)	1,632 (1.77)	-10.1 (-1.86)	1.19 (5.63)	-.015 (-.92)	-2,492. (-5.36)	.30	.989 27.4
(3) *Public 2-yr colleges* ($R_u^2 = .911$, $SE_u = 50.9$) D.W. = 1.22	.0026 (2.92)	7,849. (2.08)	160. (.12)	-.536 (-.07)	.741 (2.08)	-.054 (-2.19)	-880. (-1.43)	.43	.947 39.2
(4) *Public total* ($R_u^2 = .927$, $SE_u = 259$) D.W. = 2.02	.0060 (3.23)	34,947. (6.84)	4,407. (1.85)	-44.2 (-2.59)	2.35 (3.79)	.033 (.62)	-9,241. (-6.36)	.46	.993 75.6

(5) *Private universities* ($R^2_u=.960$, $SE_u=3.31$) D.W. = 2.25	$\underline{.0001}$ (3.47)	$\underline{278.}$ (5.57)	$\underline{150.}$ (3.58)	.191 (.65)	$\underline{.620}$ (16.78)	$\underline{-.0016}$ (−2.06)	$\underline{-115.}$ (−5.28)	.22	.994 1.32
(6) *Private 4-yr colleges* ($R^2_u=.984$, $SE=.820$) D.W. = 1.44	$\underline{.00003}$ (3.06)	$\underline{128.}$ (3.73)	13.2 (.92)	.018 (.19)	$\underline{.947}$ (8.82)	$\underline{-.0006}$ (−2.13)	$\underline{-20.9}$ (−2.76)	.48	.996 .427
(7) *Private 2-yr colleges* ($R^2_u=.889$, $SE_u=117$) D.W. = 2.02	$\underline{.000009}$ (3.68)	7.55 (.81)	4.80 (1.59)	.023 (1.77)	$\underline{.047}$ (7.44)	$\underline{-.0002}$ (−3.35)	-2.60 (−1.57)	.11	.934 .091
(8) *Private total* ($R^2_u=.971$, $SE_u=3.87$) D.W. = 1.96	$\underline{.0001}$ (2.82)	$\underline{430.}$ (5.22)	$\underline{160.}$ (2.13)	.152 (.28)	$\underline{1.46}$ (7.78)	-.0008 (−.58)	$\underline{-168.}$ (−4.35)	.99	.989 2.40

[a]Percent of population age 16-26 for universities, 16-22 for 4-yr colleges, and 16-20 for 2-yr colleges respectively.

[b]Five-year moving average rate of growth of real GNP.

[c]Number of persons aged 25 and over with one or more years of college completed.

Table 4-3
Investment by State and Local Governments in Higher Education, 1929-68 and 1946-68
(t-statistic in parentheses below coefficient; $t \geq 1.70$ for 10 percent level of significance or better.)

Investment 1929-68	Pretax personal income Y_t	College-age pop. C_{16-26}	Inequality (Gini coefficient) g_{kt}	Own (shadow) price p_{S+L}	Stock of HE capital[a] S_{Et-1}	Constant term	ρ	R^2_e (after ρ) SE_e
(9) *Public total*								
$R^2_u = .988$, $SE_u = 121$	.0044	20,578.	2,277.	1.03	.009	–6,342.	.69	.994
	(3.09)	(7.98)	(1.01)	(1.84)	(4.05)	(–6.28)		89.6
(10) *Private total*								
$R^2_u = .989$, $SE_u = 2.74$	.0001	155.9	–113.	1.54	–.000002	–21.78	.40	.992
	(2.51)	(2.90)	(–2.49)	(12.65)	(–.03)	(–.86)		2.44
Investment 1946-68								
(11) *Public total*								
$R^2_u = .986$, $SE_u = 133$	.0051	30,572.	6,917.	1.67	.007	–9,876.	.29	.994
	(1.91)	(7.83)	(2.34)	(2.97)	(1.94)	(–6.37)		90.8
(12) *Private total*								
$R^2_u = .983$, $SE_u = 3.38$	.0001	221.5	–81.9	1.54	–.000003	–42.61	.37	.987
	(1.16)	(1.72)	(–.85)	(8.92)	(–.02)	(.83)		2.94

[a]Value of the depreciated stocks, at original cost, in constant 1958 dollars from Table B-4.

Expected real future income added by higher education per young adult (Y_{Bt}^e), did not prove significant when introduced. The measurement of expectations, however, had to be based in the usual way on current and past income differentials. But alternatively, a low *actual* growth rate (g) could be expected to stimulate state investment efforts. The more siginificant negative coefficients for investment at public universities and four-year colleges in column g of Table 4-2 are consistent with this hypothesis.

The inequality coefficient (g_k) is positively associated with state investment at public colleges and universities and at private universities. This is consistent with the hypothesis that the public sector seeks a correction through public expenditure to the existing income distribution. But the effect as measured here is not a strong one.

The effective price per student in real terms paid by the state and local government (p_{S+L}) to support larger enrollments is significantly and positively associated with larger state and local investment expenditure (not enrollment). This may be partly due to higher unit costs, partly to improving quality, and partly to new enrollment encouraged by the subsidy.

The stock of human capital in the society formed through higher education (S_{Et-1}^E), when it is significant, has a negative coefficient consistent with the hypothesis that existing stocks are a short-term deterrent to further state and local investment. This stock is measured in Table 4-2 as the number of persons aged 25 and older who have completed more than one year college education. The short-term dynamic stock adjustment effect revealed here is more consistent with the stock adjustment hypothesis when the stock is measured in this way than it is when the stock is measured in value terms (in Table 4-3).

Finally, the positive autoregression coefficient (ρ) obtained for a first-order autoregressive transformation of the residuals is consistent with the hypothesis that growing resources devoted to basic research creates new knowledge and new opportunities for investment in human resources by state and local governments, as well as needs for additional replacement investment. The ρ coefficients are large enough to be significant, in contrast to the ρ coefficients found in the equations dealing with investment by households in Chapter 3. The coefficients were obtained using a Cochrane-Orcutt iterative technique, re-estimating all the coefficients in each equation at each step in the iteration to obtain new residuals and a new ρ This procedure was repeated until two successive estimates of ρ differed by less than .001, or until the number of iterations reached 20, in which case the lack of convergence has been indicated in the tables. If the effects of the creation of new knowledge are reflected more heavily in investment by state and local governments than in investment by households, it may be that the effects are largest on graduate education, which is financed primarily by endowment income and by Federal, state, and local governments.

Stability of the Parameters. Some indication of the stability of these parameters over longer periods of time may be obtained by comparing the parameters estimated for the longer 1929-68 period to those estimated for the shorter but more recent 1946-68 postwar period.

For the purpose of making these comparisons in Table 4-3, the desired growth effect (g) which was significant fewer times than any other variable in Table 4-2 was dropped. It is unlikely that stabilization or growth objectives were understood and incorporated explicitly in any major public state policy prior to 1946. Also the stock of higher educational capital was measured in value terms at original cost as described in detail in Appendix B. Use of this measure appears to weaken the stock adjustment effect, suggesting that later additions to the stock of human capital may not have any more weight than earlier additions in the adjustment process.

Comparing the parameters estimated for the longer 1929-68 period to the corresponding parameters postwar shown in the last two equations in Table 4-3, the signs in every case are identical. The coefficients are also of the same order of magnitude for each variable when the prewar period is included in the regressions. In general when the prewar years are included, the R^2 remain about the same, the intercepts are a little closer to the origin, and the net regression coefficients are a bit smaller. There appears to be as much (or more) stability in these coefficients as is generally observed in multivariate economic models of household or business decisions.

III. Conditional Predictions of Investment to 1980

Predictions of state and local expenditures on higher education are shown in Table 4-4. The predictions of real investment have been made using the sources of fluctuations and growth isolated by the regression equations in Table 4-3. Whether made using the 1946-68 or 1929-68 equations, the predictions of state and local investment at public and private institutions (shown in the first four columns of Table 4-4) are remarkably similar.

Moreover, the predictions are conditional on the policies implied by the values assigned to the policy variables, p_{S+L}, for the years up to 1980 shown in Table 4-5. Enrollment as well as the price terms are all endogenous in a model which specifies the cost side developed in the appendix to this chapter. In Table 4-5, p_{S+L} (as well as p_{T+F} and p_F) has been based on the actual data through 1968, and then on projections of "Student Charges by Institutions of Higher Education" made by George Lind in *Projections of Educational Statistics to 1980-81* (1971, p. 101-8).

State and local investment in postsecondary education includes state and local government appropriations included in the current fund revenues

Table 4-4
Conditional Predictions of Investment by State and Local Governments in Higher Education to 1980
(in millions of dollars, using regression equations from Table 4-3)

Academic year (beginning)	Constant (1958) dollars				Current dollars			
	Public institutions using (11) 1946-68	Private institutions using (12) 1946-68	Public institutions using (9) 1929-68	Private institutions using (10) 1929-68	Price index (P.C.E. deflator)	Predicted all institutions (9 + 10) in cur. $	Actual all institutions	Percent error (predicted from actual)
1969	5,096	119	5,103	118	1.235	6,448	6,722	−4.08% [a]
1970	5,355	126	5,327	125	1.290	7,033	[a]	
1971	5,687	132	5,645	130	1.360	7,854	[b]	
1972	6,209	142	6,127	140	1.340	8,711		
1973	6,782	151	6,691	149	1.440	9,850		
1974	7,200	158	7,154	156	1.480	10,819		
1975	7,707	167	7,704	164	1.510	11,881		
1976	8,193	175	8,228	172	1.540	12,936		
1977	8,715	183	8,789	181	1.581	14,182		
1978	9,200	191	9,320	189	1.619	15,395		
1979	9,686	199	9,869	197	1.661	16,720		

[a]The lag is substantial in the assembling and preparation of educational statistics. The data shown for the 1969-70 academic year were obtained prior to their publication in 1974.

[b]The spring 1970 student demonstrations may have had a temporary effect on 1970-71 and 1971-72 appropriations. See, however, the close correspondence to 1970 and 1971 appropriations as discussed below in the next section.

Table 4-5
Values Used for Policy Variables, in Conditional Predictions

| Year | State and Local Aid Per Student | |
	$p_{S+Lpublic}$	$p_{S+Lprivate}$
1969	886.46	56.80
1970	903.93	59.75
1971	921.40	62.69
1972	938.87	65.64
1973	956.34	68.58
1974	973.80	71.53
1975	991.27	74.47
1976	1008.74	77.42
1977	1026.21	80.36
1978	1043.68	83.31
1979	1061.15	86.25

Source: See text. Peter Moore also contributed valuable assistance.

of institutions, state and local support of sponsored research, state and local support of other sponsored programs, and state and local student-aid grants[f] as these items are defined in the *Financial Statistics of Institutions of Higher Education* (1968-69, p. 16).

Recent shifts toward more state grants for direct student aid tend to channel more state aid to private institutions. This is because state grants have normally been limited to tuition and fees, which provide a larger sum per student-recipient to the higher tuition private institutions. (Average full cost at private institutions was also $1,256 higher per student than at publicly controlled institutions.[g]) This practice fails to meet the needs of low-income students, whose parents are unable to cover room, board, and other living expenses for an extended period. But this tuition-aid practice is often urged by those who are less concerned about aiding students in need than about getting aid to private institutions by means that avoid institutional grants. A maintenance grant system such as that used in Britain, which involves a flat grant to the student that he can use to help with his room, board and other expenses, does not discriminate so seriously against the poor.[h]

The mix of these two plans that emerges over the next few years can affect the allocation of state aid as between public and private insitutions, but is less likely to be in addition to other state support. If anything, it is likely to diminish the rate of growth of state support, since a shift of funds both to institutions not under state control and toward aid for low-income

[f]Student aid that is not awarded by institutions (such as that awarded by state scholarship commissions) would not appear here as a receipt of institutions, but would instead be included in tuition and fee receipts.

[g]*Ibid.*, p. 7. Taken alone cost per student per year at private universities was $5,124, as compared to $3,450 at public universities.

[h]In Britain only about 12 percent of each college-age group is admitted, however.

families changes the political basis of support for appropriations bills in state legislatures. The rapid growth of public junior colleges draws on the more long-standing and predictable bases of state and local support, while simultaneously lowering out-of-pocket room and board costs. This improves the access of poor families in urban areas to postsecondary educational opportunities. But the basic problem of room, board, and other living costs (foregone earnings) remains a serious one for poor families that is only now beginning to be addressed as further thought is given to the structure of federal student aid grants.

The predictions in Table 4-4 are conditional upon the forecasts of the economic and demographic variables on which state and local investment in postsecondary education depends. The two key economic variables —which are real personal income and the price index—needed to convert predictions of real investment to current prices are as reported by the Department of Commerce through 1973. The 1974-79 values are those predicted by the Eckstein-Fromm D.R.I. econometric model of the United States. The stock of educational capital (S_{Et-1}) changes more slowly over time than do flow-type variables, making it useful in forecasting. It was projected to 1980 based on projections of the contained underlying elements described in Appendix B, although in principle a more general model explaining all components of S_{Et-1} as well as the depreciation could generate it endogenously. The Gini coefficient (g_k) also changes slowly over time, although it does indicate a decline in equality in the personal income distribution from 1929-46. This measure of inequality has been pretty stable in the post World War II years: dipping slightly toward .33 in the 1963-69 period but climbing toward its post World War II average of about .35, which is the value extrapolated to 1980. These educational stock and income inequality variables, however, are less significant than are the other determinants of new investment.

Finally, the demographic variable measuring the number of college-age young adults as a percent of the total population (C_t) is calculated from population estimates and projections made by the Bureau of the Census in its *Current Population Reports*, Series P-20. The future college-age population depends on the numbers of children already in grades 4-12, so it can be predicted to 1980 quite accurately. The growth in the 1960s of college eligibles leveled off and stopped at 19.6 percent of the population in 1973, when the last of the young adults born during the large increase in births following World War II passes beyond the normal Master's Degree level. The percentage of the population in the narrower 18-20 age range begins to decline in the 1974-75 academic year toward its 1970-71 level.

Appraisal of the Predictions and Some Qualifications. Conditional predictions of current expenditures on higher education financed by state and local governments are not available in other sources. Some comparisons can be made however to the 1969-71 estimates made by Forrest Harrison and George Lind in the U.S. Office of Education (1971), *Projections of Educational Statistics to 1980-81*, which only were done including capital outlays. The current expenditure, current dollars, estimates in Table 4-4 are 92.1 percent, 89.0 percent, and 90.2 percent of the O.E. current and capital outlay totals in 1969, 1970, and 1971, respectively. (Current expenditures were 90.8 percent of the total in 1968.) The Office of Education has not attempted any projections beyond the 1971-72 academic year of expenditures by higher educational institutions by revenue source.

M. M. Chambers (1972) collects data annually on *Appropriations of State Tax Funds for Operating Expenses of Higher Education*. His census of appropriations is not identical to expenditures by institutions; it excludes appropriations by localities, while including amounts for state scholarship commissions. Fortunately it excludes capital outlays. Dr. Chambers' data for recent years in millions of current dollars compares with our Table 4-4 estimates, shown as a percent of his figures, as follows:[1]

Year	Appropriations	Estimates using basic influences
1969-70	6,198	104.0%
1970-71	7,004	100.4%
1971-72	7,704	101.9%
1972-73	8,529	102.1%

The estimates based on underlying influences on state investment decisions are very close to actual appropriations. This suggests among other things that the effect of campus unrest, most of which would have been felt in the 1970 and 1971 budgets, was less substantial in relation to the more basic political-economic sources of support for higher education than might have been thought at the time.

In the future real personal income movements are more difficult to predict.[i] The disturbing effects of the energy crisis following difficulties in the Middle East on real personal income in 1974 and 1975, as well as the aftereffects of Watergate on governmental decision processes, for example, are not fully taken into account in the underlying estimates of real personal income. Where unpredictable events such as these have coincided with a recession, the estimates of state and local support of public institutions of higher education for 1974 and 1975 are likely to be slightly overstated.

Beyond this, the longer-run path of real personal income and hence of state and local support for higher education depends significantly on

---

[i] Shorter-run forecasts are likely to be more accurate than longer-run forecasts, in part because effective stabilization policies are not always followed.

whether or not Federal fiscal and monetary policies (as well as other national economic policies) are used wisely to maintain full employment and non-inflationary growth.

Appendix: State and Local Supplementary Enrollment Demand

A simultaneous equation model dealing with the supplementary demand for enrollment made effective by state and local governments has been estimated by restricted three-stage least squares methods with the results as shown in Table 4-6. It is the model illustrated in Fig. 4-1. For purposes of focusing on supplemental state support, the amount of support per student coming from other sources has been taken as predetermined (i.e., $p_{T+F} + p_G + p_F$ is taken as given by the data).

The coefficients of these terms representing support per student from other sources has then been restricted to equal -1.00 in the estimation process, as explained in the appendix to Chapter 3, so that the shadow price representing state and local support per student (p_{S+L}) becomes endogenous.

The results indicate that as before, growth in income, in the number of young adults, and in the real prices of inputs that must be purchased by educational institutions, are important to the state and local support of enrollments and to the amount of support per student, especially at public institutions. The amount of state and local support going to private institutions is small. The rising real cost to the state per student of supporting additional enrollments does appear to have a deterrent effect on desires to support increased enrollments at public institutions. The relation of g_k as an index of desires for equity is usually positive, but not very significant.

Table 4-6
State and Local Supplementary Enrollment Demand, 1946-68 and 1929-68
(Restricted Three-Stage Least Squares Estimates)
(Variables defined and data sources given in Appendix A^a; t-statistic in parentheses, underlined coefficients are significant at the 10 percent level.)

	Constant	R^2(1SLS)

Public Institutions, 1946-68

(13) Enrollment demand

$$q_{pub} = \underline{.010}\ Y_t + \underline{17.966}\ C_t + 2{,}517\ g_k - \underline{1.17}\ p_{S+L(pub)} + .006\ S_{Et-1}$$
$$(3.66) \qquad (5.05) \qquad (.87) \qquad (-2.45) \qquad (1.62)$$

Constant: $\underline{-5{,}358}$ (-3.52) R^2(1SLS): .994

(14) Supply (price)

$$p_{S+L(pub)} = -.081\ q_{pub} + \underline{9.20}\ w - 1.00\ (p_{T+F} + p_G + p_G + p_F)$$
$$(-1.64) \qquad (4.92) \qquad (-1.45)$$

Constant: $+216$ $(.90)$ R^2(1SLS): .884

Private Institutions, 1946-68

(15) Enrollment demand

$$q_{pvt} = .002\ Y_t + \underline{5{,}693}\ C_t + 606\ g_k + .50\ p_{S+L(pvt)} + .007\ S_{Et-1}$$
$$(1.17) \qquad (2.09) \qquad (.24) \qquad (.11) \qquad (.24)$$

Constant: -769 $(-.58)$ R^2(1SLS): .913

(16) Supply (price)

$$p_{S+L(pvt)} = \underline{.32}\ q_{pvt} + \underline{7.42}\ w - 1.00\ (p_{T+F} + p_G + p_F)$$
$$(3.99) \qquad (3.78) \qquad (-4.98)$$

Constant: $\underline{-266}$ (-4.44) R^2(1SLS): .740

Public Institutions 1929-68

(17) Enrollment demand

$$q_{pub} = \underset{(4.00)}{.005}\ Y_t + \underset{(13.24)}{18,633}\ C_t + \underset{(.41)}{571}\ g_k - \underset{(-2.00)}{.77}\ p_{S+L(pub)} + \underset{(6.01)}{.011}\ S_{Et-1} \qquad \underset{(-5.93)}{-4.282} \qquad .994$$

(18) Supply (price)

$$p_{S+L(pub)} = \underset{(.802)}{.028}\ q_{pub} + \underset{(2.55)}{3.01}\ w - \underset{(-2.59)}{1.00}\ (p_{T+F} + p_G + p_F) \qquad \underset{(5.05)}{+579} \qquad .771$$

Private Institutions 1929-68

(19) Enrollment demand

$$q_{prt} = \underset{(2.87)}{.003}\ Y_t + \underset{(.04)}{56}\ C_t - \underset{(3.57)}{37.58}\ g_k + \underset{(.45)}{1.63}\ p_{S+L(prt)} - \underset{(-.53)}{.0007}\ S_{Et-1} \qquad \underset{(2.99)}{+1.771} \qquad .972$$

(20) Supply (price)

$$p_{S+L(prt)} = \underset{(-2.31)}{-.53}\ q_{prt} + \underset{(3.58)}{13.29}\ w - \underset{(-5.78)}{1.00}\ (p_{T+F} + p_G + p_F) \qquad \underset{(4.61)}{+452} \qquad .733$$

[a] Enrollment is in thousands, real personal income (Y_t) is in millions of 1958 dollars, and the subsidy is in 1958 dollars per student.

5 Federal Investment in Higher Education

The Education Amendments of 1972 define a new approach that could become nearly as important in its eventual impact on higher education in the United States as the Land Grant Act of 1862. The new act provides for a program of basic grants to individual students based on need and related support to institutions that for the first time undertakes to extend post-secondary educational opportunities to significant numbers of students from low-income homes.

The design of the "basic grant approach" to student aid, which is essentially a sharply redesigned new public good, was first put forward in *Quality and Equality* (the Carnegie Commission Report (1968)), *Toward a Long Range Plan for the Financial Support of Higher Education* (the Rivlin Report (1969)), and then in the *Conference Report* on the act itself (House of Representative Report No. 92-1085). Its design has been discussed by R. Hartman (1972) who analyzes the problem of "targeting" the aid to those students who have the greatest need, and by the National Commission on the Financing of Postsecondary Education (1973) whose analysis considers the potential effects of alternative financing plans on total and relative enrollments at public and private institutions. The impact of the act will depend on these design aspects, but they can be adjusted by funding selected portions of the act more fully than others as will be discussed in this chapter. For example, aid is more fully "targeted" by relaxing the "half-cost" provision, and aid to private institutions is increased by aiding state student-aid plans that cover only tuition. But the ultimate impact of the act also depends on the overall level of Federal support which thus far has received less attention.

In the midst of the national discussion of these new Federal student aid and institutional aid programs, severe cuts were implemented by the Administration in Federal funding in 1973-74 and 1974-75 of on-going Federal graduate education programs. Particularly severely cut were programs in health manpower development in medicine, dentistry, nursing, and pharmacy, all following cuts earlier in National Defense Education Act programs in graduate education. Some of the financial responsibility for these may be picked up by the states as the Basic Economic Opportunity Grants are increased. But the future impact of the new Act now depends on future funding by the Office of Management and the Budget, the Office of the Secretary of the Department of Health, Education, and Welfare, and by the Congress. It is an analysis of the longer run influences on which their decisions ultimately depend that is the primary objective of this chapter.

After a brief discussion of the earlier trends in Federal support (Part I) as well as of some economic aspects of the enacted program (Part II), a behavorial model will be set out for analysis of the postwar Federal support of higher education (Part III), and regression results will be discussed (Part IV). Some tentative conclusions will be drawn about the prospects for increased funding in both the short and longer run in Part V. It also will summarize some of the constraints, as well as seek to describe some of the opportunities that define the path of actual progress toward social goals.

I. Trends in Federal Support

Federal investment in educational capital through educational institutions grew more slowly than did investment either by state and local governments or by households in many recent years, as may be seen in Fig. 5-1. The Federal investment made through direct payments to households under the G.I. Bill are treated as subsidized household investments.

In contrast, expenditures by the Federal Government for contract research and the investment that this implies in the creation of new knowledge grew more rapidly and with less interruption throughout the 1941-68 period than any of the components of investment in education. There are some joint costs (e.g., the support of graduate student research assistants) whose allocation here to the cost of research outputs may understate somewhat the value of the education thereby acquired by the students. There also has been a curtailment of Federal support of research in the 1968-73 period that has lowered the rate of growth of Federal support.

Note that the rate of growth of real investment by households in the 1946-49 postwar period was small, relative to the growth of Federal support. It presumably can be explained largely in terms of the effect of the lower effective tuition, room, and board price ($p_{T+F} + p_{R+B}$ net of p_F) and of depleted higher educational capital stocks (S_{Et-1}) on enrollments. In general, there has been growth in Federal support of higher education in the postwar period, but it has been more sporadic and from a smaller base, one which now constitutes about 5 percent of the total expenditures of colleges and universities.

II. Federal Higher Education Programs

The education Amendments of 1972 build upon and significantly extend a foundation of existing programs. The G.I. Bill following World War II was probably the most significant piece of legislation affecting higher education up to that time. The 1972 extension of this bill has raised all G.I. benefits retroactive to September 1972 by 25 percent. The National Defense Education Act of 1958 established a program of fellowships and direct loans to students; it is maintained and extended by the Education Amendments

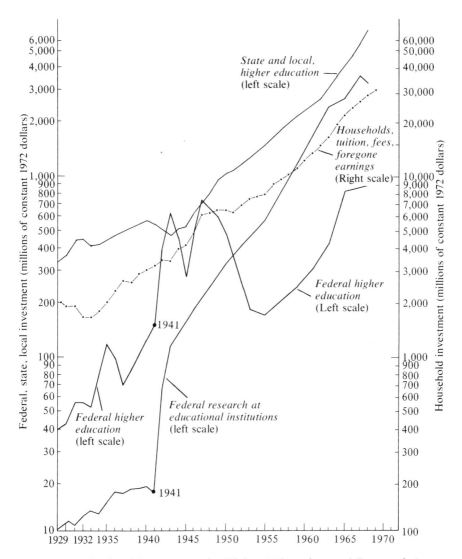

Figure 5-1 Federal Investment in Higher Education and Research (percentage rates of growth compared)

Source: See Appendix C.

of 1972 as noted below. There was also the Higher Education Facilities Act of 1963, followed by the Higher Education Act of 1965, which was, in turn, further amended in 1967 and 1968. The latter began other programs of Federal investment in human resources.

The most important new feature of the Education Amendments of 1972 is the basic grant program that provides a foundation grant for each student of from \$200 to \$1,400 depending upon his financial need as defined by his family's economic circumstances. It is intended as a foundation grant on which other programs build. But grant payments could not be made until Congress appropriated \$653.5 million to support the existing "supplemental" economic opportunity grant, work-study, and institutional student-loan programs. Beyond this, the act also provides for new cost-of-instruction aid to institutions, aid based on the number of basic grant recipients that the institutions serve. But this provision comes into effect only when Congress has appropriated sufficient funds to cover at least 50 percent of the basic grant to which each student is entitled.

So the new basic grant and institutional aid provisions are gradually "phased in," but only after the main pre-existing programs are financed. Before considering influences on the level of funding, we ought to consider the five main categories of Federal investment in educational capital and their relative scope. One indication is given by the thoughts of the House-Senate conferees as they thought ahead at the time of passage of the act and agreed upon tentative figures for fiscal 1975 and the Administration's later budget requests for fiscal 1975:

	Congress Millions, 1975	Admin. 1975
1. *Aid to students based on need:*		
(a) Basic educational opportunity grants	As appropriated	1,300
(b) "Supplemental" grants	\$200	0
(c) State student aid (50% of new state effort)	50	0
(d) Institutional programs for the disadvantaged	100	70
(e) Interest subsidy on insured student loans (\$2.0 billion limit on principal, underwritten by SLMA)	No limit	315
(f) Work-study	420	250
(g) Direct loans to students (NDEA)	400	0
2. *Categorical aid based on career objectives:*		
(a) Teacher-training programs (OE)	450	0
(b) Graduate school programs (NSF, Health manpower)	687	355
(c) Manpower training programs (Dept. of Labor)	300	0
3. *In-service training programs:*		
(a) Department of Defense (postsecondary schools, high cost-per-student service academies)	343	435
(b) AEC, CIA, NASA, Treasury and Justice Departments operate small in-service programs	n.a.	n.a.

4. *Aid linked to specific public-good demands:*

To those eligible through student voucher programs this aid is given directly to the student for him to spend where he will.

(a) G.I. Bill aid to veterans (V.A.)	1,706	2,582
(b) Social security dependents (S.S.A.)	505	856

5. *Aid to institutions; cost of education allowances:*

(a) 38 percent of all EOG, work-study, and NDSL funds awarded at the institution (rising to 50 percent for smaller institutions),		0
(b) $500 for each basic grant recipient (falling to $100 for each recipient over 1,000), triggered after existing programs and half of the basic grants are funded,		0
(c) $200 for each graduate student, (a) + (b) + (c) = 1,000		0
(d) $300 for each veteran enrolled	No limit	0
(e) Aid to developing institutions serving minorities	120	120

Future appropriations for these programs will be jointly determined by the Office of Management and the Budget and appropriations made by the Congress. The OMB in fiscal 1975, for example, fully funded the basic grants while cutting back existing programs and categorical aid (i.e., 1b, 1f, 1g, and 2a-c).[1] Congress through the Education Amendments of 1972 has protected the existing programs as indicated above, but the hand of the OMB is strengthened by the support of some members of Congress and the threat of veto of appropriations bills that do not conform to OMB proposals by the President.

Crucial features, therefore, are those provisions for "ratable reduction" and partial funding of the basic grants that are set out in the act, since partial funding or at least "half-cost" may continue. Most important, at anything less than half-funding of the basic grants, the basic grant cannot exceed 50 percent of the student's actual need. If appropriations are insufficient to satisfy even this level, not only the institutional aid is cut out but also all $200-$1,400 basic entitlements are ratably reduced.

The student's actual need is defined as the student's "actual cost" of attending including tuition and fees, room and board, books, and other living expenses, net of an expected contribution from his family. The latter is determined by his family's and his own income and assets, including in the latter all benefits received if he is a social security dependent and one-half of any veterans benefits. Even at full funding, basic grants are limited to half the cost of attending the institution. Students can supplement the "half-need" limitation of the basic grants with supplemental EOG's, state scholarships, work-study, larger family contributions, and loans.

Insufficient appropriations therefore restrict the basic grants made to the students from the poorest families by the largest absolute amounts. Since these grants can meet only half of their need and, even at full funding, only half the cost of the institution (or $1,400 less the expected family contribution, whichever is less), about half of the amount appropriated will go to students from the middle, or $6,000-13,000, income quartiles and thus is poorly targeted on those students with the greatest need.[2] The mix in the final package of aid, using state scholarships (state student incentive grants provisions), supplemental EOG's, work-study, and loans, will affect this targeting of the aid. But the current tendency for the low-income family's contributions to be a larger percent of its income, the hours of work for students from such families to be longer (a strain on a full-time student if over 10-15 hours a week), and their education debts to be larger is apt to continue. So although funding the act will go a long way, there are economic constraints, and some regressive inequalities in educational opportunity will remain. The latter is reduceable, however, by the funding and the direction given to the supplemental EOG's.

In another important effect, the half-cost provision channels a disproportionately large amount of aid to high tuition private institutions.[a] Similarly the state student incentive grants also lean heavily in the direction of aid to private institutions, because state programs normally limit grants to tuition and fees and exclude room and board costs.

Some aid to middle-income groups and to private institutions is in order, and the level of funding of these different provisions of Public Law 92-318 is one means of controlling the "mix." But one is left with the fact that private institutions do have much higher full costs per student, even though quality, the proportion of graduate students, and accounting practices do differ.[b] Caution will have to be used to avoid making the inducements to choose the high-cost private institutions too strong. That would increase the aggregate tax cost, and interfere with the maximum extension of educational opportunities. Caution will also have to be exercised to keep the aid from merely reinforcing current tendencies toward ineffective "token" grants from institutions for students with little need. Because of their large unmet need the "targeting" of the aid on the students from low-income families, students who are currently excluded, is the act's single most important feature.

---

[a] Other provisions in the act for aid to junior colleges and for institutional aid on a flat per-student basis counterbalance this to some extent.

[b] True unit-cost comparisons in the sense of cost per unit of output of "education" of constant quality are very difficult and some years into the future. The National Commission's recommendation of cost studies as a basis for Federal aid to institutions get at cost per student, but are only a first step toward measuring the costs of a given increment to test scores.

III. Public Expenditure Theory: A Positive Model for Use in Analysis

The Federal political mechanism just described may be regarded as the vehicle through which economic constraints on the attainment of social goals are transmitted. The primary goals for social investment in higher education relate to returns extending over future periods; they will be expressed first, and simply, as *growth* of real satisfactions and as *equity*. But the economic constraints on their attainment also must be made explicit if there is to be any derivation of effective demands. The economic constraints are very real, although they may sometimes be disguised by a veil of political manuveuring.

Social Goals

A multiperiod objective function expressing current and expected real satisfactions enjoyed by citizens is given in the simplest possible form below. It is analogous to the democratic state preference function, or modified welfare function, for a state government, as discussed in Chapter 4. It measures private satisfactions in terms of real incomes, assuming some imputations for nonmonetary returns.

$$W_T = W\left[\sum_{k=1}^{m} g_{kt} Y_{kt}\right] \qquad t = T, \ldots, L \qquad (5\text{-}1)$$

where Y_t = current and expected future real income including imputations,

g_{kt} = income distribution weights attached by elected officials reflecting the importance they attach to increasing the satisfactions of the kth income class,

W = a modified welfare function, or democratic state preference function, that includes the influence of social benefits (externalities).

All five categories of Federal investment in higher education are designed to contribute to the social goal of *growth* of current and expected future satisfactions (i.e., to Y_t as $t = T, T + 1, \ldots, L$). Private income returns are also returns for the society. Private returns include imputed returns to private citizens from public goods, but the overlap between private and social returns is not necessarily 100 percent, since there are also purely social benefits in the form of externalities implicit in W.[c] These take

---

[c] Some economists are denying the existence of all externalities (excluding pollution) with

the form of the discovery and development of talent, reduced crime rates and related social problems, and the strengthening of political and civic leadership from which others benefit.[d] Notice that Y_k involves returns in the form of satisfactions for all citizens, not just those in the lower-income brackets.[e] And in fact some higher education programs such as NDEA loans serve primarily middle-income groups. Finally, notice that this goal as it stands is a virtually limitless utopian ideal before any constraints from program costs and taxes have been introduced.[f]

The second goal, vertical *equity*, is expressed in the personal income distribution weights (g_{kt}). As suggested in Chapter 4, they will tend to be larger in democratic countries for each dollar of income arising in the lower-income families than for each dollar of income at the other end of the scale, since votes are distributed more equally than are private-sector incomes. The first category of higher education programs providing aid based on financial need serves this goal of vertical equity most directly. Other programs also serve it, but less directly.[g]

A third goal, that of satisfying demands for particular public goods which are included in total real income such as defense and social security, is served most directly by categories 3 and 4 of the education programs. Defense and social security are largely social goods, as is the social benefit element in education. This means that the exclusion principle, which is essential to enforcement of the prices that are necessary if private production is to occur, cannot be effectively applied. Alternatively there may be substantial cost economies making public production more feasible. The demand for defense (and veterans benefits) overlaps with the demand for education, so that some defense-related higher education programs gather support from both sources.

The Economic Constraints

The degree to which social goals can be attained is limited by the con-

---

capitalization and measurement arguments that in the author's opinion constitute an almost unbelievable defiance of common sense.

[d]Cartter (1972) has estimated private benefits at 75 percent and social benefits at 25 percent of the total with a degree of precision and comprehensiveness that surely overreaches the state of the art, while commendably encouraging work on measurement. For good discussions of social benefits of higher education, see Hartman (1972), Mundel (1972), and Bowen (1972).

[e]Reasons relating to the election of those who govern are discussed further in Chapter 4.

[f]Efficiency in the attainment of growth is therefore another matter. Resources must be invested in relation to costs where rates of return are highest, although care must be used to include nonmonetary and social returns.

[g]The "director's effect" suggests that individual programs tend to benefit the most those persons who are toward the middle of the income range that the program is designed to serve. This certainly is true at present of public higher education institutions taken as a whole. But this fact is not inconsistent with this analysis, for if the distribution of benefits is more equal

straits imposed by the total resources available in the society and by the cost of specific programs.

First, there is the constraint of the limited total resources available to the society at any given time for allocation between private goods and public goods, the latter including Federal support of higher education. This total resource constraint assumes that the Federal budget operates with a fixed net deficit, or is nearly balanced, over the recession-prosperity cycle taken as a whole. *Total personal income* before taxes for the planning period therefore represents the total resources available for allocation.[h] Maximizing total public and private satisfactions[i] subject to this constraint, an effective demand for enrollment to be added by Federal investment can be derived. When expressed as a function of the average price per student to the Federal government (p_F), this incremental investment-demand may be added vertically to the demands for higher education arising from other sectors to obtain total enrollment demand, illustrated as *DD* in Fig.5-2.

Second, there is the constraint imposed by the cost of the program. It is useful here to start with the full cost of sustaining the student at the institution, illustrated by line *pp* in Fig. 5-2.[j] Equilibrium without the Federal investment would be at E_1; by increasing the Federal subsidy (p_F) total enrollment can be increased, say to E_2, in the case of the public institutions that are illustrated. The limits to this process are that Federal investment, represented by the shaded area $p_F q_{pub}$ incurs a tax cost in dollar terms that must be met. Using either discretionary or automatic adjustments in effective tax rates,[k] taxes simultaneously incur disutility (or dissatisfaction) that must be laid off against the net benefits.

IV. Federal Investment Regression Results

Federal investment-demand functions are presented below in Table 5-1. They emphasize those influences that shift the demand curve in Fig. 5-1 outward, thereby increasing real Federal investment expenditure (the shaded area), which is the dependent variable. Changes in costs, of course,

---

than the distribution of income in the private sector, the program would still be redistributive, in relative terms.

[h] See also (4-2), and the time constraints in Chapter 2.

[i] See (4-4). It replaces the Y's in (5-1) above with q's and treats the g_k's as taste parameters for ease in derivation. This procedure releases the assumption of one fixed set of relative prices implicit in (5-1).

[j] This supply function based on production costs assumes to simplify the problem that *nonprofit institutions* merely supply enrollments at average cost rather than at marginal cost. Some students of course are charged more and others less through financial aids. An institution can choose to charge a higher average price, offering education of higher average quality, which shifts the cost function pp upward.

[k] For the tax function with rates like t_1 and to t_2 be adjusted see Eq. (4-3).

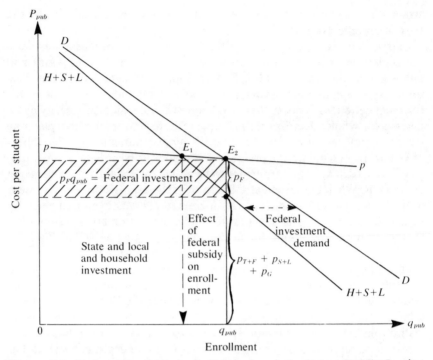

Figure 5-2 Federal Investment in Educational Capital at Public Institutions (Enrollment demands are derived demands for inputs used in the production of human capital.)

will also influence expenditure, especially increases in faculty and nonfaculty salaries, which shift the average total cost function upward. But many of these nominal cost increases are not increases in the relative costs of education, but instead reflect general conditions in the economy, so these latter are removed by deflation of investment expenditures for changes in the price level.[1] Other cost increases are induced by increased demands for education coming from households and from state and local governments. So although changes in real costs make it more difficult to get unequivocal hypotheses about demand alone, *relative* cost changes are both smaller than the nominal changes and are, furthermore, in large part demand-induced.

No predictions using regression equations of Federal investment in higher education will be attempted, because there is a sample of just one expenditure unit involved and the possibility of large transitory distur-

---

[1]The Personal Consumption Expenditures implicit deflator is used for deflation throughout. It is used for public expenditure here because it is likely to be closer to a shadow price of *final* public goods to the collectivity than is a deflator based only on factor prices.

bances. Instead, the determinants in Table 5-1 will be interpreted for the insight they offer into some of the underlying sources of support in the longer run.

Current Resources and Potential Growth

Increases in real income (Y_t) are significant in providing resources to finance increased Federal investment in higher education. Results in column 1 of Table 5-1 are fully consistent with this hypothesis.[m] The effect is similar to that for investment by households and by state and local governments. It appears to be reversible in that recessions appear to slow down or stop the rate of increase in investment in higher education after a one-year lag by all three types of expenditure decision units (e.g., see Fig. 5-1, 1931-33 and, in part, 1971-72). The marginal propensity for Federal investment out of current income at public institutions in Table 5-1 is about twice what it is at each corresponding type of private institution.

The absolute difference in returns to those with a college education over returns to those with a high school diploma (i.e., Y_{Bt}, not all of which can be attributed to the economic productivity of the additional training) is positively related to Federal investment. Although this absolute difference can and apparently does induce additional investment,[2] it has not come through here or elsewhere when other influences are taken into account by this measure. Furthermore, although new investment in higher education may be expected to make a positive contribution to the growth of real income (based on the past real income differentials used to measure Y_{Bt}), it may or may not be the most efficient route to attainment of the growth objective. Efficiency depends upon relative rates of return to alternative uses of the portion of the new resources intended for attainment of growth.

Equity

Increments in Federal aid to students based on need[n] in the past have not been significantly dependent on the degree of inequality in the income distribution (g_k). Instead aid has followed the growth of total resources (Y_t) over time, and expected potential returns (Y_{Bt}) as these students become productively employed.

---

[m] Expenditures on higher education, in turn, generate income. But this effect, which is similar to that in any consumption or investment function, can be expected to be weaker (since other things also generate income), and to occur only after a lag.

[n] This does not refer to a shift within this category to basic EOG's with the total substantially unchanged.

Table 5-1
Investment by the Federal Government in Higher Education, 1946-68
(*t*-statistic in parentheses below coefficient; significant coefficients are underlined.)

Investment (Dependent variable)	Pretax personal income Y_t	Expected monetary returns Y_{Bt}	Inequality (Gini coefficient) g_k	Veterans V	Employment rate N	Party control (Democrats) D	Stock of HE capital S_{Et-1}	Constant term	ρ	R^2 (after ρ) SE_ϵ
(1) *Public universities*										
$R_u^2 = .846$, $SE_u = 29.0$	.0017	.0459	-3,412	.0021	-15.78	9.58	-.0025	2,513	-.13	.849
D.W. = 1.81	(2.42)	(.68)	(-3.70)	(2.14)	(-1.74)	(.44)	(-2.36)	(2.50)		28.7
(2) *Public 4-yr colleges*										
$R_u^2 = .886$, $SE_u = 14.5$	.0006	.0005	143	.0035	3.39	13.82	-.0003	-482	.05	.923
D.W. = 1.71	(2.00)	(1.66)	(.36)	(4.27)	(.91)	(1.54)	(-.58)	(-1.15)		11.9
(3) *Public 2-yr colleges*										
$R_u^2 = .20$, $SE_u = 68.3$	.0003	.0110	-63	.0003	-1.27	-1.99	-.0001	-33	.95	.948
D.W. = 1.36	(3.59)	(1.57)	(-.65)	(1.08)	(-1.40)	(.97)	(-.91)	(-.32)		3.4
(4) *Public total*										
$R_u^2 = .934$, $SE_u = 32.3$	.0025	.0771	-3,533	.0068	-7.38	27.30	-.0032	1,534	-.43	.950
D.W. = 2.14	(4.39)	(1.31)	(-4.42)	(4.50)	(-.89)	(1.42)	(-3.57)	(1.68)		28.0

(5) *Private universities*										
$R_u^2 = .851$, $SE_u = 18.3$	.0007	.0720	−2,187	.0042	−2.70	17.94	−.0017	897	−.50	.895
D.W. = 2.31	(2.39)	(2.32)	(−5.20)	(5.31)	(−.61)	(1.76)	(−3.65)	(1.85)		15.3
(6) *Private 4-yr colleges*										
$R_u^2 = .824$, $SE_u = 13.8$	.0004	.0357	−530	.0043	4.54	18.49	−.0009	−317	−.26	.890
D.W. = 1.98	(1.60)	(1.45)	(−1.58)	(6.62)	(1.35)	(2.30)	(−2.44)	(−.85)		10.9
(7) *Private 2-yr colleges*										
$R_u^2 = .559$, $SE_u = 15.1$	.0001	−.0004	−12	.0003	.21	19.69	−.0001	−19	.17	.819
D.W. = 1.76	(1.89)	(−.17)	(−.38)	(3.82)	(.72)	(2.74)	(−1.86)	(−.56)		1.0
(8) *Private total*										
$R_u^2 = .860$, $SE_u = 30.0$	.0012	.1152	−2,724	.0088	3.22	37.53	−.0027	431	−.45	.912
D.W. = 2.37	(2.42)	(2.33)	(−4.05)	(6.90)	(.46)	(2.32)	(−3.69)	(.56)		23.8

Joint Demands

National demand for defense and education was an important influence upon the increases in Federal investment in higher education in 1941-42 and was seen as an effective demand-source once again through the National Defense Education Act in 1958. Similarly, the large number of veterans has propelled increased Federal investment following each war at almost all types of educational institutions, as evidenced by the "Veterans" column in Table 5-1.

Direct support of room and board through voucher payments that go to individuals for them to use as they please have constituted a long-standing and very important form of Federal support for higher education. Payments of this type made through each G.I. Bill by the Veterans Administration are shown in Table 5-2; similar but much smaller payments are made through the Social Security Administration dependents' program. There are other smaller postsecondary education programs in other departments, but there is not even any centralized collection of data on their scope[3] much less any effort to coordinate them in a more comprehensive national education policy.

Stabilization

The net relation between the employment rate (N) and real investment as given in Table 5-1 is not significant. Although higher education has not acted as an effective counter-cyclical stabilizer, it has stabilized the transition to a peacetime economy in the past by absorbing large numbers of veterans. It has un-utilized potential for cyclical stabilization.

Political Party Effects

There is some indication (see Table 5-1) that the periods in which Democrats controlled both the executive and legislative branches were the ones in which Federal investment increased most rapidly. The effect only appears to be significant for investment at private four-year and private two-year colleges. A similar variable for Republican party control was tried in regressions not reported here. However one must conclude that Federal investment through higher educational institutions has not been a strongly partisan matter. The final version of the Education Amendments of 1972 passed, for example, in the House of Representatives with a slight majority from both parties.

Higher Education Capital Stocks

Existing stocks of educational capital do appear to act as a deterrent to new Federal investment. (See the negative coefficient of S_{Et-1} in Table 5-1.) The ρ coefficient, however, is also negative in those instances where the coefficient of S_{Et-1} is negative and significant (i.e., (1), (4), (5), (6), and (8)).

It is important to distinguish excess stocks of college graduates in certain fields (e.g., teaching, engineering, physics, aerospace) that arise because of cyclical declines and structural shifts, from long-run secular overproduction (or underproduction) of college graduates in general. Firms always tend to slack off in their new hiring of engineers and other college graduates in recessions. The continuing shortages in some fields such as medicine, and the failure of rates of return to fall over time in the U.S. also weigh against long-run oversupply.

V. The Challenge in the New Federal Role in Higher Education

By far the most important new challenge addressed by the Education Amendments of 1972 lies in the steps being taken to open postsecondary educational opportunities for the first time to significant numbers of students from low-income families. If this is to be successful it is necessary that the financial aid be targeted better on those who need it, and that the quality of most institutions be strengthened. It is very important that there be creative and innovative development of new approaches that motivate this type of student.

Improved targeting of aid requires elimination of the half-cost, half-need provision, or at the very least, its replacement with some kind of a sliding scale. It also requires a refined operation of the Federal need-analysis system and/or use those that are operated by the American College Testing Program and by the College Scholarship Service. It must obtain the parents' income and asset information directly from the parent while he refers to his tax records, contain built-in checks for accuracy in the reporting of assets, and not be satisfied with student's estimates of these items—which are well known to be extremely inaccurate.

As this new group of urban poor are enrolled it is not sufficient only that workable curricula are developed. There is need to relate curriculum and apprenticeship training to national as well as local manpower needs, meeting shortages where rates of return are high. This would include opening entry to skilled trades and vocations from plumbers to doctors, circumventing barriers to entry that have often become formidable.

Table 5-2

Federal Investment in Higher Education Made Through Veterans Benefits (in millions of current dollars)

Year[a]	Total amount paid to		World War II veterans[b]		Korean (1952-64) and Post-Korean (1966-74) bills		Reporting allowance institutions
	Individuals	Institutions	Individuals	Institutions	Veterans	Dependents	
1946	459.0	331.1	459.0	331.1			
1947	481.0	509.3	481.0	509.3			
1948	553.4	486.4	553.4	486.4			
1949	541.4	446.9	541.4	446.9			
1950	403.5	338.3	403.5	338.3			
1951	266.3	248.2	266.3	248.2			
1952	168.8	119.5	112.1	118.3	56.7		1.2
1953	203.9	57.7	45.4	55.0	158.4		2.7
1954	314.0	29.2	17.5	24.4	296.5		4.8
1955	416.0	18.0	5.6	11.4	410.4		6.6
1956	457.0	9.9	.6	2.8	454.2	2.2	7.1
1957	426.0	6.8	.09	.1	421.2	4.7	6.7

1958	354.3	5.8	.02	.2	347.8	6.5	5.6
1959	242.0	4.0	.006	.1	233.1	8.9	3.9
1960	157.9	2.6	−.006	.1	145.5	12.4	2.5
1961	99.8	1.5	−.006	.02	82.9	16.9	1.5
1962	65.9	.9	.002	.02	44.8	21.1	.9
1963	46.9	.6	.001	−.005	25.1	21.8	.6
1964	32.1	.3	.002	.002	8.9	23.2	.3
1965	28.0	.2				28.0	.2
1966	246.9	.001			215.9	31.0	.001
1967	370.2	1.4			334.9	35.3	1.4
1968	468.4	1.8			431.1	36.7	1.8
1969	710.1	2.3			665.1	45.0	2.3
1970	1,179.7	3.0			1,117.3	62.4	3.0
1971	1,381.3	3.6			1,312.5	68.8	3.6
Total[c]	10,171.4	2,648.3	2,983.6	2,591.4	6,762.9	424.9	56.9

Source: Data generously provided by Roland C. Hartman and Edward R. Silberman, director, Management and Budget Service, Veterans Administration.

[a] Given for academic years, listed by first half of the academic year (i.e., data shown for 1946 applies to 1946-47 fiscal year).

[b] Payments of 29.6 percent to individuals and 58.3 percent of payments to institutions made under this act were used for higher education. Annual figures not available on this basis were obtained by applying these percentages to each column involving World War II veterans.

[c] All totals are for 1944 through 1971.

The attempts to develop curricula meaningful to the student can draw, in part, on the successful experiences in agriculture and engineering that emerged from the Land Grant Act. But its success also depends on recognition of the different characteristics of students that come from poor urban families. Educational capital basically is produced by the family, and the model offered by the parent, as well as parental guidance and support, are very important. For seriously disadvantaged students the new act does seek to replace this in part with institutional services and guidance. But simultaneously there is the serious need for more basic research on the production of educational capital by the family. It is a *production and investment* process extending over the life cycle that most emphatically includes preschool, intermediate, and college levels.

Another new challenge presented by this act lies in the possibilities implicit in it for virtually eliminating some of the worst aspects of unemployment. There is the possibility of varying the rate of funding of the basic opportunity grants in response to the unemployment rate in the 18-20-year-old age bracket so that the basic grants also act as a built-in stabilizer. The unemployment rate among 16-19-year-olds often reaches 15 percent, and it is normally about three times the rate for all civilian workers. Colleges could draw many new entrants out of the labor markets at times when unemployment is high (thereby improving markets for others). This would support investment in the accumulation of skills at times when foregone earnings costs are low and hence rates of return on the investment in relation to these costs are high. Stabilization effects would work automatically in the other direction in periods of full employment and of inflationary pressures—since larger amounts of skilled, productive manpower would be released into labor markets when they are tightest. The stabilization effects of Veterans' benefits following wars could be integrated with counter-cyclical stabilization effects of modified EOG's toward attainment of this more broadly defined stabilization goal.

The most obvious challenge presented by the new Federal role lies in meeting society's desire that higher education make significantly positive and efficient contributions toward the attainment of growth defined to include the nonmonetary private and social returns discussed above. This requires new work on calculating relative rates of both monetary and nonmonetary return for use in improving the efficiency of allocation decisions. There is some evidence, for example, that rates of return are highest for resources invested in preschool education, in improving the quality of secondary education in poor and rural areas, in training more doctors,[o] in

---

[o]The argument that there is only a maldistribution of doctors seems to overlook the fact that average incomes of urban specialists of about $120,000, of general practitioners of about $60,000, and long waiting lists are economic symptoms of acute shortages in an area where demands are income-elastic and growing rapidly.

supporting good students from low-income homes, and in improving the quality of junior colleges. There is serious need for research to expand the measures of rates of return to graduate degree programs to include imputations for nonmonetary, social returns through improved measurement of the social benefits of research. The price of the failure to do this will be distortion of social decisions due to errors of omission. The efficient attainment of real growth also implies Federal support for improving the efficiency of the entire process of producing educational capital. Beyond this, Federal support for the creation of new knowledge through research opens new higher return investment opportunities.

In conclusion, the situation that exists is itself a challenge inviting the development of a more comprehensive national education-economic policy. The investments in human resources now scattered among the Veterans Administration, Department of Labor, Social Security Administration, and Office of Education need to be drawn together in the USOE as well as in the budget in a more integrated approach. Furthermore, the production of educational capital by households occurs over its entire life cycle, and it is not surprising that progress with some of the problems in postsecondary education depends on making progress with those same problems at the primary and secondary levels. Finally, an integrated policy dealing with the economic aspects of educational policy needs to diffuse the race issue which has interfered with educational policy in the past, and stress the basic goals of real income growth, equity, and cyclical stability, which tend to be held in common by all citizens.

6 Federal Investment in Research at Institutions of Higher Education

New knowledge is created primarily by the work of individuals engaged in a wide range of different kinds of research. Higher education embodies this new knowledge in individuals, attaches it to pre-existing knowledge and an orientation to creativity: together they are important to the maintenance and progress of civilization.

There is an interdependence between the allocation of resources to research and to education. New knowledge created by basic research, about one-half of which is done in universities, presents new opportunities for high-return investment in educational capital. This embodiment of the new knowledge is necessary if the knowledge is to be applied and made effective.

In an excellent survey by Z. Griliches (1971) of empirical work on the returns to investment in research, the internal rates of return implied tend to be quite high (12-50 percent), in spite of conservative assumptions. He also notes the lag of 5-8 years before the products of basic research begin to affect the average productivity of an industry or economy. Therefore we are unlikely to see the effects of the current curtailment of basic research support on productivity growth immediately, but instead can expect to be plagued by its effects in the 1978-85 period.

Less is known about the support of that research done at universities. But because it is in part a joint product with education, and creates new opportunities for investment in education, it is appropriate that this chapter analyze the support for those types of research most closely interdependent with educational capital formation.

Basic research must be supported almost entirely by governments and foundations because the returns are almost entirely in the form of social benefits that cannot be collected by private agents through application of the price mechanism's exclusion principle. It differs from the patentable inventions of applied research in this respect.

Because the benefits from basic research are largely social benefits, the returns are very hard to measure accurately. T.W. Schultz and Zvi Griliches, however, have estimated rates of return to society from agricultural research on hybrid corn, sorghum, poultry, fertilizers, and agricultural extension based on the value of inputs *saved,* at 35-57 percent per dollar invested.[1] Comprehensive estimates of return to research in other disciplines such as educational psychology (e.g., improved efficiency in learning), economics (e.g., elimination of depressions), government (e.g., improved workability of social programs), or medicine (e.g., less illness) are not available, but they are likely to be high.

It is clear that most advances in knowledge do not contribute directly to the growth of *measured* national income. The contribution is indirect, showing up through improved quality of the newer labor force for example, or through improvements in the quality of final products,[a] or through similarly unmeasured improvements in social welfare. That portion of the advance in knowledge showing up in measured income growth is that which reduces cost, roughly estimated by Denison at one-fourth of the U.S. growth rate for the 1950-62 period.[b] There is no way of knowing how much basic versus applied research contributes to this residual; yet, returns to research do exist, as evidenced also both by the widespread support of research by firms who must meet market tests and by public support related to social benefits, even though much evidence pertinent to allocative efficiency is lacking.

Because of the interdependence of research with the process of investing in higher education and because returns to this research in the form of income growth and improved social welfare do exist, we shall turn now to the allocation of resources to the support of university-based research. In Part I the allocation of resources to university-based research is described. A model is presented in Part II to explain Federal effective demands for university-based research. It is followed in Parts III and IV with estimates of the interdependent system. Part V is a summary of the conclusions.

I. The Effective Demand for University-based Research

About 3.5 percent of national income in the United States is spent on research. This is higher than in Europe where the percentages are:[2]

Belgium	1.2%
Germany	1.5%
Netherlands	1.7%
France	1.8%
United Kingdom	2.5%

A large part of the research effort in the United States is devoted to military and space research, although space research has declined sharply. U.S. nondefense research expenditures (omitting military and space research) at

---

[a] Applied end results usually are made possible by developments at a more basic level.
[b] That is, 0.76 percentage points. See Denison (1967, p. 281, and 1973).

current exchange rates are still about two and one-half times as large as the average for these European countries. These cross-section comparisons suggest that the effective demand for research is quite income elastic.

Within the United States, the largest single source of demand is through the Federal government, which finances almost three-fifths of all research.[3] Of this, less than 10 percent normally goes to colleges and universities.[4]

The Support for Academic Research

Academic research is also supported by some state funds and by foundation grants. But it is difficult to separate the use of state funds and endowment funds for research from funds used to support graduate education.[5] Federal- and foundation-supported research are usually underwritten, however, with contract funds identified with specific research objectives that can be separated in the accounts of institutions.

Fig. 6-1 illustrates the spectacular growth of federally supported research at both public and private colleges and universities from 1928 through 1967, with declines in the period from 1968 through 1974. Prior to World War II, Federal research support going to colleges and universities was relatively small, and was limited mainly to the research activities of state agricultural experiment stations. It will be noticed in Fig. 6-1 that Federal research support going to public and to private institutions has been approximately equal in amount. It also is apparent that Federal investment in research has not exhibited highly volatile responses to cyclical fluctuations in either the 1932, 1938, 1949, 1954, 1958, or 1971 recession periods.

The data on Federal support of university-based research are developed in Appendix C. The major sources are the U.S.O.E. *Biennial Survey of Education* (which is the oldest known current series on research expenditures), the bulletins on *Land Grant Colleges and Universities,* and the National Science Foundation *National Patterns of R. & D. Resources.*

The growth in Federal investment in the creation of new knowledge at universities has been much more rapid than the growth of personal income, as also may be seen clearly in Fig. 6-1. This suggests further that research demands over time have a high long-run income elasticity.

Externalities and Growth of Basic Research

More than three-fourths of all funds spent by colleges and universities for

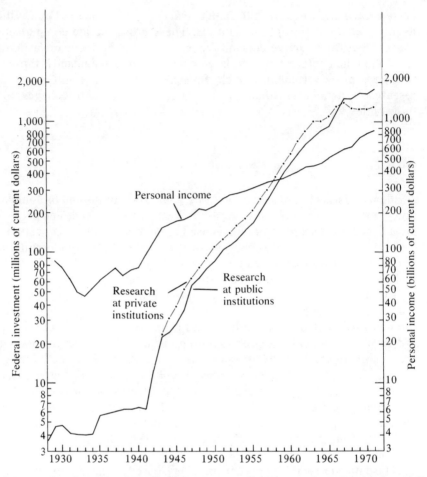

Figure 6-1 Growth of Federal Investment in Research at Institutions of Higher Education

Source: Appendix C, and Division of Science Resources Studies, National Science Foundation (for the last three years).

research support basic, rather than applied, research. As indicated previously the externalities that arise are largely social benefits from which the investor cannot collect a monetary return. So private firms have a limited incentive to support basic research, and prefer applied research that is more closely related to marketable applications. Furthermore, since findings of basic research must first be incorporated in applied research, the findings need to be widely and freely shared, and the eventual returns to basic research are then much longer in coming. Put another way, profit-

Table 6-1

Rates of Increase in Basic and Applied Research by Performing Sector, 1953-70

(annual growth rate in percent)

Sector	Basic research	Applied research
Universities and colleges	15.7	7.8
Affiliated research centers	13.9	9.3
Other nonprofit institutions	13.8	11.7
Federal government	10.5	8.0
Industry	9.9	9.8
Total	13.1	9.2

Source: National Science Foundation, *National Patterns of R & D Resources, 1953-71* (NSF 70-46), p. 3.

making institutions will underinvest in basic research from society's point of view since there is no way for them to collect all of the returns.

The rates of increase of expenditure for basic research up to 1970 have been higher at universities (15.7 percent) than in industry (9.9 percent) as may be seen in Table 6-1 above. But percentage increases have generally been higher for basic than for applied research at all types of profit and non-profit institutions.

These growth rates for basic research when converted to real terms are still over two times as high as the sustainable rate of growth in real gross national product. They suggest that basic research taken alone has had a high secular income elasticity of demand.

Content and Distribution of Federal Investment in Research

Most of the Federal support for research at universities and colleges comes from the Department of Health, Education, and Welfare and the Department of Defense. These two departments account for about 40 percent and 25 percent respectively, or two-thirds of the total. The remaining third comes from the National Science Foundation, National Aeronautics and Space Administration, Atomic Energy Commission, Department of Agriculture, Department of the Interior, and Department of Commerce. There has been a shift in emphasis in recent years with space and education research declining in absolute amount, and health research (which has always been the largest) increasing.

These agencies support research at universities in differing degrees. Over 75 percent of the National Science Foundation research funds go to universities, whereas less than 5 percent of the Department of Defense research and development funds go there. Most defense research is applied research performed by industry, whereas the NSF supports basic research and science education.

Military research is another instance of joint demand, in that the demand for defense research at universities is a byproduct of the effective demand for defense.[c]

Federal support for research is heavily concentrated in a few institutions. There are in the U.S. some two thousand institutions of higher learning of which 20, or about 1 percent, get 60 percent of the Federal funds. The data developed in Table C-1 separate expenditures at universities, four-year colleges and two-year colleges, revealing that almost all of the federally supported research (i.e., 84-90 percent) was performed at universities. The eight universities receiving the largest amount of Federal research and development funds were (in descending order), MIT, Michigan, Stanford, Columbia, UCLA, Illinois, Harvard, and Berkeley.[6]

II. The Model; Federal Effective Demands for University-based Research

The Federal government again is assumed to be an agent acting largely in response to the desires in the electorate for greater monetary and non-monetary satisfactions. It is reasonable to assume that some of these satisfactions can be increased through efforts to advance knowledge through research. It is the major influences on the public agents who determine the allocation of public funds to nonprofit research which will be considered here. There is another set of decision makers, those who act as research entrepreneurs in obtaining these funds and using them. This second set of agents is the primary focus of Schultz's recent inquiry (1971, pp. 217-46). In one sense his work supplements this section which deals with influences on the supply of research funds, an aspect that he does not directly consider.

Expected Growth and Externalities

Increased social satisfactions and their distribution have been expressed in a modified welfare function (or democratic state preference function) as follows:[10]

$$W_T = f\left[\sum_{k=1}^{n} g_{kt} Y_{kt}\right] \qquad t = T, \ldots, L \qquad (6.1)$$

---

[c] Defense research performed by industry is very large, accounting for 30 percent of all R & D expenditure.

[d] See Chapters 4 and 5.

Research is expected to yield future returns in the form of real private income (Y_t) for many families in the electorate over periods $T + 1, . . ., L$. It is also expected to yield social benefits shared by all and expressed in f. The distributional impacts of the private benefits from the research (e.g., sickle-cell anemia vs. cancer research) appear in the g_{kt} weights. Also weights favoring a longer planning horizon would tend to favor basic rather than applied research.

Current resources constrain the amounts available for research of all kinds. This assumes restrictions on borrowing. Borrowing for this purpose, for example, is restricted by borrower's risk because returns to basic research involve long-run social benefits that are quite uncertain. The constraint also assumes fixed tax shares,[e] so that total tax receipts which most directly constrain investment in research are in turn a function of personal income. Under these assumptions, Federal investment in the creation of new knowledge through research (I_{Rt}) is ultimately a function of current real personal income (Y_t), as shown in Eq. 6.2 below.

Since advances in knowledge are a prime source of growth of future income (Y_t, $t = T + 1, . . ., L$), desired investment in research may also be hypothesized to be a positive function of these expected net returns. The desire for normal growth will be measured by the gap between the desired rate of economic growth (taking the desired rate $g^* = 4.2$ a sustainable rate) and the actual growth rate g, or $(g^* - g)_{t-1}$. This ignores efforts to raise the sustainable rate g^*. This much, however, can be set out as the first two terms in a linear-first approximation:

$$I_{Rt}^* = \alpha_1 Y_t + \alpha_2 (g^* - g)_{t-1} + \alpha_3 W_{t-1} + \alpha_4 \qquad (6.2)$$

W_{t-2} seeks to reflect intensification of the reach for defense and national power. It is a dummy variable that switches from zero to one following Sputnik at the time the military-space technology race began. It is intended to reflect the element of joint demand between demands for research and desires for defense or national power.

Stocks of "Disembodied" Knowledge

It is possible to conceive of a stock of knowledge created by research of all kinds (S_{Kt}). It resides primarily in major libraries and materials in print. Its existence is distinct from attempts to embody this knowledge in persons, which is the role of investment in education.

Investment in research is an attempt to increase this stock of "disem-

---

[e]Equal proportional sacrifice is probably a more accurate characterization of our entire current Federal tax system than is equal marginal sacrifice (i.e., minimum aggregate sacrifice).

bodied'' knowledge. It is useful to define new research in relation to the portion of the stock of existing knowledge that has been created by research as follows:

$$I_{Rt} = [S_{Kt} - (1 - \delta)S_{Kt-1}] \qquad (6.3)$$

Specific investment in research—for example, the large-scale Manhattan Project, to develop the atom bomb in World War II, or the investment needed to place a man on the moon—can be regarded as investment designed to close a gap between actual knowledge $(1 - \delta)S_{Kt-1}$ and some specific desired level (S_{Kt}^*). But although frequently only part of the adjustment occurs in any one year, this has not contributed to significant short-run cyclical volatility in investment in Federal support of university-based research, as may be seen in Fig. 6-1. Contracts once made normally are carried to completion. This weighs against postulating a stock adjustment process as a central element in the analysis of demand, although not against defining research in relation to the stock of knowledge as a useful organizing concept.

Storage of this existing stock of knowledge (S_{Kt}) in libraries and minimizing its loss through depreciation (δ) do constitute an important social concern, however. The Education Amendments of 1972 authorize the appropriations for libraries that are shown in Table 6-2.

Obsolescence differs from depreciation in that it may be a positive function of new research. Rosen (1971) has suggested that the rate of obsolescence of scientific knowledge is quite high, although it is obsolescence of knowledge after it has been embodied in educational capital of which he speaks, i.e., of $(1 - \delta)S_{ET-1}$. He does not explicitly relate this rate to investment in new research.

But disembodied knowledge presents formidable measurement problems, even if it were to be measured at original cost. Much knowledge is created in other countries, it is heterogeneous, and obsolescence rates are more easily conceived of in relation to embodied knowledge. For these reasons it is best to omit S_{Kt-1} from regressions, while retaining the focus on

Table 6-2
Appropriations Authorized for Libraries
(in millions of dollars)

		1972	1973	1974	1975
A.	College library resources	$18	$52.5	$59.5	$70
B.	Library training and research	12	22.5	25.5	30
C.	Library of Congress	9	12	15	19

investment in research as an explicit effort to add to the stock of existing knowledge.

III. Empirical Tests of Influences on Investment in Research

These major influences on real Federal investment in research at institutions of higher education which were summarized in Eq. 6.2 are tested using time series data in Table 6-3. Investment in research performed at public universities, colleges, junior colleges, and all public institutions combined is considered by regression equations (1)-(4), and equations (5)-(8) deal with comparable types of private institutions.

The main results are, first, that Federal investment in research at all types of higher educational institutions does depend significantly on growing real income. This is consistent with the hypothesis that research is a normal public good, and with the higher secular income elasticity noted earlier. Second, the financial support for research also depends significantly on the excess of desired over actual growth rates, at least at universities. Third, W'_{t-2} as an index of efforts to advance military and space technology turned out to be a less important factor than might have been expected.

Emphasis should be placed only on those Table 6-3 regressions dealing with research at public and private universities, where almost all of the organized research is conducted. The statistical properties of these equations, (1) and (5), are quite good. It does seem reasonable that desired growth and the military-space race drop away as positive influences on research effort at four-year colleges and junior colleges. Beyond this point, the equations dealing with research at junior colleges and at private four-year colleges, (3), (6), and (7), are best ignored. Research at junior colleges was practically nonexistent prior to 1966, and the data series underlying equation (6) contains too much serial correlation in the residuals.[f]

The ρ coefficient is positive, and $\rho = .33$ to $.36$ in the university research equations. There is from investment in graduate education the likelihood of a positive feedback effect that makes available larger numbers of skilled research workers able to do research, a feedback effect that has not been taken into account. The statistics are bad on investment in graduate education, but there is a clear upward trend in the number of persons in the population as measured by Census estimates with five or more years of college education. Increasing the numbers of persons with advanced training certainly operates to restrain increases in cost while improving the

---

[f]Several explanatory variables were tried that did not work out and are not discussed here. Most notably $G_{T/G}$, or Federal transfer payments as a percent of the total budget as an index of social, as distinguished from defense, concerns, was tried but was never significant.

Table 6-3
Investment in Research at Institutions of Higher Education by the Federal Government, 1946-68
(*t*-statistic in parentheses below each coefficient; significant coefficients are underlined.)

Investment I_R (Dependent variable)	Real personal income Y_t	Gap, desired over actual growth rate $(g^* - g)_{t-1}$	National power (military space race) W'_{t-2}	Constant term	ρ	$\bar{R}^2$ (after ρ) SE_ϵ
(1) *Public universities*						
$R_u^2 = .960$, $SE_u = 66.26$	.0032	19.52	85.71	−846	.36	.981
D.W. = 1.90	(12.13)	(2.59)	(1.74)	(−8.59)		45.82
(2) *Public 4-year colleges*						
$R_u^2 = .429$, $SE_u = 24.74$	.0004	1.02	a	−150	.85	.955
D.W. = 1.75	(5.43)	(.96)		(−.374)		6.92
(3) *Public 2-year colleges*						
$R_u^2 = $ n.a., $SE_u = 42.80$	.0001	.20	a	b	1.01	.846
D.W. = .85	(3.26)	(.74)				2.01
(4) *Public total*						
$R_u^2 = .954$, $SE_u = 79.15$	.0035	18.81	80.32	−968	.46	.980
D.W. = 1.90	(10.90)	2.11	(1.38)	(−7.69)		52.44

(5) Private universities $R^2_u = .954$, $SE_u = 55.30$ D.W. = 1.82	$\dfrac{.0024}{(10.40)}$	$\dfrac{14.69}{(2.16)}$	70.51 (1.58)	$\dfrac{-638}{(-7.33)}$	.33	.973 42.14
(6) Private 4-year colleges $R^2_u = $ n.a., $SE_u = 735.$ D.W. = .68	$-.0011$ (-1.64)	-2.67 $(-.53)$	66.02 (1.86)	$\dfrac{1,181}{(2.07)}$	.96	.937 33.85
(7) Private 2-year colleges $R^2_u = .850$, $SE_u = .326$ D.W. = 1.41	$\dfrac{.0001}{(9.57)}$	.055 (1.79)	a	$\dfrac{-3.20}{(-6.86)}$	.62	.955 .179
(8) Private total $R^2_u = .365$, $SE_u = 303$ D.W. = 1.06	$\dfrac{.0018}{(5.15)}$	2.53 (.29)	a	b	.94	.969 66.89

Sources: Appendices A and C.

$^a W'_{t-2}$, the least significant variable, was dropped before the equation was reestimated.
^{b} The constant term was not significantly different from zero and was suppressed.

capacity to do effective research. Perhaps the contribution of graduate education to research underlies the $\rho \simeq .36$,

$$(.36u_{t-1} + \epsilon_t) = [.36S_{EGt-1} + \epsilon_t] \tag{6.4}$$

where S_{EGt-1} is the stock of postgraduate education.

IV. A Model with Interdependence between Higher Education and Research

It has been suggested above that investment in higher education depends in part on new higher return opportunities to invest, using the new knowledge created by basic research. Similarly, investment in research is only practicable by using human resources created by investment in higher education.

This suggests the dependence of investment in higher education on investment in the creation of new knowledge through research (I_{Rt}, instead of ρ). Its essence is shown in the higher education investment equations 6.5, 6.6, and 6.7 and in the joint dependence of investment in research on investment in higher education in 6.8:

$$I_{Ht} = f_5 (. \ . \ ., I_{Rt}) \tag{6.5}$$

$$I_{S+Lt} = f_6 (. \ . \ ., I_{Rt}) \tag{6.6}$$

$$I_{Ft} = f_7 (. \ . \ ., I_{Rt}) \tag{6.7}$$

$$I_{Rt} = f_8 [. \ . \ ., (I_{Ht} + I_{S+Lt} + I_{Ft})] \tag{6.8}$$

This simultaneous equation model therefore links the investment in research considered in this chapter to the investment in higher education considered in Chapters 3-5. Using the main results drawn from Chapters 3-6, the joint dependence of education and research is tested in the estimates made by restricted three-stage least squares that are presented in Table 6-4. I_{Ht}, I_{S+Lt}, and I_{Ft} are treated as jointly dependent variables, but their coefficients are forced by the restriction in the estimating process to be equal to one another as shown by the .756 coefficient estimated for each in Eq. 4 in Table 6-4.

The significance of both current income and young adults (or veterans) holds up in these simultaneous equation estimates. The positive and usually significant coefficients for investment in research are consistent with

Table 6-4
The Joint Dependence of Investment in Education and Research
(t-statistic is shown below each coefficient in parentheses; millions of constant 1958 dollars.)

Investment in:	Current income	Young adults (C_{18-26}) or veterans (V)	Desired growth (Y_{Bt}, g^*) or equity (g_k)	Constant term	Investment in research, education
(1) Higher education, households	$\underline{.032}\ Y_t$ (7.83)	$+\underline{54456}\ C_{18-26}$ (7.67)		$\underline{-12360}$ (−7.21)	$\underline{+2.53}\ I_{Rt}$ (5.05)
(2) Higher education, state and local	$\underline{.013}\ Y_t$ (11.37)	$+\underline{21074}\ C_{18-26}$ (8.50)	$+\underline{5721}\ g_k$ (2.79)	$\underline{-7988}$ (−7.14)	$+1.778\ I_{Rt}$ (1.55)
(3) Higher education, federal	$\underline{.009}\ Y_t$ (4.61)	$+\underline{.039}\ V_t$ (7.76)	$+.027\ Y_{Bt}$ (.53)	-779 (−1.49)	$+\underline{.112}\ I_{Rt}\quad -13.7\ (1\ -\ \delta)S_{Et-1}$ (.93) (5.04)
(4) Research[a]	$.003\ Y_t$ (1.08)		$+19.64\ (g^* - g)_{t-2}$ (1.06)	-1214 (−1.49)	$+.756\ (I_H + I_{S+L} + I_F)$ (1.45)

Sources: See Appendix A for sources and for the definitions of the variables.

[a]Research in (4), and in (1), (2), and (3), was deflated with the Personal Consumption Expenditures deflator (as were all other economic variables), in contrast to the FPGS deflator used earlier in this chapter. Switching to the latter would very possibly cause the significance of Y_t and $(g^* - g)_{t-2}$ in (4) to conform more closely to earlier results.

the hypothesis that new research does create new investment opportunities, for households (see Table 3-4) and for state and local governments (see Table 4-2) at least. It is not important in the equation explaining Federal investment in higher education. Investment in higher education makes a less satisfactory addition to the research equation (4 in Table 6-4); when it is introduced, it substitutes, in part, for highly significant income and desired growth effects.[g]

We may conclude that this source of simultaneity does not disturb any of our other results. Although other types of tests of this subtle hypothesis are needed, it also offers some evidence consistent with the proposition that investment in research does create new educational capital investment opportunities.

V. Summary of Conclusions

Research in institutions of higher education supported by the Federal government is concentrated in a few universities. It is dependent upon real income growth, and exhibits a very high gross secular income elasticity.

Research simultaneously contributes to advances in knowledge, and through this to growth. Because its relation to growth is widely recognized, it may sometimes be called upon (e.g., in the 1960s) to increase growth. But this effect, if it exists, is weak.

The measures that were tried of the effect of intensified demands for military-space technology did not prove significant. However, recent NSF data for total R & D support to all universities show increases up through 1969, followed by a flattening out in 1969-74, especially in 1970.[h] 1970-71 saw the beginning of the end of the space race, Vietnam, and campus disturbances, and was also a recession period. The restrictions continued through the 1974-75 fiscal year budget, including the Nixon Administration's restrictions on Federal support of the related opportunities for investment in graduate education. But the restrictions on Federal *research* support are likely to be less significant in the long-run than the positive effect of the continuing growth of real income.

Finally there is some tentative evidence of interdependence between investment in higher education and investment in research. Research creates new knowledge that generates obsolescence of some existing

---

[g] When the number of persons in the population with 5 or more years of higher education was substituted for this recent investment, it together with current income was highly significant.

[h] Unpublished data supplied by the Universities and Nonprofit Institutions Studies Group, Division of Science Resources Studies, National Science Foundation. The total is for all institutions, but does not include NIH programs that NSF classifies under "other science activities."

knowledge, and hence of some human capital, while at the same time creating opportunities to invest profitably in new educational capital. There is some suggestion that these opportunities are seized upon by households. As postsecondary educational opportunities are further extended to students who are from low-income families, this contribution of new knowledge by research has the potential of preventing diminishing returns to educational capital.

7 Conclusions

Higher education has been viewed in a new light in this study, as an investment in human resources with the household regarded as the basic producer of educational capital. This is important, for not only does the family provide the emotional support and offer a model for guidance with greater or lesser efficiency from preschool through graduate school years, but it also provides the bulk of the investment.

Higher educational institutions fill a necessary supporting role by supplying formal education inputs. Governmental units also support the process by correcting underinvestment (or overinvestment) and furthering equity. Research has a key role in the creation of new knowledge that offers (and finds) new high return opportunities for investment in educational capital, countering the onset of diminishing returns to this type of investment.

I. Major Findings

It is a basic result that investment in higher education turns out to be a positive function of current personal income not only for households, but also for state and local governments and for the Federal government. This result, at least for households, is intuitively obvious and frequently alluded to, but others have not specifically worked it out. This study develops an analytical model of the family's life cycle subject to short term constraints on borrowing and on access to future returns in Chapter 2, that together with the analysis of public expenditure decisions in Chapters 4 and 5 explains why current income is logically important. Current resources are empirically more important than expected future earnings per student in all cases, including investment by families (Chapter 3), by state and local governments (Chapter 4), or by the Federal government (Chapter 5). Most investigators are likely to accept the influence of income on investment in education as reasonable, and many have mentioned it almost in passing (together with the feedback, but nonsimultaneous, effect of education as an important contributor to economic growth). But the theory presented here, as well as the empirical results, give income a central role with both statistical and analytical content.

The income elasticities of investment demands for research are even higher than they are for postsecondary education. Together with the preceding income effects on education, this suggests that in a growing economy, investment in postsecondary education can be expected to continue to expand even though enrollments decline, and eventually expansion of research can be expected to resume as an offset to diminishing returns.

The number of young adults in the college-age bracket, which is a measure of aggregate investment opportunities, is the second important determinant of all types of investment in higher education by households (see Table 3-2) and by state and local governments (see Table 4-3). It is replaced by a four-year moving total of recently discharged veterans as the second most important determinant of Federal investment. The graduation from college of those who were part of the post-World War II wave of births, and the recession-related decline in income, operated to curtail finances at public and private institutions alike in 1971-74. This should ease whenever job markets are good and full employment fiscal and monetary policies are followed. However, educational planners would do well to use the lower demographic projections to plan on curtailment of capital expenditure and slower rates of growth of real investment in higher education.

Other variables are more marginally significant in specific situations. High long-run interest rates have been negatively related to investment by households at private institutions (Chapter 3). Rising private school tuitions have increased revenues at these institutions from families (Chapter 3) along with continuing restrictions on admission. There is some evidence of a negative short-term reduction in public sector investment when existing stocks of educational capital get high (see Tables 4-2 and 5-1). But this is often accompanied by a positive trend that has been removed from the residuals, a trend that tentatively has been interpreted as a creation of new investment opportunities through research. Data has been developed on research expenditures at different types of universities (Appendix C) which reveals that the high secular income elasticity mentioned above is sometimes accompanied by some response of rates of investment in research to deviations between actual and desired rates of growth.

The limitations to time series analysis are well recognized. But they do reveal effects that can be revealed in no other way, and suggest hypotheses for further testing with microeconomic data. Such tests are underway.

II. Growth, Stability, and Equity: Implications for Policy

The Education Amendments of 1972, summarized in Chapter 5, may well be as important as, if not more important than, the Land Grant Act of 1862 in their impact in the long run on higher education in the United States. The

Land Grant Act extended postsecondary education to the sons of farmers and to children from middle-income homes, creating new curricula in agriculture, engineering, and business in the process. The Education Amendments of 1972 undertake to extend postsecondary educational opportunity to students from low-income families.

This Act presents many challenges, not the least of which lie in the imaginative testing of workable curricula and in the administration of the act so that it effectively aids those with greatest need. There is the simultaneous Administration effort, for example, to discontinue and to decentralize some existing Federal higher education programs to the states, linked with a battle over revenue sharing. The Act itself furthermore will divert large amounts of the money through the half-cost provision (see Chapter 5) to the high-cost private schools. Private institutions are less strongly church related now, and in the author's opinion do deserve and need some public support. They have felt financial pressures recently similar to the falling revenue receipts per student that have troubled the public institutions. These pressures have been rooted primarily in the slower rates of growth of endowment fund income and slackening of demand (Chapter 3). But the high tax cost of excessive use of private institutions through the half cost provision as a means of extending educational opportunity (because of the high per student cost in private institutions) needs to be taken seriously into account.

It is concluded that the crisis in educational finance facing public and private institutions alluded to in the introductory chapter is in part a passing phase, for there are several undercurrents of long-run growth. Adjustments need to be made for the slowdown in the rate of increase in the numbers of young adults in the oncoming college generations. But there are important effects from rising income. There are implications in the gradual extension of postsecondary education to low-income homes. And the production of new knowledge by research also suggests a slower but continuing expansion of real investment in higher education as new opportunities for investment in human capital are created.

The challenges presented by the revolution that is underway in the subject of educational finance, however, remain very real. As basic social science disciplines are brought to bear on the problems of education, whole new ways of looking at and doing things that go beyond narrower efforts to do old things better are increasingly likely to emerge. In addition to the current attention being given to measuring costs, I should like to summarize three possibilities developed in more detail in the text.

First, there is the broad challenge of improving investment decisions, and through this the allocation of resources, toward the end of achieving humane growth. This involves locating where there are higher rates of return, using a broader criteria of monetary plus nonmonetary (and private plus social) returns, and then taking steps to increase investment at those points. If there is overinvestment elsewhere, it should be curtailed. Calculating more broadly conceived rates of return and finding out where they are highest in both education and research are two very large and difficult tasks. Important contributions are being made to this by Schultz (1971) and (1972), the NRC Panel on the Benefits of Higher Education, and others. Two very limited aspects of attempts to improve calculated rates of return are the incorporation of nonmonetary private benefits in the analysis offered in Chapter 2 of family decision-making, and the incorporation of social benefits in the model of public decision-making offered in Chapter 4. But there is much to be done in merely calculating the contribution of various education and research inputs to measured growth.

Second, there is the challenge of finding ways of utilizing the continuing expansion of junior college enrollments to help stabilize the high 13-18 percent unemployment rates among young adults aged 17-20 during recessions. Specific suggestions have been made in Chapter 5 as to how this might be done by use of the BEOG's while also reaching unemployed blocks. The release of larger numbers of more skilled persons onto labor markets during periods of overfull employment, then, would help stabilize further by easing shortages and aiding productivity during the periods when the most help is needed toward easing inflationary pressures.

Third, there is the challenge of research on means of securing equity in access to educational opportunity for each new generation. Specific suggestions have been made relating to the importance of modifying the half-cost provision and more fully funding the basic and supplemental economic opportunity grants referred to in Chapter 5. This is related to the debate over low public school tuitions, discussed in the appendix to Chapter 3. Unfortunately it has proceeded without much reference to the out-of-pocket room, board, and other living costs, or to the total stock of educational capital. The issue has been dominated by competitive relationships between the public and private sectors, and within the public sector as low-cost junior colleges compete with the senior public institutions with lower out-of-pocket room, board, and tuition costs.

But is it is not just the growth of educational capital stocks which low tuitions encourage, but also the extension of higher educational opportunities to the poor. This operates toward reducing the inequality in the personal distribution of income in the next generation. Vertical equity in benefits is also a challenge, because its realization depends on recognition of the different characteristics of students that come from poor urban families. This, in turn, is based on understanding the process of production of educational capital by households.

In sum, there is the challenge offered by the need for development of a more coherent national higher education policy. There is the need for focus on the concept of investment in educational capital as a unifying concept. The present state of affairs is a mixture of pressure group special pleadings and of relatively limited hard research by economists, educational psychologists, and specialists from other "outside" basic disciplines that is so vital to the development of new approaches. There is need to find ways to avoid the "off again, on again" element in Federal policies that create such havoc in the higher education community and make no contribution to economic stability. There is need to coordinate and perhaps to collect together some responsibility for widely scattered higher education programs and data now located in many different agencies. And most important, there is need to relate education programs more coherently to broadly held desires for economic growth (efficiency) and intergenerational equity.

Appendix A
List of Variables and Data Sources

The source notes below refer to items in Part II of the list of References to "Government Documents and Related Data Sources." The source notes are not repeated for each variable where there is duplication, but in all cases follow the list of variables that are all drawn from the same source. Measures in real terms are deflated by use of the Personal Consumption Expenditures (P.C.E.) implicit deflator unless indicated to the contrary.

I_t = *Investment in higher education* in period t. Different components of this investment appear with subscripts, and sources, that are given later on in this list.

q_{it} = *Quantity of the ith market good* in period t. When the *ith* good is some component of formal higher education (as will be clear from the context), q equals enrollment, and the subscript refers to the *ith* type of institution as indicated next below.

q_{pub} = *Enrollment in all public institutions* of higher education: public universities and four- and two-year colleges.

q_{pvt} = *Enrollment in all private institutions* of higher education: private universities and four- and two-year colleges.

> *Source* (of enrollment data): 1929-54: U.S.O.E. *Biennial Survey of Education* (1962). 1955-73: U.S.O.E. *Opening Fall Enrollments in Higher Educational Institutions* (1973).

p_{it} = *Price of the ith market good* in period t. When the *ith* good is some component of formal higher education (as will be clear from the context), p equals the own-price, and the subscripts refer to the *ith* type of institution, or component, as indicated below.

p_{jt} = *Price of a substitute* for the *ith* good in period t.

p_{pub} = *Price per student at public institutions* in constant 1958 dollars, at full cost. For components of full cost, see subscripts below. For type of public institutions, see table stubs where price terms are used.

> p_{T+F} = *Tuition and fees per student* at public institutions $(p_{T+F}q_{pub}/q_{pub})$.
>
> p_{S+L} = *State and local support per student* $(p_{S+L}q_{pub})$.
>
> p_F = *Federal support per student* $(p_F q_{pub}/q_{pub})$.

141

p_G = *Gifts and endowment income per student* $(p_G q_{pub}/q_{pub})$.

p_{pvt} = *Price per student at private institutions* in constant 1958 dollars. For components of full cost, see subscripts below. For universities, four-year and two-year colleges, and all private institutions, see table stubs.

p_{T+F} = *Tuition and fees per student* at private institutions $(p_{T+F}q_{pvt}/q_{pvt})$.

p_{S+L} = *State and local support per student* $(p_{S+L}q_{pvt}/q_{pvt})$.

p_F = *Federal support per student* $(p_F q_{pvt}/q_{pvt})$.

p_G = *Gifts and endowment income per student* $(p_G q_{pvt}/q_{pvt})$.

Source (of price data above): See sources for investment expenditure given below, and method of computing index of prices in parentheses above.

I_{Pub} = *Total investment in higher education at public institutions* (total and major components in millions of constant 1958 dollars, P.C.E. deflator), $(p_{pub}q_{pub})$.

I_{T+F} = *Real investment by households through tuition and fees* at public institutions $(p_{T+F}q_{pub})$.

I_{S+L} = *Real investment by state and local governments* at public institutions, broken down into investment at public universities, or four- or two-year institutions as indicated where used.

I_F = *Real Federal investment in higher education* excluding research (see Appendix C and $p_{FV}q_{pub}$ as defined below)—broken down into investment at public universities, as indicated where used.

I_G = *Real investment from gifts and endowment income* at public institutions.

I_{pvt} = *Total investment in higher education at private institutions* (total and all major components in millions of constant 1958 dollars, P.C.E. deflator) $(p_{pvt}q_{pvt})$.

I_{T+F} = *Real investment by households through tuition and fees* at private institutions, $(p_{T+F}q_{pvt})$.

I_{S+L} = *Real state and local investment* at private institutions, broken down into investment at private universities, four- or two-year colleges as indicated where used.

I_F = *Real Federal investment in education* excluding research (see Appendix C) at private institutions—broken down into investment at private universities, four-year or two-year colleges as indicated where used. See also I_{FV} below.

I_G = *Real gift and endowment income* of private institutions.

Source (of all investment expenditure data above): 1929-1969 U.S. Office of Education *Biennial Survey of Education* (1962), Chapter 4, "Statistics of Higher Education," after which its name was changed to U.S.O.E. *Financial Statistics of Higher Education: Current Funds Revenues and Expenditures* (1973). The concepts are those in Table 3 of each issue. Specifically, 1927: pp. 34,40; 1929: pp. 54-55; 1931: pp. 32-33; 1933: pp. 38-39; 1935: pp. 40-41; 1937: pp. 50-51; 1939-41: pp. 38-39; 1943: p. 42; 1945: p. 48; 1947: p. 58; 1949: p. 36; 1951: p. 48; 1953: p. 10; 1955: p. 10; 1957: p. 8; 1959: p. 12; 1961: p. 34; 1963: p. 4; 1965: p. 11; 1966: p. 14; 1967: pp. 12-13; 1968: p. 16; 1969 and later unpublished data supplied by C. George Lind of the National Center for Educational Statistics. For I_F see Appendix C.

I_H = *Total real investment by households in higher education*, in millions. Public institution (*pub*) or private institution subscripts are added when appropriate. The components are:

I_{T+F} = *Net tuition and fees paid by households*, ($p_{T+F}q_{pub}$ or $p_{T+F}q_{pvt}$, the same as above).

I_{R+B} = *Room and board* at public ($p_{R+B}q_{pub}$) or private ($p_{R+B}q_{pvt}$) institutions.

I_{EFE} = *Excess foregone earnings* beyond room and board costs at public ($p_{EFE}q_{pub}$) or private ($p_{EFE}q_{pvt}$) institutions.

I_{FV} = *Veterans and social security dependents'* benefits paid to households by the federal government at public ($p_{FV}q_{pub}$) and at private ($p_{FV}q_{pvt}$) institutions. These are included in tuition and fee and room and board payments made by households above.

Source (of investment expenditures by households above) I_{T+F}: same as I_{T+F} farther above, so see the detailed sources listed there; I_{FV}: see Table 5-2; I_{R+B}: computed using a price index for room and board costs (and for total out of pocket costs to the household) for 1929-64 from E. D. West et. al. p. 38, and for 1965-73 from U.S.O.E. *Projections of Educational Statistics* (1971) and later issues. These are specific to public and private institutions. They are multiplied by enrollment (i.e. $p_{R+B}q_{pub}$ and $p_{R+B}q_{pvt}$) to obtain I_{R+B} at each type of institution. I_{EFE} at public and private institutions are computed by adjusting real average weekly earnings in manufacturing (from the *Statistical Abstract*) for a 25-week school year by employment rates. The resulting foregone earnings per student are multiplied by public and private institution enrollments, respectively. Room and board is then subtracted to get the excess foregone earnings residual.

$I_{R(pub)}$ = *Total Federal expenditures on research at public institutions of higher education* (in constant 1958 dollars and all deflated by Federal Purchases of Goods and Services deflator).

$I_{R(pvt)}$ = *Total Federal expenditures on research at private institutions of higher education* (in constant 1958 dollars and all deflated by Federal Purchases of Goods and Services deflator).

Source (of data on investment in research): see Appendix C.

S_{Et-1} = *The stock of higher educational capital* as of the end of period $t-1$ measured at original cost.

Source: Appendix B, Table B-4, lagged one year.

S_{Et-1}^c = The stock of higher educational capital as of the end of period $t-1$ measured as the number of persons aged 25 and older with at least one year of college.

Source: U.S. Bureau of the Census, *Current Population Reports,* Series P-20, Nos. 6, 15, 99, 121, 138, 158, 169, 182, 194, and 207.

S_{Et}^a = *The stock of all educational capital*, including primary and secondary.

Source: Appendix B, Table B-1.

$Y_{Dt} = $ *Real disposable personal income.*

> *Source*: U.S. Office of Business Economics *National Income and Product Accounts (1972).*

$Y_t = $ *Real personal income.*

> *Source*: *Ibid.*

$Y_t^e = $ *Expected real disposable personal income* for years $t = T+1$, on. Rather than by using a distributed lag on past income, this was measured directly by an index of income expected in the future in relation to current income as of February each year as reported to Michigan Survey Research Center interviewers, and was computed as the net percent expecting an increase.

> *Sources*: 1949-59 *Federal Reserve Bulletins* (1973) (March issues, e.g., 1959, p. 253), 1960-69 *Survey of Consumer Finances*, Michigan Survey Research Center.

$Y_{Bt}^e = $ *Average annual increment to expected real personal income attributable to a bachelor's degree.* This is net of annual real personal income expected by a high school graduate. Expectation measures are based on the hypothesis that they reflect current actual income differentials.

> *Source*: Of actual differentials: 1946-70: U.S. Bureau of the Census *Statistical Abstract of the U.S.* (1972); 1939, 1946 are in *1962* issue, p. 119; 1949, 1956 in *1970*, p. 111; 1965, 1966 in *1968*, p. 112; 1967, 1968 in *1970*, p. 111; 1969, 1970 in *1972*. See also *AER*, December 1960.

$C_t = $ *Young adults of college-eligible age as a percent of the population*; upper age allows for graduate school, lower for state planning. Age ranges used in explanatory variables are:

> C_{18-26} for total investment by households, including returning veterans.
>
> C_{16-26} for state investment at universities.
>
> C_{16-22} for state investment at four-year colleges.
>
> C_{16-20} for state and local investment at two-year colleges.

> *Source*: U.S. Bureau of the Census, *Current Population Reports* (1972), Series P-25, Nos. 311, 314, 385, 416, 441, and 448.

$S_{Pt-1} = $ *Psychological stocks of tastes and habits for higher education*, measured as the number of persons (parents) aged 35-64 who have completed four or more years of college.

> *Source*: U.S. Bureau of the Census, *Current Population Reports*, (1972), Series P-20.

g_{kt} = *Implicit income distribution weights, measured collectively, as Gini coefficient of inequality in the distribution of income*, calculated by quintiles.

> *Sources*: 1929-63 H. Miller, *Income Distribution in the U.S.*, p. 21; 1964-70 U.S. Bureau of the Census, *Current Population Reports*, Series P-60, No. 80, p.28.

g_t = *Actual growth rate of real Gross National Product.*

> *Source*: A five-year moving average of annual percentage increases in real GNP as calculated from the U.S. Office of Business Economics (1972) National Income and Product data. The average is computed for years $T - 3$ through $T + 1$ to apply to the current year T.

δ = *Obsolescence rate applying to the stock of educational capital*, (which, only in Chapter 2, includes depreciation from retirements and death). This is estimated as part of the regression co-efficient $\theta(1-\delta)$ from the data.

ρ = *A coefficient measuring autoregression in the residuals* by a first-order autoregressive scheme. Rho, ρ, is postulated to be a crude measure of the stimulus to investment provided by new knowledge created by research.

s_t = *Percent of the household's total work-time devoted to the production of educational capital.*

w_t = *Index of faculty salaries, nonfaculty salaries, and the price of supplies and services* purchased by educational institutions.

> *Source*: Weights of .43 for faculty salaries, .28 for nonfaculty salaries, and .29 for the price of supplies and services are from J. D. Millett, *Financing Higher Education in the U.S.*; 1929-67 data from J. O'Neill (1971), p. 81; 1967-71 faculty salaries from *AAUP Bulletin*, June 1971, p. 240; nonfaculty salaries from U.S. Office of Business Economics (1972) July 1971, p. 36; Price of supplies data from the Wholesale Price Index for fuel, paper, and paint, in Ibid. For 1972-80: After conversion to 1958 base, indices were projected to 1980 based on growth rates of comparable deflators as predicted by the DRI econometric model.

r = *long-term real interest rate*. Measured as the interest rate on new first mortgages deflated by the Personal Consumption Expenditures implicit deflator.

> *Source*: 1929-47 Morton, *Urban Mortgage Landing*, p. 173; 1948-72 *Economic Report of the President*; 1973-80 as predicted by DRI model.

r_M^e = *Ex ante private rate of return from investment in higher education*, an internal rate of return.

> *Source*: Calculated as described in Part IV, Chapter 2 above from survey data described in McMahon and Wagner (1973).

V_t = *Change in the number of veterans under age 35 in civil life*, a four-year moving total.

> *Source*: 1929-55: *Historical Statistics of the U.S.*, Series Y787-800, p. 738; 1956-69 U.S. Bureau of the Census, *Statistical Abstract* (1973).

Q_{et} = *Gross additions to the stock of educational capital produced through higher education* (see I_h).

P_{et} = *Shadow price of Q_{et} to households*. (This is not measured directly, but see p_{T+F}, p_{R+B}, and p_{EFE} under I_H above).

D = *Control by Democratic party*. A dummy variable; D = one, in years Democrats control both executive and legislative branches, D = zero, in years they control none or one branch only.

> *Source: Statistical Abstract*.

R = *Control by Republican party*. A dummy variable: R = one, in years Republicans control both executive and legislative branches, R = zero, in years they control none or one branch only.

> *Source: Statistical Abstract*.

N = *Percent of labor force employed*. For example, for 5 percent unemployment, N = 95.0.

> *Source*: U.S. Executive Office of the President, *Economic Report of the President* (1974).

$(g^* - g)$ = *The gap between the desired (or sustainable) rate of economic growth and the actual rate*. The former is taken to be 4.2%, the latter is measured as a moving average of the actual rate over the *preceding* five years. Specifically

$$(4.2\%) - (g_{t-3}) = 4.2 - \left(\sum_{t=-5}^{-1} g_t \right) /5$$

W = *Wartime dummy variable* intended to reflect, in part, greater external threats. W = one for war years, W = zero for nonwar years.

W_{t-2} = *Post-Sputnik period.* A special emphasis on both space research and military preparedness occurred that was strengthened by the Viet Nam escalation. A dummy variable with W = zero for 1946-62, W = one for 1963 onward.

F_t = *Federal grants in aid* to state and local governments, no measure for which is needed here.

B_t = *State and local borrowing*, no measure needed here.

R_t = *All other state and local revenue*, other than that from application of a sales tax rate (t_1) or of an income tax rate (t_2), of state and local governments, no measure for which is needed.

μ = *A rate of discount for borrower's risk*. It is an average of the expected rates for $t = T, \ldots, L$.

γ_1 = *A rate of discount for lender's risk*. This also is an average of the expected rates.

θ_t = *A short term adjustment coefficient.*

u_t = *A disturbance term.*

ϵ_t = *A disturbance term.*

Appendix B
Annual Data on the Stock of
Educational Capital, 1928-72

I. Estimates of Total Educational Capital

Estimates of the total stock of educational capital in the United States during the 1928-72 period that was created by formal education were constructed and based upon the real costs in 1958 dollars of the resources invested in primary, secondary, and higher education. These costs include the tuition and fees, tax, and gift-supported costs of the institution-controlled resources used for instruction, the earnings foregone by students, expenditures on books, expenditures on school supplies, and commuting expenses. This appendix reports the data, explains the methods by which they were constructed, and gives the underlying data sources.

The method employed in general is that developed by Schultz (1971) as reported in his *Investment in Human Capital*, chap. 8. Therefore the results for 1928-1972 after allowance for the minor adjustments in concept appropriate to our purposes (described below) are directly comparable to T.W. Schultz's benchmark estimates for 1940 and 1957, but include the intervening years and extend the estimates through 1972. The method estimates the stock of educational capital as the annual real cost of education per person in 1958 dollars times the number of constant (equal length) school years completed by those members of the population aged 14 years old and over. This total stock of all educational capital, S_{Et}^a, which includes that formed through primary and secondary schooling, is shown in Table B-1 in column 2 (for 1928-45) and column 6 (1946-72). The latter is the product of column 4 (average cost) and column 5 (school years completed), which are shown separately for the postwar years.

The only important difference between Schultz's data and the estimates derived in this appendix is that Schultz (1971) measures the stock of educational capital embodied in the population as the product of the annual cost per member of *labor force* (ibid. p. 128, col. 2) and the total constant schools years completed by the population (ibid., p. 126, col. 4). The estimates presented here compute and use the average annual cost of education with respect to the *population* rather than with respect to the labor force. This puts the results on a consistent basis. The educational capital stock formed by the entire population including housewives is society's total stock from the point of view of the analysis of decisions to invest, including investment in education for women. The result is that a more rapid growth of educational capital in the postwar years is revealed; S_{Et}^a is 51 percent of Schultz's estimate in 1945 and grows to 91 percent of his

Table B-1
Stock of Educational Capital, 1928-72 at Original Cost (constant 1958 dollars)

(1) Prewar years	(2) Stock of all educational capital (billions of dollars) S_{Et}^a	(3) Postwar years	(4) Cost in 1958 $ of one school year, average of all levels [Table B-3, Col. (8+9+10) ÷ (7)]	(5) Total constant school years completed (in millions)	(6) Total stock of all educational capital (billions, 1958 $ S_{Et}^a
1928	188				
1929	195				
1930	201				
1931	210				
1932	218				
1933	226				
1934	235				
1935	243				
1936	251				
1937	260				
1938	268				
1939	276				
1940	285				
1941	296				
1942	308				
1943	320				
1944	331				
1945	343				

Year			
1946	355	868	409
1947	378	902	419
1948	399	921	433
1949	438	946	463
1950	489	970	504
1951	522	990	527
1952	572	1,030	555
1953	617	1,046	590
1954	657	1,068	615
1955	670	1,094	612
1956	719	1,119	643
1957	754	1,146	658
1958	797	1,181	674
1959	855	1,209	707
1960	891	1,225	728
1961	954	1,272	750
1962	1,022	1,298	788
1963	1,079	1,336	807
1964	1,179	1,373	859
1965	1,300	1,416	918
1966	1,419	1,455	975
1967	1,534	1,494	1,026
1968	1,632	1,539	1,061
1969	1,444	1,288	1,121
1970	1,697	1,453	1,168
1971	1,814	1,491	1,217
1972	1,999	1,530	1,306

estimate in 1957. It reflects the shift from low-cost elementary schooling of homemakers and others who are included in the population but not in the labor force toward higher-cost secondary and college training. The remaining difference is accounted for by Schultz's data being in 1956 rather than in 1958 prices. The third and final difference is that although our data are listed also by academic year, the designation is for the beginning rather than the ending half.

Other measures of the value of the stock of educational capital in terms of its marginal productivity (as measured by earnings under the assumption that labor is paid the value of its marginal product) are less relevant to a capital stock adjustment model on the grounds that human capital cannot be liquidated by resale. Nevertheless, the failure to take depreciation and obsolescence of society's stock of educational capital into account (apart from mortality, which is naturally taken into account) is a definite weakness of this original resource-cost measure of the size of the current stock.

Table B-2 shows the calculation of average annual resource costs of education in constant dollars, which is put on a per-student basis in Table B-3, columns 8-10, before being averaged for use in the calculation shown in column 4 of Table B-1. These average annual resource costs in Table B-2 include annual earnings foregone by high school and college students in the postwar years as shown in columns 3 and 7. They were calculated by multiplying the 11 earning-equivalent weeks of high school students and 25 earning-equivalent weeks of college students, as discussed in Schultz (1971, p. 85), by the average weekly earnings of all manufacturing workers from the *Historical Statistics of the United States*, p. 92, Series D 626-34, and later issues of the *Statistical Abstract*. These measures of average weekly earnings were then adjusted for changes in the rate of unemployment taken from the *Economic Report of the President*. Next, total foregone earnings adjusted for unemployment were obtained by multiplying these average weekly earnings by enrollment in secondary schools, as described in U.S.O.E., *Digest of Educational Statistics*, 1970, p. 27, and U.S.O.E., National Center for Educational Statistics, *Projections of Educational Statistics to 1979-80, 1970 Edition*, 1971, p. 20, and in colleges and universities as found in U.S.O.E., *Biennial Survey of Education in the U.S.*, chap. 4; U.S.O.E., *Opening (Fall) Enrollment in Higher Educational Institutions*; and U.S.O.E., National Center for Educational Statistics, *Projections of Educational Statistics to 1979-80, 1970 Edition*, 1971, p. 23. Expenditures for books and other private expenses such as commuting, shown in columns 4 and 8 of Table B-2, are estimated as 5 percent of total foregone earnings at the secondary level and 10 percent at the college level by Schultz (1971, p. 94, n. 5, and p. 95, n. 5). In general, years beyond the last year for which data is available are extrapolated on the basis of the previous five-year average annual rate of growth.

The net institutional cost of public elementary and secondary schools shown in columns 1 and 2 of Table B-2 then was estimated by first deducting capital outlays from gross expenditures (i.e., capital outlays, U.S. Bureau of the Census, *Historical Statistics of the U.S. Colonial Times to 1957*, p. 209; Research Division of N.E.A., *Estimates of School Statistics, 1967-68*, Research Report 1967-R 19; and gross expenditures, U.S. Bureau of the Census, *Statistical Abstract of the U.S.*, 1952, Table 143, and later issues). Implicit interest and depreciation charges, calculated as 8 percent of the value of property (1929-58: U.S.O.E., *Biennial Survey of Education in the U.S.*, chap. 2, Table 1, and 1959-67: U.S.O.E., *Statistics of State School Systems*) were then added to this net cost to obtain the total institutional cost of public elementary and secondary schools. This public total was then multiplied by the ratio of gross expenditures for private versus public elementary and secondary schools (gross expenditures for private elementary and secondary schools are given by U.S. Bureau of the Census, *Statistical Abstract of the U.S.*, 1952, Table 143, and later issues). This yielded an estimate of the total institutional cost of *private* elementary and secondary schools. Next, these *public* and *private* totals were combined to obtain the overall institutional cost of all elementary and secondary schools in the same proportion as estimated by Schultz (1971, p. 91, Table 6.3, cols. 9, 10, 11).

The total institutional cost of colleges and universities shown in column 6 of Table B-2 was estimated as the sum of implicit interest and depreciation charges, calculated as 8 percent of the value of property (U.S.O.E., *Historical Statistics, of the U.S. Colonial Times to 1957*, p. 213; U.S.O.E., *Higher Education Finances, Selected Trend and Summary Data*, 1968, p. 3; and U.S.O.E., *Financial Statistics of Institutions of Higher Education: Property, 1965-66*, p. 27, and later issues), plus current income used for instruction. The latter is from the following sources: for state and local governments, and the Federal Government, U.S.O.E., *Biennial Survey of Education in the U.S.*, chap. 4; U.S.O.E., *Financial Statistics of Institutions of Higher Education: Current Revenue and Expenditures*, 1960, p. 12, and later issues; for tuition and fees, ibid., p. 15, and earlier issues; and for endowment earnings, private gifts and grants, organized activities related to instructional departments, and miscellaneous activities, U.S.O.E., *Historical Statistics of the U.S. Colonial Times to 1957*, p. 212, Series H 339-350, and U.S.O.E., *Statistical Abstract of the U.S.*, 1962, p. 132, and later issues.

The total adjusted earnings foregone by high school and college students plus their expenditures for books and for commuting were added to the respective total institutional costs at each level shown in columns 1, 5, and 9 in Table B-2. These costs and the institutional costs of elementary schools have been converted to 1958 dollars using the Personal Consump-

Table B-2
Total Annual Resource Costs of Education, 1946-75
(in millions of constant 1958 dollars)

	Elementary	Secondary				Higher			
Year	(1) Total	(2) Institutional	(3) Foregone earnings	(4) Other (e.g., books)	(5) Total (2+3+4)	(6) Institutional	(7) Foregone earnings	(8) Other (e.g., books)	(9) Total (6+7+8)
1946	4,082	2,346	4,094	205	6,644	1,708	2,515	252	4,474
1947	4,264	2,419	4,283	214	6,916	1,926	3,316	332	5,573
1948	4,568	2,547	4,455	223	7,225	2,223	4,138	414	6,775
1949	5,136	2,827	4,450	222	7,499	2,457	4,169	417	7,042
1950	5,725	3,096	4,830	241	8,167	2,622	4,490	449	7,561
1951	5,963	3,197	5,128	256	8,581	2,589	4,395	439	7,423
1952	6,438	3,421	5,450	272	9,143	2,689	4,225	423	7,337
1953	7,295	3,842	5,928	296	10,067	2,859	4,604	460	7,923
1954	8,341	4,354	5,976	299	10,629	3,052	4,651	465	8,168
1955	8,438	4,367	6,439	322	11,128	3,315	4,993	499	8,807

Year									
1956	9,291	4,765	7,137	357	12,259	3,597	5,175	518	9,289
1957	10,021	5,094	7,595	380	13,068	3,939	5,718	572	10,229
1958	10,714	5,397	7,579	379	13,356	4,299	5,744	574	10,618
1959	11,385	5,658	8,416	421	14,496	4,662	6,729	673	12,063
1960	12,196	6,007	9,000	450	15,457	5,088	7,185	718	12,991
1961	12,959	6,297	9,553	478	16,328	5,596	7,762	776	14,134
1962	13,907	6,696	10,635	532	17,863	6,180	8,775	878	15,832
1963	15,122	7,215	10,966	548	18,728	6,829	9,180	918	16,927
1964	16,474	7,788	12,149	607	20,545	7,601	10,848	1,085	19,534
1965	18,338	8,551	12,928	646	22,126	8,780	12,490	1,249	22,519
1966	20,096	9,284	13,603	680	23,567	9,736	13,677	1,368	24,781
1967	21,670	9,919	13,994	700	24,613	10,914	14,872	1,487	27,273
1968	22,694	10,244	14,750	738	25,731	12,167	16,471	1,647	30,266
1969	24,726	11,109	15,454	773	27,336	13,199	17,683	1,768	32,649
1970	26,266	11,746	15,659	783	28,188	14,590	18,174	1,817	34,582
1971	27,754	12,296	15,930	796	29,021	16,085	18,919	1,892	36,895
1972	30,201	13,254	16,753	838	30,845	18,326	20,322	2,032	40,680
1973	32,362	14,068	17,330	866	32,265	20,708	21,580	2,158	44,446
1974	34,502	14,786	17,735	887	33,408	23,347	22,437	2,244	48,028
1975	36,766	15,758	18,403	920	35,080	26,578	23,592	2,359	52,529

Table B-3
Annual Cost of Education per Member of the Population Aged 14 Years and Over, 1946-75
(in constant 1958 dollars)

Year	Annual Cost per Student[a]			Median School Yrs. Completed, Pop.				Annual Cost per Person		
	(1) Elementary	(2) Secondary	(3) Higher	(4) Elementary	(5) Secondary	(6) Higher	(7) Total (4+5+6)	(8) Elementary (1×4÷7)	(9) Secondary (2×5÷7)	(10) Higher (3×6÷7)
1946	200	1,072	2,670	8.0	1.3	.35	9.7	1,600	1,442	924
1947	205	1,098	2,600	8.0	1.4	.35	9.7	1,637	1,528	909
1948	210	1,129	2,590	8.0	1.4	.37	9.8	1,671	1,597	956
1949	226	1,172	2,670	8.0	1.4	.39	9.8	1,800	1,681	1,049
1950	245	1,256	2,844	7.9	1.5	.41	9.8	1,943	1,831	1,172
1951	247	1,300	2,982	7.9	1.5	.44	9.8	1,961	1,920	1,300
1952	256	1,345	3,162	7.9	1.5	.46	9.9	2,022	2,001	1,445
1953	277	1,418	3,266	7.9	1.5	.46	9.9	2,196	2,135	1,492
1954	306	1,436	3,223	7.9	1.5	.46	9.9	2,420	2,180	1,489
1955	298	1,427	3,310	7.9	1.5	.46	9.9	2,362	2,186	1,523
1956	318	1,459	3,466	7.9	1.5	.46	9.9	2,522	2,254	1,612
1957	333	1,468	3,470	7.9	1.6	.46	10.0	2,639	2,295	1,613

Year										
1958	348	1,452	3,461	7.9	1.6	.49	10.0	2,755	2,301	1,682
1959	361	1,510	3,572	7.9	1.6	.50	10.0	2,860	2,429	1,800
1960	375	1,515	3,626	7.9	1.6	.52	10.1	2,970	2,458	1,893
1961	394	1,512	3,661	7.9	1.6	.54	10.1	3,116	2,473	1,977
1962	415	1,553	3,792	7.9	1.7	.56	10.1	3,284	2,565	2,128
1963	441	1,535	3,767	7.9	1.7	.56	10.2	3,487	2,587	2,124
1964	471	1,631	3,946	7.9	1.7	.57	10.2	3,726	2,810	2,226
1965	517	1,702	4,075	7.9	1.8	.60	10.2	4,084	2,906	2,339
1966	558	1,759	4,180	7.9	1.8	.62	10.3	4,413	3,120	2,487
1967	599	1,800	4,257	7.9	1.8	.65	10.3	4,729	3,181	2,657
1968	620	1,825	4,372	7.9	1.8	.66	10.4	4,930	3,249	2,828
1969	670	1,885	4,472	7.9	1.8	.68	10.4	5,328	3,415	2,938
1970	714	1,892	4,545	7.9	1.8	.70	10.4	5,672	3,448	3,086
1971	762	1,897	4,615	8.0	1.8	.71	10.5	6,063	3,490	3,207
1972	841	1,952	4,824	8.0	1.9	.73	10.5	6,691	3,626	3,430
1973	914	1,992	5,007	8.0	1.9	.74	10.6	7,277	3,734	3,640
1974	989	2,001	5,166	8.0	1.9	.76	10.6	7,871	3,786	3,839
1975	1,069	2,040	5,414	8.0	1.9		10.6	8,516	3,896	4,109

[a]Totals from Table B-2, Columns 1, 5, and 9 divided by the number of students at each level.

tion Expenditure implicit price deflator, U.S. Office of Business Economics, *National Income and Product Accounts of the U.S. 1929-65*, 1966 Supplement to the *Survey of Current Business*, p. 162, and later July issues, and U.S. Office of Business Economics, *Survey of Current Business*, September 1971, p. 13. These costs were then divided by the respective enrollment levels. Sources of these costs are: U.S.O.E., *Biennial Survey of Education in the U.S.*, chap. 1, p. 24, and later issues, and U.S.O.E., National Center for Educational Statistics, *Projections of Educational Statistics to 1979-80, 1970 Edition*, 1971, p. 20. The resulting annual real costs per student are shown in columns 1-3 in Table B-3. These costs per student were then multiplied by the average number of school years completed by the population at each level of education, shown in columns 4-6 in Table B-3 from U.S. Bureau of the Census, *Current Population Reports*, Series P-20, no. 6, and later reports, and U.S. Bureau of the Census, *Statistical Abstract of the U.S.*, 1956, p. 111, and later issues. The resulting costs per person at each level were summed and then divided by the overall average number of school years completed, shown in column 7 of Table B-3, to estimate the average annual real cost of education inclusive of all levels, shown in columns 8-10 of Table B-3, in Schultz [1971, p. 127, Table 8.3 (1957 labor force only)] and Table B-1.

The resulting average cost of education for one year shown in Table B-1, column 4, was then multiplied by the total number of constant school years completed by the population (14 years old and over) shown in Table B-1, column 5, to estimate the total real value of the stock of educational capital (S_{Et}), which is the desired result, shown in Table B-1. The following procedure was used to adjust the length of the school year to a constant 1940 base. First, the population was divided into six age groups (14-24, 25-34, 35-44, 45-54, 55-64, 65 years and over). The median number of school years attained by each age group as reported in U.S. Bureau of the Census, *Current Population Reports*, Series P-20, No. 6, and later issues, and U.S. Bureau of the Census, *Statistical Abstract of the U.S.*, 1956, p. 111, and later editions, was then multiplied by an index measuring the length of the school year in which one-half of their education was completed, taken from U.S. Bureau of the Census, *Historical Statistics of the U.S., Colonial Times to 1957*, p. 207, and U.S. Bureau of the Census, *Statistical Abstract of the U.S.*, 1962, p. 121, and later issues. Next, the constant median number of school years completed by each age group was multiplied by the total number of persons in each group, figures taken from U.S. Bureau of the Census, *Current Population Reports*, Series P-25, No. 311, and later issues. These results were then summed to obtain the total number of constant school years completed by the entire population aged 14 years and over.

Constant school years completed were computed for 1928-72, but all of the necessary cost data is not available for the pre World War II years. The values of the educational capital stock for 1928-45 were therefore obtained by interpolating between Schultz's benchmark years from Schultz (1971, p. 129, Table 8.5, col. 3) and then adjusted for level by the ratio at the 1946 link year.

II. Estimates of the Stock of Higher Educational Capital

Because this study is limited to the investment demand for higher education, it is the stock of educational capital created by higher education only that is most directly relevant to the adjustment of existing stocks of educational capital in the society. New estimates of these, eliminating stocks created by primary and secondary education are presented in the second and last columns of Table B-4 for the pre World War II and postwar years respectively.

For the post World War II years, the total number of years of higher education completed by the population 14 years old and over, shown in column 8 of Table B-4, was estimated. First, the number of persons 14 years old and older who had completed 1-3 years college, in Column 4, was multiplied by an average of 2 years completed by this group, to get column 5. Then the number completing at least four years of college (in column 6) was multiplied by 4, a conservative average of the number of years they completed, to obtain column 7, which was added to column 5 to get the total in column 8. These population statistics were obtained from the U.S. Bureau of the Census, *Current Population Reports*, Series P-25, Nos. 21, 43, and 385, and Series P-20, Nos. 6, 15, 79, 121, 138, 158, 169, 182, 194, 207, and 229.

To obtain the stock of higher educational capital in column 10, the total number of years of higher education completed in column 8 was multiplied by the average annual cost per student of higher education in constant 1958 dollars, shown in column 9, and taken from Table B-3, column 3.

For the prewar years, since the computation just described is not possible, an estimate was made by multiplying the total stock of educational capital as given by Table B-1 by .242, the link percentage in the overlapping 1946 year. This will overestimate somewhat the stock of higher educational capital in the earlier years, where its size relative to that of the primary and secondary educational capital stock is likely to be smaller than it was in 1946. The 1973-79 projections are not based on analysis of causal influences but instead exhibit extrapolations of underlying trends.

The estimates in Table B-4 also assume that the college school year has not changed significantly over time.

Table B-4

Stock of Higher Educational Capital, 1929-79 at Original Cost (in billions of constant 1958 dollars)

(1) Prewar years	(2) Higher educational capital S_{Et}	(3) Postwar years	(4) Persons age 14+ with 1-3 yrs college (millions)	(5) Years completed by 1-3 yr persons (millions)	(6) Persons age 14+ with 4 yr college (millions)	(7) Years completed by 4-yr persons (millions)	(8) Total years of H.Ed. completed by population (millions)	(9) Annual cost of H.Ed. per student (in dollars) (from B-3)	(10) Higher educational capital S_{Et}
1928	45.50								
1929	47.19								
1930	48.64								
1931	50.82								
1932	52.76								
1933	54.69								
1934	56.87								
1935	58.81								
1936	60.74								
1937	62.92								
1938	64.86								
1939	66.79								
1940	68.97								
1941	71.63								
1942	74.54								
1943	77.44								
1944	80.10								
1945	83.01								

Year							
1946	6.7	13.4	4.7	18.8	32.2	2,670	85.97
1947	7.0	14.0	4.8	19.2	33.2	2,600	86.32
1948	7.4	14.8	5.2	20.8	35.6	2,590	92.20
1949	7.6	15.2	5.6	22.4	37.6	2,670	100.39
1950	8.0	16.0	6.1	24.4	40.4	2,844	114.90
1951	8.4	16.8	6.6	26.4	43.2	2,982	128.82
1952	8.8	17.6	7.1	28.4	46.0	3,162	145.45
1953	8.9	17.8	7.1	28.4	46.2	3,266	150.89
1954	9.0	18.0	7.3	29.2	47.2	3,223	152.12
1955	9.0	18.0	7.4	29.6	47.6	3,310	157.56
1956	9.1	18.2	7.6	30.4	48.6	3,466	168.45
1957	9.2	18.4	7.7	30.8	49.2	3,470	170.72
1958	9.7	19.4	8.2	32.8	52.2	3,461	180.66
1959	10.3	20.6	8.6	34.4	55.0	3,572	196.46
1960	10.9	21.8	8.9	35.6	57.4	3,626	208.13
1961	11.7	23.4	9.3	37.2	60.6	3,661	221.86
1962	12.3	24.6	9.9	39.6	64.2	3,792	243.45
1963	12.5	25.0	10.2	40.8	65.4	3,767	246.36
1964	12.7	25.4	10.3	41.2	66.2	3,946	261.22
1965	13.4	26.8	10.8	43.2	68.6	4,075	279.54
1966	14.4	28.8	11.4	45.6	72.4	4,180	302.63
1967	15.4	30.8	11.9	47.6	76.4	4,257	325.23
1968	15.7	31.4	12.6	50.4	81.2	4,372	363.12
1969	16.8	33.6	13.2	52.8	84.2	4,472	376.54
1970	17.6	35.2	13.7	54.8	88.4	4,545	401.78
1971	18.4	36.8	14.3	57.2	92.4	4,615	426.43
1972	19.2	38.4	14.8	59.2	96.0	4,824	463.10
1973	20.7	41.4	15.4	61.6	100.0	5,007	500.70
1974	20.7	41.4	15.9	63.6	105.0	5,166	542.43
1975	21.5	43.0	16.5	66.0	107.4	5,414	581.46
1976	22.3	44.6	17.1	68.4	111.4	5,588	622.50
1977	23.1	46.2	17.6	70.4	115.0	5,762	662.63
1978	23.9	47.8	18.2	72.8	119.0	5,936	706.38
1979			18.7	74.8	122.6	6,110	749.09

Appendix C
Annual Data on Federal Investment in University-based Research

This appendix presents newly developed estimates of Federal investment in research done at institutions of higher education. Previously only scattered figures have been available on research done outside of industry, mostly in publications of the U.S. Office of Education and of the National Science Foundation. But considerable additional attention was needed to get these collected into one place and put on as consistent a basis as possible for the entire time period.

Estimates are shown in Table C-1, columns 2 and 6, for Federal support research at institutions of higher education for the academic years 1928 through 1968. Academic-year data are dated in Table C-1 as of the first half of each academic year. Federally supported research at public and private institutions in the postwar years is shown separately in columns 7 and 11. These, in turn, are broken down by research at universities, four-year colleges, and two-year junior colleges in columns 8-10 and 12-14. The sources for 1943-68 are as follows: U.S. Office of Education, *Biennial Survey of Education*, chap. 4, "Statistics of Higher Education," 1943: Table 3, p. 42; 1945: Table 3, p. 48; 1947: Table 3, p. 58; 1949: Table 2, p. 36; 1951: Table 2, p. 48; 1953: Table 3, p. 10; 1955: Table 3, p. 10; 1957: Table 3, p. 8; U.S.O.E., *Financial Statistics on Institutions of Higher Education*, 1959: Table 3, p. 12; U.S.O.E., *Higher Education Finances*, 1961: Table 2, p. 34; Ibid., 1963: Table 2, p. 4; National Center for Educational Statistics, *Financial Statistics for Institutions of Higher Education*, 1965: Table 2, p. 11; Ibid., 1966: Table 3, p. 14; Ibid., 1967: Table 3, pp. 12-13, and Ibid., 1968: Table 3.

Before 1951 total Federal research expenditures were used from these sources for two categories only, funds for public institutions and funds for private institutions, because the definitions classifying universities and four-year colleges changed in 1951. Starting in 1951, the data are the same as those given by these publications for the following categories: (1) public universities, (2) public four-year colleges, (3) public two-year junior colleges, (4) private universities, (5) private four-year colleges, and (6) private two-year junior colleges. In order to allocate the funds granted to public and private institutions between 1943 and 1951 to the types of institutions mentioned above, percentages based on 1951 definitions were used. For example, the percentage that each type of institution represented in the total public research figure in 1951 was calculated, and these percentages were applied to the total for public institutions for the period 1943-50.

163

Table C-1

Federal Investment in Research at Institutions of Higher Education, 1928-68

(in millions of current dollars)

(1) Prewar years	(2) Total public	(5) Postwar years	(6) Total	Public institutions				Private institutions			
				(7) All public	(8) Univ.	(9) 4-year	(10) 2-year	(11) All private	(12) Univ.	(13) 4-year	(14) 2-year
1928	3.6	1943	47.0	22.2	21.3	0.9	0.0	24.8	15.4	9.4	0.0
1929	4.6	1944	56.8	24.6	23.6	1.0	0.0	32.2	20.0	12.2	0.0
1930	4.8	1945	67.0	27.3	26.1	1.1	0.0	39.7	24.6	15.1	0.0
1931	4.2	1946	92.1	39.5	37.9	1.6	0.0	52.6	32.6	20.0	0.0
1932	4.1	1947	118.9	53.4	51.2	2.2	0.0	65.5	40.6	24.9	0.0
1933	4.1	1948	143.1	63.5	60.7	2.6	0.1	79.6	49.4	30.2	0.0
1934	4.2	1949	167.8	74.0	70.8	3.1	0.1	93.8	58.2	35.6	0.0
1935	5.4	1950	200.5	89.0	85.2	3.7	0.1	111.5	69.2	42.3	0.0
1936	5.8	1951	232.5	103.4	99.0	4.3	0.1	129.1	80.1	49.0	0.0
1937	6.0	1952	263.7	114.8	109.6	5.1	0.1	148.9	94.5	54.3	0.0
1938	6.1	1953	295.5	127.0	121.1	5.9	0.0	168.5	109.0	59.5	0.0
1939	6.1	1954	337.2	150.1	144.8	5.3	0.0	187.1	119.7	67.3	0.1
1940	6.2	1955	379.1	173.4	168.5	4.8	0.0	205.7	130.4	75.1	0.2
1941	6.2	1956	471.0	217.4	211.5	6.0	0.0	253.6	157.1	96.1	0.3
		1957	563.2	261.6	254.5	7.1	0.0	301.6	184.0	117.2	0.5
		1958	710.7	326.9	316.6	10.3	0.0	383.8	245.9	138.3	0.6
		1959	858.4	392.3	378.8	13.5	0.0	466.1	306.0	159.4	0.7
		1960	1083.1	486.5	467.5	19.0	0.0	596.6	370.6	225.2	0.8
		1961	1307.6	580.6	556.2	24.4	0.0	727.0	435.2	291.0	0.8
		1962	1571.3	686.1	656.7	29.3	0.0	885.2	512.0	372.0	1.3
		1963	1835.0	791.5	757.2	34.3	0.0	1043.5	588.7	453.1	1.7
		1964	1969.3	869.7	823.0	46.3	0.3	1099.6	637.0	461.0	1.6
		1965	2103.7	947.8	888.8	58.4	0.6	1155.9	685.4	469.0	1.6
		1966	2510.4	1217.7	1114.5	94.8	8.4	1292.7	875.6	415.0	2.1
		1967	2917.4	1487.8	1340.3	131.3	16.2	1429.6	1065.8	361.1	2.7
		1968	2774.9	1480.2	1317.2	137.5	25.5	1294.7	1005.8	285.1	3.8

Prior to 1966, the *Biennial Survey of Education* gives figures on Federal support for research only for every other year; the estimates for the years between biennial surveys were interpolated.

Finally, in the post World War II years Federal funds for research at institutions of higher education as described above did not include that portion of Land Grant Act funds used for research at agricultural experiment stations. The latter therefore was obtained separately from the U.S.O.E. *Digest of Educational Statistics*, 1963, chap. 2, p. 83, Table 80, and later issues. Most of these funds (96.3 percent) went to public universities. However, the 1956-58 issue of the *Biennial Survey* (chap. 4, sec. 2, Table 14, p. 27) is the basis for a percentage breakdown among public institutions (columns 7-10), which then was used for allocating total Land Grant Act research funds among types of public institutions in the postwar years.

Although U.S.O.E. data are probably the best, if not the only, source of R and D expenditures by colleges and universities prior to 1951, there is no *Biennial Survey* data on research at colleges and universities for the years prior to World War II. Federal research support to institutions of higher education prewar however was relatively small and was limited mainly to the research activities of state agricultural experiment stations. The data shown for 1928-41 were drawn, therefore, from the U.S.O.E. Bulletin No. 28, *Land-Grant Colleges and Universities*, 1930, p. 56, Table 13, and later issues, and applied to Federal research funds provided under the land grant acts. These went to the 69 land grant institutions, 68 of which are public, plus Cornell University, where the New York State College of Agriculture is located. The prewar totals in column 2 therefore are totals for Land Grant Act research at public institutions.

For the 1928-41 period, the land grant acts were the Hatch, Adams, Purnell, Jones-Bankhead (1936), and Agricultural Adjustment Acts. For the two academic years beginning in 1929 and 1930, total Federal expenditures for institutions of higher education had to be divided between research and nonresearch by using the 1928 and 1931 research percentages (28.4 percent and 27.1 percent respectively). Jones-Bankhead Act Federal expenditures on higher education had to be separated into research and nonresearch for 1935-41 by application of the 1946 percentage (16.85), the year the relevant breakdown first became available. Funds from the other land grant acts were added to the Jones-Bankhead research funds to obtain the total.

Historical Statistics of the United States, chap. W, "Research and Development, General Note," pp. 609-14, has a good survey of related data sources. As indicated there, the oldest known current series on research expenditures is that on organized research by institutions of higher education, 1930-42 in U.S.O.E. *Statistics of Higher Education: Receipts, Ex-*

penditures, and Property 1953-4, 1957, p. 131, but this reveals nothing about Federal support in relation to that from foundations, endowment funds, and state government. Joseph H. Schuster, study director at the National Science Foundation, who has been very helpful in developing the data presented here, also recommends U.S.O.E. over the National Science Foundation as about the only source for the years prior to 1953.

Appendix D
Data-Collecting Instruments

A STUDY OF THE COLLEGE INVESTMENT DECISION

Questionnaire: Stage I (Nonfreshmen)

Directions: We hope this questionnaire will provide you an interesting and complete overview of the investment you are making for yourself while you are in college. To be a useful study that can help all students, however, each question must be answered. Please *circle the correct response* for each appropriate item. If a question asks for a monetary amount, enter a 0 (zero) if it does not apply to you. Please *do not leave blanks.* Thank you.

1. Are you currently attending college? *(Circle one.)*

   Full time .1 . . . . *(Go to Question 2A.)*
   Part time . . . . .2 . . . . *(Go to Question 2A.)*
   Not enrolled in college . . . . . . .3 . . . . *(Skip to Question 19.)*

2A. What is the name of the college you are **now** attending?

   _____

B. In what state is it located?

   _____

C. Do you plan to attend this college next year? *(Circle one.)*

   Yes 1
   No 2

3. When you complete your formal schooling, what occupation do you plan to pursue? *(Please select the occupation from the list enclosed with this questionnaire and write the appropriate code number below.)*

   ___ ___   ___ ___

4. What is the highest academic degree that you intend to obtain? *(Circle one.)*

   None 1
   Associate (or equivalent) 2
   Bachelor's degree (BA, BS, etc.) 3
   Master's degree (MA, MS, etc.) 4
   PhD or EdD 5
   MD, DDS, DVM (Medical) 6
   LLB, or JD (Law) 7
   BD (Divinity) 8
   Other 9

5. How important to you is each of the five following reasons for continuing your education? Although the reasons are not mutually exclusive, think carefully about the relative importance of each reason compared to the others. *(Circle one for each item.)*

	Very Important	Somewhat Important	Not Very Important	Not Important
A. To get a better job that earns a higher income	1	2	3	4
B. To enjoy greater personal satisfaction	1	2	3	4
C. To serve society	1	2	3	4
D. To serve the next generation by more competently rearing children	1	2	3	4
E. The guidance and advice of my parents	1	2	3	4

6. How important to you is each of the following potential benefits from your college education? *(Circle one for each item.)*

	Very Important	Somewhat Important	Not Very Important	Not Important
A. Meeting and conversing with interesting people	1	2	3	4
B. Finding a husband (wife) with good financial prospects	1	2	3	4
C. Locating a suitable career	1	2	3	4
D. Providing volunteer civic and intellectual leadership	1	2	3	4
E. Nonmonetary job satisfaction	1	2	3	4
F. Finding a husband (wife) with college-developed values	1	2	3	4
G. Earning a good income in your chosen career	1	2	3	4
H. A continuing interest in reading and new ideas	1	2	3	4
I. Guiding and educating your own children	1	2	3	4
J. Becoming more broadminded, concerned about others, and more tolerant	1	2	3	4

7. Approximately how much money did your parents spend on you for clothing and supplies (e.g., sheets, pillows, typewriter, radio, etc.) from July 1971 through January 1972?

   $_____ .00

8A. Do you contribute money to your parents to help them pay bills or provide for your brothers and sisters?

   Yes . . . . .1 . . . . *(Answer Question 8B.)*
   No . . . . .2 . . . . *(Skip to Question 9.)*

B. Approximately how much per month do you pay your parents?

   $_____ .00 per month

9. Where do you now live while attending college? *(Circle one.)*

   With parents or relatives 1
   Nonuniversity housing (not with parents or relatives) 2
   In residence hall, fraternities, or sororities .3
   Other university housing 4

167

10A. Do you have any brothers or sisters (living at home and/or away from home)?

Yes ....1 .... *(See note below.)*
No ....2 .... *(Skip to Question 11.)*

If yes to Question 10A:

> Questions 10B and 10C inquire about the age and college experience or plans of your brothers and sisters. They are to be answered in the box or matrix that appears between these two questions.

B. What is the age of each of your brothers and/or sisters? *(List the ages in the first column of the box below and indicate whether it is a brother or sister in the second column.)* *

Question 10B		Question 10C	
Age	Brother = 1 Sister = 2 (Circle one.)	Number of College Years Completed	Number of College Years to Go
	1　2		
	1　2		
	1　2		
	1　2		
	1　2		
	1　2		

*If you have more than 6 brothers and sisters, list the information for the oldest 6.

C. How many years has each of your brothers and/or sisters completed and how many years do you estimate that each has to go in college? *(List the college years completed in the third column and the years to go in the fourth column of the above box.)*

11. Is your college on a semester, quarter, or trimester system? *(Circle one.)*

Semester 1
Quarter 2
Trimester 3

12. Are you single or married? *(Circle one.)*

Single 1
Married (spouse not a student) ....2 *(See instruction below.)*
Married (spouse also a student) ......3 *(See instruction below.)*

> **Married Students:** Include the expenses of all your family members in each item in Question 13. If your spouse is also a student, be sure to include his or her tuition expense in Question 13A and books and supplies expenses in Question 13B.

13. The following questions are concerned with your expenses while attending college this academic year. In the first column for each item, list the expenses you actually incurred during the first term (semester, trimester, or quarter), and in the second column estimate your expenses for the rest of the academic year (second semester, second trimester, or second and third quarters). Do NOT include summer school expenses. THIS QUESTION IS VERY IMPORTANT. PLEASE ANSWER CAREFULLY REFERRING TO YOUR COLLEGE CATALOG OR FINANCIAL RECORDS (checkbook, receipts, etc.).

	I Actual Expenses (1st Semester, 1st Trimester, or 1st Quarter)	II Estimated Expenses (2nd Semester, 2nd Trimester, or 2nd and 3rd Quarters)
A. Tuition	$____.00	$____.00

(Show total, as indicated in your college catalogs, before the deduction of any tuition waiver. Amount of any waiver received should be shown in Item 14B.)

B. Books and Supplies	$____.00	$____.00

(Include the cost of books and supplies you purchased for class, plus the cost of books, records, tapes, etc., you purchased for your personal use.)

C. Board and All Food	$____.00	$____.00

(Include cost of meals covered by board job. Include meals you purchased that are not included in board charges. Married students include dependents.)

D. Room or Housing Costs	$____.00	$____.00

(Include cost of rent that you earn through work.)

E. Medical, Dental, Health	$____.00	$____.00

(Include medical insurance costs and other medical or dental bills you paid that were not covered by insurance.)

F. Value of Durable Goods Purchased	$____.00	$____.00

*(Include the **purchase price** of any durable goods [auto, cycle, TV, Hi-Fi, refrigerator, etc.] that you bought or will buy during this academic year.)*

G. Debt Repayment	$____.00	$____.00

(Include the amount paid for installment loans [e.g., car payments] and any other loan payments you have made or will make during the academic year.)

H. Travel, Transportation, Insurance	$____.00	$____.00

(Include travel to and from college, trips taken while at school [e.g., ski trips], transportation at college, and gas and maintenance expense. Include cost of auto or cycle insurance, and life insurance premiums.)

I. All Other Expenses

1. New clothing purchased	$____.00	$____.00
2. Entertainment (movies, dances, parties, etc.)	$____.00	$____.00
3. Laundry and dry cleaning	$____.00	$____.00
4. Personal care (cosmetics, shampoo, etc.)	$____.00	$____.00
5. Liquor, beer, Cokes, snacks	$____.00	$____.00
6. All other expenses (except taxes)	$____.00	$____.00

14. The following items are concerned with the sources of funds you used or will use to meet the expenses listed in Question 13 above. Again, this question is *very important* so please answer it carefully. If you received no funds from the sources listed, indicate this by writing a $0 (zero) in the appropriate blank.

	I Actual Expenses (1st Semester, 1st Trimester, or 1st Quarter)	II Estimated Expenses (2nd Semester, 2nd Trimester, or 2nd and 3rd Quarters)
A. Parents' Contribution	$____.00	$____.00

*(Include direct payments they made for your college expenses, any allowance you received, and any money you **borrowed** from your parents.)*

B. Scholarship or Grant	$____.00	$____.00

(Include local, state, or college scholarships or grants. Include tuition or fee waiver.)

C. Student Loan	$____.00	$____.00

*(Include loans from the college, the government, and banks to cover your college expenses for this year. Do **not** include auto or similar durable goods loans.)*

D. Job	$____.00	$____.00

(Include value of meals earned in board job and rent earned in housing unit as well as cash income.)

E. New Debt Incurred $_____.00 $_____.00

*(Do **not** include debt listed as student loan in Question 14C above. Include all other debt incurred (installment loans, etc.) during the academic year.)*

F. Change in Assets   +   +

                   –   –
$_____.00 $_____.00

(From September 1, 1971, through end of the 1st semester (quarter or trimester) indicate the net change in your assets (savings and/or stocks and bonds) in Column I. In Column II estimate the change in your assets for the rest of the academic year. Be sure to circle the plus or minus sign indicating whether your assets increased or decreased.)

G. Other Income $_____.00 $_____.00

*(Include income from GI Bill, Social Security, welfare, the parents of your spouse (unless spouse is also a student), interest or dividends, or other income. Do **not** include borrowing or tax refunds.)*

H. Married Students: Income of Spouse $_____.00 $_____.00

(Include income from employment of spouse. If spouse is also a student, include contribution made by spouse's parents, scholarship, job at school, student loan spouse incurred this year, and other income spouse received.)

15A. Did your parents borrow money to help you pay for your college expenses this year?

Yes ....1 .... *(Answer Question 15B.)*
No ....2 .... *(Skip to Question 16.)*

B. Approximately how much did they borrow?

$_____.00

16. On a 4.0 grade system, what is your approximate cumulative grade point average at the present time? (A = 4.0 and F = 0.0; round to nearest tenth.)

___.___

17. When you enrolled, or just before you enrolled in college, did either of your parents take a new or additional job to help pay for your college expenses?

Yes 1
No 2

18. Approximately how much money did you *save* from your job last summer (1971)?

$_____.00

19. Using the occupation list and codes provided, complete Question 19A if you are *currently enrolled.* If you are not currently enrolled in college, complete Question 19B.

A. If you dropped out of school today, what type of occupation or job would you most likely be working in?

____ ____ ____ .... *(Skip to Question 20.)*

B. In what occupation are you currently employed? *(Code in the space below. If unemployed, circle "1" below.)*

____ ____ ____

Not employed ...1

20. What is the amount of annual income (before taxes) you expect to earn when you complete your formal schooling?

$_____.00 per year

21A. What is the amount of annual income (before taxes) you expect to earn 25 years from now? *(Provide your best estimate (assuming no inflation) even if you are very uncertain.)*

$_____.00 per year

B. How certain are you that 25 years from now you will be earning the amount of income you estimated? *(Circle one.)*

I am very certain (probability above .75) 1
I am reasonably certain (probability between .50 and .75) 2
I am somewhat uncertain (probability between .25 and .50) 3
I am very uncertain (probability less than .25) 4

22. What statement below best characterizes your opinion about the general wage level over the next 25 years in the occupation you intend to pursue? When answering this question, do **not** consider or include the effects of any promotions you may receive. *(Circle one.)*

The average wage level will increase at about the same rate
that inflation occurs in the economy 1

The average wage level will increase at a faster rate
than inflation in the economy 2

The average wage level will increase at a slower rate
than inflation in the economy 3

23. How many years of formal schooling has each of your parents completed? *(Include elementary school, high school, and college.)*

Father or Guardian _____ Mother or Guardian _____

24. What type of college did your parents attend? *(Answer for both.)*

	Father	Mother
None	1	1
Private	2	2
Public	3	3
I don't know	4	4

25. Is your father and/or mother employed in a job that earns income? *(Answer for both.)*

	Father or Guardian	Mother or Guardian
Employed	1	1
Unemployed	2	2
Deceased	3	3

26. What is your father's and/or mother's occupation? *(Code from the occupation list provided. If unemployed or deceased, indicate the occupation in which they were most recently employed.)*

Father or Guardian __ __ __ Mother or Guardian __ __ __
(Housewife code = 002)

27. What is the age of each parent, if living?

Father's Age _____ Mother's Age _____

28. Approximately how many years have your parents been employed in a job that earned income? *(Answer for both.)*

	Father or Guardian	Mother or Guardian
Never employed	1	1
1-10 years	2	2
11-20 years	3	3
21-30 years	4	4
More than 30 years	5	5
I don't know	6	6

29. What was the size of the town you grew up in? *(Circle one.)*

Farm 1
Rural nonfarm 2
Small town (population 2,500-50,000) 3
Large town (population 50,000-250,000) 4
Large city (population over 250,000) 5
Suburb of city with population over 250,000 6

30. Since the time your parents first left school to begin work, what statement(s) below best describes the amount of additional education that each has had? *(Circle all that apply. Be sure to respond for both your father and mother if you live with both.)*

	Father or Guardian	Mother or Guardian
No structured educational experience	1	1
Attended occupational business or trade conferences and/or received military training	2	2
Received formal training program provided by employer (on the job training)	3	3
Enrolled in one or more adult education courses	4	4
Enrolled in one or more college courses but did not receive an additional degree	5	5
Returned to school for an additional degree	6	6

31A. Has any member of your family visited a doctor or been in the hospital during the last year? **(Married Students:** *If you received support from your parents, include them as part of your family.)*

Yes ....1 *(Answer Question 31B.)*
No ....2 *(Skip to Question 32.)*

B. In the blanks below please indicate your best estimate of your family's health care experience over the last year.

	Yourself	Your Spouse and Children *(if married)*	Your Parents, Brothers, and Sisters
Number of days in the hospital	___	___	___
Number of visits to the doctor (omit dentists)	___	___	___
Cost of surgery (if any)	___	___	___
Approximate cost of special drugs or special medical equipment	___	___	___

32. Do your parents have medical insurance on—

	You	Themselves
Yes	1	2
No	1	2

Thank you for your cooperation. It will help us to identify the true costs of college and document the need for financial aid. *Please return the questionnaire* to us in the enclosed, self-addressed, stamped envelope.

INSTRUCTIONS

Please Read Before Completing Questions 13 and 14

Questions 13 and 14 are concerned with your expenses and sources of money to pay for these expenses while attending college this year. Question 13 attempts to identify all the expenses you encountered while going to college. Question 14 attemps to identify the income, or sources of money, you used to pay these expenses. It is important to realize that THE TOTAL AMOUNT OF MONEY LISTED IN EACH COLUMN OF QUESTION 14 MUST EQUAL (or exceed) THE TOTAL EXPENSES YOU LISTED IN QUESTION 13. That is the total amount of expenses you indicate in Question 13 must not be greater than the total amount of money you will use to pay them as indicated in Question 14.

The fact that each student has different costs which are met by different means makes the accuracy of YOUR response very important.

Questions 13 and 14 are designed to help you assess "what happened" during the first term this year, and to help you estimate how you will finance the rest of the year. Thus, Question 13 asks you what you spent during the first term and Question 14 asks how you paid these expenses. What amount did your parents pay—either to you or to the college (Q. 14A)? How much was derived from a scholarship or grant (Q. 14B)? From a student loan (Q. 14C)? Did you have a job while attending school and if so how much did you earn (Q. 14D)? If you have savings (assets), was it necessary to used these savings, or part of them to pay for your expenses (Q. 14F)?

In any case, recognize that by one means or another (your income, the contributions of your parents or relatives, or your debt) these expenses were paid. If there are sources of funds that are not included in the items listed in Question 14, please note *their nature* and *amount* either on a separate page or in the column containing Question 14.

We cannot overemphasize the importance of these two questions. The ultimate value, however, rests with each individual student, with you. Thank you for taking care to answer them.

OCCUPATION CODING LIST

RETIRED/NO EARNED INCOME
001 Retired
002 Housewife
003 Disabled
004 Deceased

PROFESSIONAL/TECHNICAL
101 Accountants
102 Architect
103 Artist
104 Author, editor
105 Chemist
106 Clergyman
107 College professors and administrators
108 Doctor, dentist
109 Engineer
110 Engineering technician
111 Lawyer or judge
112 Musician
113 Natural scientist
114 Pharmacist
115 Social scientist
116 Social/welfare workers
117 Teachers (elementary/secondary)
118 Technicians (medical/dental)
119 Technicians (electronic)
120 Other professional
121 Other technical

MANAGERS, OFFICIALS, PROPRIETORS
201 Government officials and administrators
202 Manufacturing manager (salaried)
203 Proprietor (self-employed—manager)
204 Retail manager (salaried)
205 Other salaried manager

FARMING
301 Owner operator
302 Tenant farmer
303 Sharecroppers

CLERICAL
401 Bookkeepers
402 Typist, stenographer, secretary
403 Mailmen, postal clerks
404 Other clerical work

SALES WORKERS
501 Insurance agents, underwriters
502 Real estate agents, brokers
503 Wholesale sales
504 Retail sales clerks
505 Manufacturing sales
506 Other sales work

CRAFTSMEN, FOREMEN
601 Bakers
602 Blacksmiths, forgemen
603 Boilermakers

CRAFTSMEN, FOREMEN [continued]
604 Cabinetmakers, carpenters
605 Compositors, typesetters
606 Cranemen, derrickmen
607 Electricians
608 Foreman, manufacturing
609 Foreman, nonmanufacturing
610 Linemen, servicemen
611 Locomotive engineers, firemen
612 Machinist
613 Masons, stonecutters
614 Mechanic, aircraft
615 Mechanic, other
616 Metal workers
617 Painter
618 Plasterers, cement finishers
619 Plumbers, pipefitters
620 Stationary engineers
621 Structural metal workers
622 Tailors, furriers
623 Tinsmiths, coppersmiths, etc.
624 Toolmakers, die makers
625 Other craftsmen

OPERATIVES
701 Apprentices
702 Assemblers
703 Attendants, auto and parking
704 Brakemen, switchmen
705 Bus, truck, tractor drivers
706 Filer, grinder
707 Furnacemen, smeltermen
708 Laundry and dry cleaning
709 Meat workers (except slaughter)
710 Mine workers
711 Power station operators
712 Sailors and deckhands
713 Sawyers, spinners, weavers
714 Stationary firemen
715 Welders and flame cutters
716 Other operative

SERVICE WORKERS
801 Barbers, cosmetologists
802 Charwomen, janitors
803 Cooks, domestic
804 Firemen, fire protection
805 Guards, watchmen
806 Policemen and sheriffs
807 Waiters, bartenders, counter workers
808 Other service workers

LABOR (except mining)
901 Fishermen, oystermen
902 Longshoremen, stevedores
903 Lumbermen
904 Labor, other (not elsewhere specified)
905 Farm labor

A STUDY OF THE COLLEGE INVESTMENT DECISION
Questionnaire: Stage II (Freshmen)

Directions: We hope this questionnaire will provide you an interesting and complete overview of the decisions you have made about going to college. To be a useful study that can help others, however, each question must be answered. Please *circle the correct response* for each appropriate item. If a question asks for a monetary amount, enter a 0 (zero) if it does not apply to you. Please *do not leave blanks.* Thank you.

1. Are you currently attending college? *(Circle one.)*

   Full time ....1.......... *(Go to Question 2A.)*
   Part time ....2.......... *(Go to Question 2A.)*
   Not enrolled in college ....3......... *(Skip to Question 17.)*

2A. What is the name of the college you are **now** attending?

   _____

B. In what state is it located?

C. Do you plan to attend this college next year? *(Circle one.)*

   Yes 1
   No 2

3. When you complete your formal schooling, what occupation do you plan to pursue? *(Please select the occupation from the list enclosed with this questionnaire and write the appropriate code number below.)*

   ___ ___ ___

4. How important to you is each of the five following reasons for continuing your education? Although the reasons are not mutually exclusive, think carefully about the relative importance of each reason compared to the others. *(Circle one for each item.)*

   Very Important
   Somewhat Important
   Not Very Important
   Not Important

   A. To get a better job that earns a higher income 1 2 3 4

   B. To enjoy greater personal satisfaction 1 2 3 4

   C. To serve society 1 2 3 4

   D. To serve the next generation by more competently rearing children 1 2 3 4

   E. The guidance and advice of my parents 1 2 3 4

5. How important to you is each of the following potential benefits from your college education? *(Circle one for each item.)*

   Very Important
   Somewhat Important
   Not Very Important
   Not Important

   A. Meeting and conversing with interesting people ...1 2 3 4

   B. Finding a husband (wife) with good financial prospects 1 2 3 4

   C. Locating a suitable career 1 2 3 4

   D. Providing volunteer civic and intellectual leadership 1 2 3 4

   E. Nonmonetary job satisfaction 1 2 3 4

F. Finding a husband (wife) with college-developed values 1 2 3 4

G. Earning a good income in your chosen career 1 2 3 4

H. A continuing interest in reading and new ideas 1 2 3 4

I. Guiding and educating your own children 1 2 3 4

J. Becoming more broadminded, concerned about others, and more tolerant 1 2 3 4

6. What is the highest academic degree that you intend to obtain? *(Circle one.)*

   None 1
   Associate (or equivalent) 2
   Bachelor's degree (BA, BS, etc.) 3
   Master's degree (MA, MS, etc.) 4
   PhD or EdD 5
   MD, DDS, DVM (Medical) 6
   LLB, or JD (Law) 7
   BD (Divinity) 8
   Other 9

7. Approximately how much money did your parents spend on you for clothing and supplies for school (e.g., sheets, pillows, typewriter, radio, etc.) from June 1972 through September 1972?

   $ _____

8. When you enrolled, or just before you enrolled in college, did either of your parents take a new or additional job to help pay for your college expenses? *(Circle one.)*

   Yes 1
   No 2

9. Where do you now live while attending college? *(Circle one.)*

   With parents or relatives 1
   Nonuniversity housing (not with parents or relatives) 2
   In residence hall, fraternities, or sororities 3
   Other university housing 4

10A. Do you have any brothers or sisters (living at home and/or away from home)? *(Circle one.)*

   Yes ....1 .... *(See note below.)*
   No ....2 .... *(Skip to Question 11.)*

If yes to Question 10A:

> Questions 10B and 10C inquire about the age and college experience or plans of your brothers and sisters. They are to be answered in the box or matrix that appears following these two questions.

B. What is the age of each of your brothers and/or sisters? *(List the ages in the first column of the box below and indicate whether it is a brother or sister in the second column.)* *

C. How many years of college has each of your brothers and/or sisters completed and was the institution publicly or privately controlled? *(List the college years completed in the third column and the institution type in the fourth column of the box below.)*

	Question 10B		Question 10C		
Age	Brother = 1 Sister = 2 *(Circle one.)*		Number of College Years Completed	Public = 1 Private = 2 *(Circle one.)*	
	1	2		1	2
	1	2		1	2
	1	2		1	2
	1	2		1	2
	1	2		1	2
	1	2		1	2

*If you have more than 6 brothers and sisters, list the information for the oldest 6.

11. Is your college on a semester, quarter, or trimester system? *(Circle one.)*

Semester 1
Quarter 2
Trimester 3

> The following two questions are concerned with your estimate of the expenses of attending institutions other than the one you are presently attending and the offers of financial assistance you may have received from these same institutions.

12. Please list the names of those colleges which you considered attending and the state in which they are located (other than the one you are currently attending). IF MORE THAN TWO, LIST THE TWO YOU MOST SERIOUSLY CONSIDERED ATTENDING.

a. _____
                                    State
b. _____
                                    State

13. Complete the following box or matrix with respect to each of the colleges listed in 12 (above).

	COLLEGE	
	a	b
Estimate the total cost of attending this college for one year, including room and board (excluding summer school).		
Did you apply for financial aid (Yes or No)?		
What was the amount of scholarship aid offered to you?		
How much was offered to you in the form of loans?		
What was the amount of work-study assistance offered?		

14. The following questions are concerned with the college you are currently attending. Where possible, use exact amounts. Otherwise, estimate as best you are able. This question is very important, so please consider it carefully. If you receive no funds from the sources listed, please indicate this by writing $0 (zero) in the appropriate blank (all questions refer to the 1972-73 academic year).

A. Estimate the total cost of attending this college for one year, including room and board (excluding summer school).

$_____

B. Parents' Contribution: How much will your parents contribute toward your education this year in the form of allowance, payments made directly to the college on your behalf, and loans they make to you?

$_____

C. Work/Earnings: How much will you earn from the following *during the school year?*

$_____ Work-study program
$_____ Other job or jobs

D. Scholarships and Grants: What amounts will you receive from each of the following sources?

$_____ Scholarship (awarded by state)
$_____ Scholarship (awarded by college)
$_____ Scholarship (other than above)
$_____ Economic Opportunity Grant

E. Loans (other than from parents): What amount will it be necessary for you to borrow from the following sources?

$_____ National Defense Loan
$_____ Federally Insured Loan
$_____ College loan fund (other than above)
$_____ Other loans (specify_____)

F. Savings: What is the amount of your savings that you will need to *spend* to help pay this year's expenses?

$_____

G. Other Income: How much will you receive from the following sources during this school year?

$_____ G.I. Bill
$_____ Vocational Rehabilitation
$_____ Social Security
$_____ Welfare
$_____ Other (interest, dividends, support, etc.)

H. Spouse: If married, how much will your spouse contribute to your college expenses this year?

$_____

15A. Did your parents borrow money to help you pay for your college expenses this year? *(Circle one.)*

Yes . . . . .1 . . . .*(Answer Question 15B.)*
No . . . . .2 . . . . *(Skip to Question 16.)*

B. Approximately how much did they borrow?

$_____

16A. What was the major emphasis of your high school program? *(Circle one.)*
College preparatory 1
Vocational 2

B. What was your rank in your high school class? (*Example:* If you were 53rd in your class of 100, write 53 in the first blank and 100 in the second.) Please give your best estimate.

_____ out of _____ total in class

17A. Do you contribute money to your parents to help them pay bills or provide for your brothers and sisters? *(Circle one.)*
Yes ....1 ....*(Answer Question 17B.)*
No ....2 ....*(Skip to Question 18.)*

B. Approximately how much per month do you pay your parents?

$_____ per month

18. Approximately how much money did you *save* from your job last summer (1972)?

$_____

19. Using the occupation list and codes provided, complete Question 19A if you are *currently enrolled.* If you are not currently enrolled in college, complete Question 19B.

A. If you dropped out of school today, what type of occupation or job would you most likely be working in?

___ ___ ___ ....*(Skip to Question 20.)*

B. In what occupation are you currently employed? *(Code in the space below. If unemployed, circle "1" below.)*

___ ___ ___

Not employed ...1

20. What is the amount of annual income (before taxes) you expect to earn when you complete your formal schooling?

$_____ per year

21A. What is the amount of annual income (before taxes) you expect to earn 25 years from now? *(Provide your best estimate [assuming no inflation] even if you are very uncertain.)*

$_____ per year

B. How certain are you that 25 years from now you will be earning the amount of income you estimated? *(Circle one.)*
I am very certain (probability above .75) 1
I am reasonably certain (probability between .50 and .75) 2
I am somewhat uncertain (probability between .25 and .50) 3
I am very uncertain (probability less than .25) 4

22. What statement below best characterizes your opinion about the general wage level over the next 25 years in the occupation you intend to pursue? When answering this question, do **not** consider or include the effects of any promotions you may receive. *(Circle one.)*

The average wage level will increase at about the same rate that inflation occurs in the economy 1

The average wage level will increase at a faster rate than inflation in the economy 2

The average wage level will increase at a slower rate than inflation in the economy 3

23. How many years of formal schooling has each of your parents completed? *(Include elementary school, high school, and college.)*

Father or Guardian _____ Mother or Guardian _____

24. What type of college did your parents attend? *(Answer for both.)*

	Father	Mother
None	1	1
Private	2	2
Public	3	3
I don't know	4	4

25. Is your father and/or mother employed in a job that earns income? *(Answer for both.)*

	Father or Guardian	Mother or Guardian
Employed	1	1
Unemployed	2	2
Deceased	3	3

26. What is your father's and/or mother's occupation? *(Code from the occupation list provided. If unemployed or deceased, indicate the occupation in which they were most recently employed.)*

Father or Guardian ___ ___ ___ Mother or Guardian ___ ___ ___
(Housewife code = 002)

27. What is the age of each parent, if living?

Father's Age _____ Mother's Age _____

28. Approximately how many years have your parents been employed in a job that earned income? *(Answer for both.)*

	Father or Guardian	Mother or Guardian
Never employed	1	1
1-10 years	2	2
11-20 years	3	3
21-30 years	4	4
More than 30 years	5	5
I don't know	6	6

29. What was the size of the town you grew up in? *(Circle one.)*

Farm 1
Rural nonfarm 2
Small town (population 2,500-50,000) 3
Large town (population 50,000-250,000) 4
Large city (population over 250,000) 5
Suburb of city with population over 250,000 6

30. Since the time your parents first left school to begin work, what statement(s) below best describes the amount of additional education that each has had? *(Circle all that apply. Be sure to respond for both your father and mother if you live with both.)*

	Father or Guardian	Mother or Guardian
No structured educational experience	1	1
Attended occupational business or trade conferences and/or received military training	2	2
Received formal training program provided by employer (on the job training)	3	3
Enrolled in one or more adult education courses	4	4
Enrolled in one or more college courses but did not receive an additional degree	5	5
Returned to school for an additional degree	6	6

31A. Has any member of your family visited a doctor or been in the hospital during the last year? **(Married Students:** *If you received support from your parents, include them as part of your family.)*

Yes . . . . .1 *(Answer Question 31B.)*
No . . . . .2 *(Skip to Question 32.)*

B. In the blanks below please indicate your best estimate of your family's health care experience over the last year.

	Yourself	Your Spouse and Children *(if married)*	Your Parents, Brothers, and Sisters
Number of days in the hospital	___	___	___
Number of visits to the doctor (omit dentists)	___	___	___

Cost of surgery (if any) ___ ___ ___

Approximate cost of special drugs or special medical equipment ___ ___ ___

32. Do your parents have medical insurance on—

	Yes	No
You	1	 2
Themselves	1	 2

Thank you for your cooperation. It will help us to identify the true costs of college and document the need for financial aid. *Please return the questionnaire* to us in the enclosed, self-addressed, stamped envelope.

Instruction/Worksheet
for the Family Financial Statement

GENERAL — TO THE FINANCIAL AID APPLICANT:

1. Complete all four pages of this worksheet. Read and follow the instructions as you proceed.

2. **Then** transfer the information you have placed on pages one, two and three of this worksheet to the appropriate sections of the enclosed Family Financial Statement. Instructions for transferring the information are contained on page three (Block Z) of this worksheet. **Use soft lead pencil.**

3. Mail this completed worksheet to your first choice institution. Additional copies of page 4 are available from your high school counselor to be mailed to your additional choice schools.

4. **Mail the Family Financial Statement to ACT** in the envelope provided. **Do not fold** the Family Financial Statement. **Include the appropriate fee (see page 3).**

STATE CODES

(Use Code of Your State of Residence)

Ala.	01
Alaska	02
Ariz.	03
Ark.	04
Calif.	05
Colo.	06
Conn.	07
Del.	08
D.C.	09
Fla.	10
Ga.	11
Hawaii	12
Idaho	13
Ill.	14
Ind.	15
Iowa	16
Kans.	17
Ky.	18
La.	19
Maine	20
Md.	21
Mass.	22
Mich.	23
Minn.	24
Miss.	25
Mo.	26
Mont.	27
Nebr.	28
Nev.	29
N.H.	30
N.J.	31
N.M.	32
N.Y.	33
N.C.	34
N.D.	35
Ohio	36
Okla.	37
Oregon	38
Pa.	39
R.I.	40
S.C.	41
S.D.	42
Tenn.	43
Tex.	44
Utah	45
Vt.	46
Va.	47
Wash.	48
W. Va.	49
Wis.	50
Wyo.	51
Canada	53
All Others	55

A APPLICANT'S NAME (Last Name First)

Blocks A, B, and C: Applicant's name (last name first), home address and home city. Begin in the **first** box of each block and leave empty boxes between the parts of your name, between the parts of your address and between the parts of your home city (if appropriate).

B APPLICANT'S HOME ADDRESS—HOUSE NUMBER AND STREET (where you now receive mail)

C APPLICANT'S HOME CITY (where you now receive mail)

D HOME STATE CODE*

E ZIP CODE (where you now receive mail)

F APPLICANT'S SEX

G APPLICANT'S DATE OF BIRTH — MONTH DAY YEAR

H APPLICANT'S SOCIAL SECURITY NUMBER

Blocks D through K: Enter the appropriate information. *The State Code for Block D should be obtained from the list at the left. In Block I, '13th year' is the first year after high school, etc.

Block L: Enter the number of applicant's brothers and sisters who are dependent on applicant's parents and will be full-time students in college or a postsecondary vocational-technical school and those **under 21 years of age** who will **not** be in college or a postsecondary vocational-technical school in 1972-73.

Block M: Enter the age of the family member primarily responsible for earning the family income. If the applicant receives NO support from his parents and has not been claimed by them as a tax exemption for at least one year, leave this block blank.

Block N: Enter as many as three college, school or agency codes. A list of these codes is enclosed. If you are entering more than one code, you should list them in the order of preference—the code of your first choice college or school should be listed first, etc. You may request additional reports later.

I APPLICANT'S EDUCATIONAL LEVEL—FALL, 1972: 13th YEAR / 14th YEAR / 15th YEAR / 16th YEAR / 17th YEAR / 18th YEAR / OTHER / H.S.

J APPLICANT IS: SINGLE / MARRIED / DIVORCED / SEPARATED / WIDOWED

K NUMBER OF CHILDREN DEPENDENT ON APPLICANT

K IF THE APPLICANT HAS WRITTEN THE ACT TEST, INDICATE THE TIME IT WAS WRITTEN: BEFORE SEPT 1969 / BETWEEN SEPT 1969 AND SEPT 1970 / BETWEEN SEPT 1970 AND SEPT 1971 / BETWEEN SEPT 1971 AND SEPT 1972 / I HAVE NEVER WRITTEN IT

F MALE / FEMALE

L NUMBER OF APPLICANT'S BROTHERS AND SISTERS DEPENDENT ON APPLICANT'S PARENTS WHO WILL: BE IN COLLEGE 1972-73 / NOT BE IN COLLEGE 1972-73

M AGE OF MAIN FAMILY EARNER

N LIST CODES OF COLLEGES, SCHOOLS, AND SCHOLARSHIP AGENCIES TO RECEIVE THIS REPORT (SEE ENCLOSED LISTING FOR CODES): FIRST / SECOND / THIRD

Blocks O through V: Enter the appropriate response to each question.

O During the Period Sept. 1, 1972 through May 31, 1973, Applicant will be: FULL-TIME STUDENT / HALF-TIME STUDENT / LESS THAN HALF-TIME STUDENT

P When Does Applicant Want Financial Assistance? (Mark Only One Answer): Sept. 1972 through May 1973 / Fall 1972 only / Winter 1973 only / Spring 1973 only / Summer 1973 only

P What is Applicant's Final Educational Goal?: Less than one year / Two year degree / Four year degree / Master's degree / PhD or Professional degree

Q IS APPLICANT A U.S. CITIZEN? YES / NO

R DOES APPLICANT LIVE WITH PARENTS OR GUARDIANS? YES / NO

WILL APPLICANT RECEIVE ANY FINANCIAL ASSISTANCE (INCLUDING ROOM, BOARD, MONEY, ETC.) EXCEEDING $200 IN VALUE FROM PARENTS OR GUARDIANS BETWEEN SEPT 1971 AND MAY 1973? YES / NO

S On Parents' or Guardians' Federal Income Tax Return is the Applicant Listed as an Exemption? 1971 TAX RETURN? YES / NO 1972 TAX RETURN? YES / NO

T MARRIED APPLICANTS: During the Period Sept. 1, 1972 through May 31, 1973, Will Applicant's Husband or Wife Be a Full-time Student? YES / NO

YEAR APPLICANT'S HUSBAND OR WIFE WILL GRADUATE FROM COLLEGE: 1972 / 1973 / 1974 / 1975 / BEYOND 1975

U APPLICANT'S PARENTS ARE: MARRIED / DIVORCED / SEPARATED / WIDOWED / DECEASED / OTHER

V OCCUPATION OF THE MAIN FAMILY EARNER (MARK ONLY ONE ANSWER): WAGES OR SALARY / BUSINESS OWNER / FARM OWNER / OTHER

page 1

Reporting Income - Blocks W AND X

GENERAL

List here adjusted gross income on federal tax form, federal income tax, exemption and other income information for the MOST RECENT YEAR FOR WHICH A FEDERAL TAX RETURN WAS FILED plus additional information requested. The word "PARENTS" means the persons upon whom the applicant is financially dependent; for example, father, stepfather, male guardian; mother, stepmother, or female guardian. **Parents'** income information should be included if the applicant wishes to qualify for federal financial aid programs. The applicant's parents should place their income information in the unshaded column; the shaded column is for applicant and (if he is married) spouse income information. For **each** column enter responses to all questions following these instructions.

NOTE: To enter numbers for the following questions, place one number in each small box. The numbers should end in the last (right-hand) box of each row of boxes. EXAMPLES:

Enter $320.18 this way: | 3 | 2 | 0 |
Enter $1,851.14 this way: | 1 | 8 | 5 | 1 |
Enter $10,972.77 this way: | 1 | 0 | 9 | 7 | 2 |

W PARENTS' INCOME	DO NOT SHOW CENTS	**X** APPLICANT'S INCOME*
FEDERAL TAX RETURN LAST FILED FOR TAX YEAR: ○ 1970 ○ 1971 ○ NEITHER (SEE INSTRUCTION 5) (INSTRUCTIONS 1 THROUGH 5 REFER TO THE YEAR INDICATED ABOVE.) WAS THIS A ○ YES JOINT RETURN? ○ NO		THE APPLICANT'S 1971 AND 1972 INCOME INFORMATION SHOULD BE REPORTED BELOW: IS (WAS) APPLICANT'S 1971 TAX FORM A ○ YES JOINT RETURN? ○ NO
ADJUSTED GROSS INCOME FROM ABOVE TAX YEAR (SEE INSTRUCTION 1)	**Instruction 1:** 'Adjusted Gross Income'—**PARENTS**—if the tax year is 1970, copy from line 18 of Federal Form 1040; if tax year is 1971, copy your adjusted gross income from your 1971 federal tax form. If you did not file jointly, you should add your adjusted gross incomes and list the sum. If you are separated or divorced, father should list adjusted gross income and, if applicant lives with mother, mother should include her adjusted gross income. **APPLICANT**—copy your adjusted gross income from your 1971 federal tax form. If you are married and did not file a joint return with your husband or wife, add your adjusted gross income to that of your spouse and list the sum. If 1971 tax form is not yet filed, estimate your 1971 adjusted gross income.	ADJUSTED GROSS INCOME FROM 1971 TAX YEAR (SEE INSTRUCTION 1)
FEDERAL INCOME TAX PAID IN ABOVE TAX YEAR (SEE INSTRUCTION 2) EXEMPTIONS CLAIMED	**Instruction 2:** 'Federal Income Tax Paid'—**PARENTS**—if tax year is 1970, copy from line 25 of Federal Form 1040; if tax year is 1971, copy your total income tax as calculated on your 1971 federal tax form. **APPLICANT** should copy the total income tax as calculated on his or her 1971 federal tax form; estimate the amount if the 1971 form has not yet been filed. **DO NOT COPY TAX WITHHELD ON W-2 FORM. Married persons not filing joint returns should add their two tax amounts and report the sum.** **Instruction 3:** 'Exemptions Claimed'—**PARENTS**—if tax year is 1970, copy from line 11 of Federal Form 1040; if tax year is 1971, copy the exemptions claimed on 1971 federal tax form. **APPLICANT** should copy exemptions claimed (or to be claimed) on 1971 federal tax form. **Married persons not filing joint returns should add their two exemption figures and report the sum.**	FEDERAL INCOME TAX PAID IN 1971 TAX YEAR (SEE INSTRUCTION 2) EXEMPTIONS CLAIMED
OTHER INCOME RECEIVED IN ABOVE TAX YEAR (SEE INSTRUCTION 4)	**Instruction 4:** 'Other Income Received In Last Tax Year'—for the tax year checked at the top of the column, parents should list all income received that was NOT subject to taxation. Examples of this type of income include any income on which no federal tax form was required, social security, veteran's benefits, sick pay, pensions, dependents' allowance, earnings on nontaxable bonds, value of rent-free housing, etc. All child support payments should be included here, **unless** father's income is included above in adjusted gross income. Parents should **NOT** include in this box any income from these sources which the applicant will include in Block X. **Instruction 5:** **IF A TAX RETURN WAS NOT FILED FOR 1970 OR 1971:** Parents should list in 'Other Income' box all income received during the last 12 months and proceed to Instruction 6.	DOES THE INCOME ABOVE FOR APPLICANT (or applicant's husband or wife) INCLUDE EARNINGS FROM THE COLLEGE WORK-STUDY PROGRAM? ○ YES ○ NO
ESTIMATED INCOME FOR ○ 1971 ○ 1972 (SEE INSTRUCTION 6)	**Instruction 6:** 'Estimated Income'—**PARENTS**— if you stated your last tax return was filed for tax year '1970,' list your estimated 1971 total income; if you stated your last tax return was filed for tax year '1971,' list your estimated 1972 total income. Indicate whether the estimate is for 1971 or 1972. **APPLICANT**—estimate your total income for 1972.	APPLICANT'S ESTIMATED INCOME FOR 1972 (SEE INSTRUCTION 6)
IF APPLICANT'S MOTHER WORKED DURING 1971 INDICATE TOTAL AMOUNT SHE EARNED (SEE INSTRUCTION 7)	**Instruction 7:** If applicant's mother worked during 1971, she should indicate the total amount of her 1971 earnings in the box at the left. If this form is being completed during 1971, she should estimate her total 1971 earnings. Applicant should complete the question at the right, indicating source(s) of income and the total amount, as requested.	INDICATE IF APPLICANT WILL RECEIVE MONEY FROM ANY OF THE FOLLOWING DURING THE PERIOD SEPT. 1, 1972 THROUGH MAY 31, 1973: (It is possible to receive benefits from more than one source—grid all that provide you funds) ○ STATE REHABILITATION ○ MANPOWER DEVELOPMENT ○ WAR ORPHANS WELFARE ○ VETERANS'-GI BILL ○ SOCIAL SECURITY ○ ASSISTANCE FROM SOURCES OTHER THAN PARENTS, JOBS, OR CODES IN BLOCK N. ○ INDICATE THE TOTAL AMOUNT APPLICANT WILL RECEIVE FROM THE ABOVE SOURCES BETWEEN SEPT. 1, 1972 AND MAY 31, 1973.

page 2

* IF APPLICANT IS MARRIED, INCLUDE INFORMATION FOR HUSBAND AND WIFE

Reporting Assets - Block **Y**

GENERAL

Report your assets using the following instructions. Please check your calculations carefully. Parents' assets information should be included if applicant wishes to qualify for federal financial aid programs.

Instruction 8:

PARENTS' SAVINGS AND INVESTMENTS

Parents' Savings	$ _____
PLUS Market Value of Parents' Stocks/Bonds	(+) $ _____
Equals	(=) $ _____
MINUS Debts against Stocks and Bonds	(−) $ _____
Equals **PARENTS' SAVINGS AND INVESTMENTS**	$ _____

Y | ASSETS INFORMATION

PARENTS SAVINGS AND INVESTMENTS
(SEE INSTRUCTION 8)

Instruction 9:

MARKET VALUE OF PARENTS' HOME (do not give value here if it will be included in farm or business)

The approximate **resale value** of the parents' home should be listed for this item. If parents rent, this should be listed as zeros.

MARKET VALUE OF PARENTS' HOME
(SEE INSTRUCTION 9)

Instruction 10:

NET VALUE OF PARENTS' FARM OR BUSINESS (do not include value of home if it was listed under MARKET VALUE OF PARENTS' HOME)

Current Market Value of Farm or Business (including farmhouse(s), building(s), machinery, animals, etc.)	$ _____
MINUS Outstanding Debts of Farm or Business	(−) $ _____
Equals Value of Farm or Business	(=) $ _____
MULTIPLY above amount by Your share of ownership (%) of Farm or Business (100% equals 1.00)	(×) _____ %
Equals **NET VALUE OF FARM OR BUSINESS**	$ _____

NET VALUE OF PARENTS' FARM OR BUSINESS
(SEE INSTRUCTION 10)

Instruction 11:

MORTGAGE ON PARENTS' HOME

The outstanding mortgage against the market value of the parents' home (shown in Instruction 9) should be listed here.

MORTGAGE ON PARENTS' HOME
(SEE INSTRUCTION 11)

Instruction 12:

PARENTS' OTHER ASSETS

Value of Trusts	$ _____
PLUS Market Value of Other Real Estate not listed before (e.g., lots, apartments, second home, etc.)	(+) $ _____
Equals Other Assets	(=) $ _____
MINUS Outstanding Mortgage on Other Real Estate (do not include business, farm, or home mortgage)	(−) $ _____
Equals **PARENTS' OTHER ASSETS**	$ _____

PARENTS' OTHER ASSETS
(list only those not included before)
(SEE INSTRUCTION 12)

Instruction 13:

APPLICANT'S ASSETS

(Include only those assets that are in the applicant's name. **If applicant is married, include assets of applicant's husband or wife.)**

Savings of Applicant	$ _____
PLUS Market Value of Stocks and Bonds in Applicant's Name	(+) $ _____
PLUS Value of Trusts in Applicant's Name	(+) $ _____
Equals	(=) $ _____
MINUS Outstanding Debts **Other than** Auto, Home Mortgage, or Business Debts	(−) $ _____
Equals **APPLICANT'S ASSETS**	$ _____

APPLICANT'S ASSETS
(SEE INSTRUCTION 13)

Z

Now, using the following instructions, transfer to the enclosed Family Financial Statement the information you have completed thus far.

Your Family Financial Statement will be processed by an electronic device which will record the information that you indicate by blackening (gridding) circles and squares in the grid areas. Complete the form carefully. USE A SOFT LEAD PENCIL. DO **NOT** USE INK OR BALL POINT PEN. In each block, clearly print the appropriate information in the boxes above the grid area. Then below each box, blacken completely the circle with the corresponding letter or number. If you are leaving **any** box blank, **grid** the small space square ⬚ s below that box. In some cases, no boxes appear above the grid area; you should merely grid the proper response. Make your marks **heavy and black.** Avoid stray marks and smudges. See the sample in Figure 1.

Grid zeros to indicate "none" to any item. To indicate that any item does not apply, grid **all** the space squares for that item. You should respond to **every** question on the form to ensure a complete and accurate analysis.

Then complete the Signature section of the Family Financial Statement, enclose the fee and it is ready for mailing to ACT.

FEE	ONE REPORT—$3	ADDITIONAL—$1 EACH

One report is sent to each code you listed in BLOCK N.
Make check payable to the American College Testing Program.
gram.   One Code - $3   Two Codes - $4   Three Codes - $5

We certify that to the best of our knowledge the information contained in this statement is correct and complete. We authorize The American College Testing Program to transmit the information to the college(s), school(s), or agency(ies) indicated and agree that they have our permission to verify it. We also agree to release copies of our U.S. or State Income Tax Returns, upon request to The American College Testing Program, or to the college(s), school(s), or agency(ies) coded herein.

Father or Male Guardian   Social Security No.

Mother or Female Guardian   Social Security No.

Applicant   Applicant's Husband or Wife
                                        MO.   DAY   YR.

Date signed:

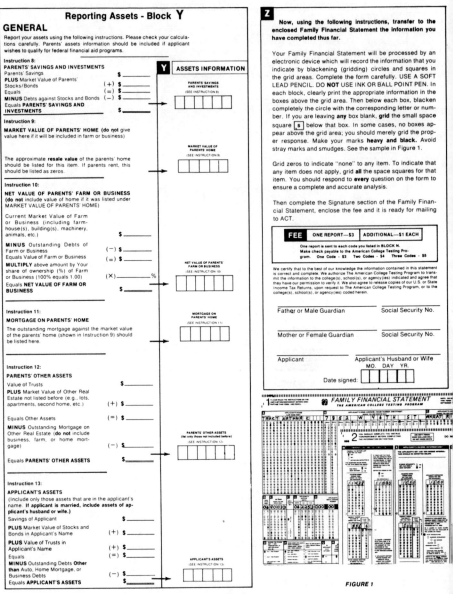

FAMILY FINANCIAL STATEMENT
THE AMERICAN COLLEGE TESTING PROGRAM

FIGURE 1

COLLEGE COPY - SUPPLEMENTAL INFORMATION SHEET *

Some institutions may use this form as a financial aid application. To provide more information about yourself, you may wish to answer the following questions. Please note, however, that many colleges and scholarship agencies will require you to file an application for financial aid.

INDICATE FINANCIAL AID PREFERENCE, IF CHOICE IS AVAILABLE (Check all that apply): ☐ Scholarship ☐ Grant ☐ Long-Term Loan ☐ Work Study Job ☐ Any Assistance Available	Telephone Number(s) at Which You May Be Reached	Campus Residence: ☐ Off-Campus Housing ☐ Campus Housing ☐ With Parents ☐ With Relatives	Your Major or Intended Major Field:

HAVE YOU PREVIOUSLY RECEIVED: A National Defense Student Loan? ☐ YES ☐ NO If so, how much?_____ An Educational Opportunity Grant? ☐ YES ☐ NO If so, how much?_____ Other Federal Aid? ☐ YES ☐ NO If so, source?_____ A State Grant or Scholarship? ☐ YES ☐ NO If so, how much?_____	HAVE YOU ANY SERIOUS PHYSICAL DISABILITY? ☐ YES ☐ NO If so, please list:_____	ARE YOU: A Veteran? ☐ YES ☐ NO A Commuting Student? ☐ YES ☐ NO A Resident for Tuition Purposes? ☐ YES ☐ NO

If the school or college you will attend during 1972-73 has more than one campus, which will you attend? _____	IF YOU OWN OR WILL DRIVE A CAR ON CAMPUS, GIVE MAKE, MODEL, YEAR: _____	IF YOU ARE NOT A U.S. CITIZEN, GIVE: Visa Type _____ Number _____ Date _____

Nature of Father's Work _____ How long with present employer?_____Years Where employed:_____ Nature of Mother's Work_____ How long with present employer?_____Years Where employed:_____	Where is applicant employed? _____ Where is spouse employed? _____ In what state are your parents legal residents? _____	Are you a transfer student? ☐ YES ☐ NO If so, list colleges attended:_____ Your high school:_____ How long have they resided there? _____

COMMENTS: Please explain any unusual circumstances or data concerning your family financial situation. Attach additional pages if necessary.

APPLICANT'S INCOME FOR SEPTEMBER 1972—MAY 1973	APPLICANT'S EXPENSES FOR SEPTEMBER 1972—MAY 1973
(Married students and independent students should give income and expenses for September 1972 through August 1973.)	

Family or friends	$_____	Housing	$_____
Gov't Sources (other than loans) G.I. Bill. Rehab., V.A. Soc. Sec. etc.	$_____	Food	$_____
Source _____ Amt./Mo _____		Medical	$_____
Source _____ Amt./Mo _____			
Earnings of spouse (net, after taxes and retirement)	$_____	Transportation	$_____
Savings, Insurance, etc	$_____	Tuition and fees	
Applicant's summer earnings (net after living expenses)	$_____	Self $_____	
Applicant's earnings while in school	$_____	Spouse (if married) $_____	$_____
Fellowship, scholarship or grants from non-college sources for 1972-73	$_____	Books, etc	$_____
Source _____		Personal (clothing, recreation, etc)	$_____
Loans, from other sources for 1972-73	$_____	Babysitting/Child Care	$_____
Source _____		Other	$_____
Other sources of income	$_____	Specify Purpose _____	
Source _____		TOTAL EXPENSES	$_____
TOTAL INCOME	$_____	NET NEED (Subtract total income from expenses)	$_____

page 4

* High School Seniors. Additional copies of this page of the Instruction/Worksheet are available from your counselor—you should send copies to each of your college and school choices.

Notes

Chapter 1
Introduction: Investment in Human Resources

1. The Carnegie Commission Report on *The New Depression in Higher Education–Two Years Later* has suggested a plateau of "fragile stability." See E. F. Cheit (1973, p. 51).

2. See Eckstein (1961) for some examples.

Chapter 2
The Basic Theory of Decisions to Invest in Higher Education

1. See for example, Jorgenson (1971, p. 1111).

2. The intercorrelation between the measure used for psychological stocks $(S_{P_{t-1}})$ —i.e., primarily the education of the head of the family—and for the student's initial educational capital stock $(S_{E_{t-1}})$ suggests combining the two into a single stock-habit effect, designated simply βS_{t-1}. Habits often prevail later with $\beta > 0$. See the stock-habit effect developed by Houthakker-Taylor (1970, p. 10) and references to the economic literature on habit formation in consumer behavior (p. 282).

3. A third possibility, that of a collective family indifference curve and allocations within the family are considered by Samuelson (1956, pp. 1080-86) in connection with "Social Indifference Curves."

4. See McMahon and Wagner (1973, p. 9, cols. 1, 3, 4, and 8).

5. See Basman (1956) for proofs concerning the effects of changes in the α's.

6. Although we have introduced modifications, see also Ben-Porath (1967) on production costs.

7. See Michael (1972).

8. See Hirshleifer (1958), Fig. 1, p. 330 which illustrates how some borrowing used to finance additional investment (distance SR') can increase multiperiod utility $(U_1 \text{ to } U_2)$.

Chapter 3
Investment by Families in Higher Education

1. See the report of the U.S. National Commission on the Financing of

Postsecondary Education (1973), *Financing Postsecondary Education in the United States,* Chapter 1. See also 92nd Congress, *Education Amendments of 1972,* (1972), p. 50.

2. See the National Commission's Report (1973), especially its normative evaluation of alternative financing plans. (Chapter 7), "The Incidence of Financial Distress" (Chapter 5), proposals for cost measurement (Chapter 8), and "Recommendations" (Chapter 9).

3. For growth effects see E. Denison (1973), A. Krueger (1968), and H. Johnson (1964). For effects on the distribution of personal income see G. Becker (1967), S. Kuznets (1966), and T. W. Schultz (1972). For consideration of some aspects of the quality of life see H. Bowen (1971), and L. Solomon and P. Taubman (1973).

4. For a summary of enrollment projections see the U.S. National Commission (1973), Chapter 1, Table 3, and the related discussion.

5. See Eq. (2-23), or R. Freeman (1971), for example.

6. See G. Psacharopoulos (1973), pp. 36-7.

7. Technical note to the Carnegie Commission's (October 1973) final report, Projection II.

Chapter 4
State and Local Investment in Higher Education

1. M. M. Chambers (1972, p. 3, and earlier issues).

Chapter 5
Federal Investment in Higher Education

1. U.S. Executive Office of the President (1974), *The Budget of the United States Government,* Fiscal 1975, pp. 413, 429, 430, and 904. Category 1 was budgeted at $913 million in 1972-73.

2. For specific estimates of how the half-cost provision "targets" aid less effectively to low-income students, see Robert Hartman (1972, pp. 465, 474, and Appendix B).

3. See also R. Freeman (1971).

4. The National Commission on the Financing of Postsecondary Education has, through research staff, attempted to collect such data.

Chapter 6
Federal Investment in Research at Institutions of Higher
Education

1. T.W. Schultz, "The Allocation of Resources to Research" (1971, p. 243).

2. From Freeman and Young, *The Research and Development Effort*, O.E.C.D.

3. *Economic Report of the President* (1974).

4. National Science Foundation *Federal Support to Universities and Colleges*, 1963-66, p. 7.

5. See James Dyal's dissertation on the costs of graduate education at the University of Illinois.

6. National Science Foundation *Federal Support to Colleges and Universities*, pp. 7, 38. See also Harris et al. (1965, p. 87).

References

I. Books and Articles

Arrow, Kenneth J. "The Economic Implications of Learning by Doing." *Review of Economic Studies* 29 (June 1962): pp. 155-73.

Astin, Alexander W. "Higher Education Benefits Associated with Social Class, Ability, and College Quality." Panel on *The Benefits of Higher Education*. Woods Hole, Mass.: National Research Council, July 1972.

Basman, R. L. "A Theory of Demand with Consumer Preferences Variable." *Econometrica* 24 (1956): 47-58.

Becker, Gary S. *Human Capital*. New York: National Bureau of Economic Research, 1964.

_____ . "A Theory of the Allocation of Time." *Economic Journal* 75 (September 1965): 493-517.

_____ . *Human Capital and the Personal Distribution of Income: An Analytical Approach*. W. S. Woytinsky Lecture. University of Michigan 1967.

_____ . *Economic Theory*. New York: Alfred A. Knopf, 1971.

_____ . "The Allocation of Time over the Life Cycle." In G. Ghez and G. S. Becker, Report No. 7217, Center for Mathematical Studies in Business and Economics, University of Chicago, April 1972.

Becker, Gary S., J. Mincer, and B. R. Chiswick. *Human Capital and the Personal Income Distribution*, National Bureau of Economic Research, forthcoming.

Ben-Porath, Yoram. "The Production of Human Capital and the Life Cycle of Earnings." *Journal of Political Economy* 75 (August 1967): 352-65.

Bishop, John. "The Private Demand for Places in Higher Education." MS. College Scholarship Service. New York: Department of Economics, New York University, 1972.

Bowen, H.R. *The Finance of Higher Education*. Berkely: Carnegie Commission on Higher Education, 1968.

_____ . "Appendix on the Social Benefits of Higher Education." In *Financing Higher Education*, edited by M. D. Orwig, pp. 168-70. Iowa City: American College Testing Program, 1971.

_____ . *Who Benefits from Higher Education and Who Should Pay*, Research Report No. 5. Washington D.C.: American Association for Higher Education, 1972.

Bowles, Samuel. "Schooling and Inequality from Generation to Generation." *Journal of Political Economy* Supplement 80, 3 (1972): S219-51.

Bowman, Mary Jean. "Education and Economic Growth." In *Economic Factors Affecting the Financing of Education,* Vol. 2, edited by R.L. Johns, I. J. Goffman, K. Alexander, and D. H. Stollar, pp. 83-120. Gainesville: National Educational Finance Project, 1970.

Brazer, Harvey, F., and M. David. "Social and Economic Determinants of the Demand for Education." In *Economics of Higher Education,* edited by S. J. Mushkin, pp. 21-57. Washington D.C.: U.S. Office of Education, 1962.

Brown, T. M. "Habit, Persistence and Lags in Consumer Behavior," *Econometrica* 20, no. 3 (1952). pp. 355-71.

Buchanan, J. M. *The Demand and Supply of Public Goods.* Chicago: Rand McNally, 1968.

Campbell, R., and B. N. Siegel. "The Demand for Higher Education in the United States, 1919-64." *American Economic Review* 57, (June 1967): 482-94.

Cartter, Alan, "The After Effects of Putting the Blind Eye to the Telescope." Paper delivered at American Association of Higher Education Meetings, March 1970, at American Association of Higher Education, Washington D.C.

Cavanaugh, Wm. J. *Student Expense Budgets of Colleges and Universities for the 1971-72 Academic Year.* Princeton: College Scholarship Service, March 1971.

_____ . *1961-62 College PCS Study.* Princeton: College Scholarship Service, 1971.

Chambers, M. M. *Appropriations of State Tax Funds for Operating Expenses of Higher Education, 1972-1973* Washington D.C.: National Association of State Universities and Land Grant Colleges, 1972.

Cheit, E. *The New Depression in Higher Education.* New York: Carnegie Commission on Higher Education, 1971.

_____ . *The New Depression in Higher Education–Two Years Later.* New York: Carnegie Commission on Higher Education, 1973.

_____ . *Quality and Equality, New Levels of Federal Responsibility* New York: Carnegie Commission on Higher Education, 1968. Committee for Economic Development. *The Management and Financing of Colleges.* Research and Policy Committee (October 1973).

Denison, Edward F. *Why Growth Rates Differ.* Washington D.C.: The Brookings Institution, 1967.

_____. *"Sources of Growth Accounting as the Basis for Long Term Projection."* MS for International Economic Association Conference, December 1972 at Moscow.

_____. *Accounting for U.S. Economic Growth, 1929-1969.* Washington D.C..: The Brookings Institution, 1973.

Duesenberry, J.S. *Income, Saving, and the Theory of Consumer Behavior* Cambridge: Harvard University Press, 1952.

Eckstein, O. "A Survey of Public Expenditure Criteria." In N.B.E.R. *Public Finances: Needs, Sources, and Utilization,* 439-94. Princeton: Princeton University Press, 1961.

Feldman, P., and S. Hoenack. "Private Demand for Higher Education." *The Economics and Financing of Higher Education.* U.S. Congress, Joint Economic Committee, Compendium of Papers. pp. 375-95. Washington D.C.: U.S. Government Printing Office, 1969.

Folger, J. K., H. S. Astin, and A. E. Bayer. *Human Resources and Higher Education.* Staff Report of the Commission on Human Resources and Advanced Education. New York: Russell Sage Foundation, 1970.

Freeman, Richard B. *The Market for College-Trained Manpower.* Cambridge: Harvard University Press, 1971.

Galper, H., and R. M. Dunn, Jr. "A Short-Run Demand Function for Higher Education in the U.S." *Journal of Political Economy* 77 (September-October 1969): 765-77.

Ghez, G., and G. S. Becker. "The Allocation of Time and Goods over the Life Cycle." In G. Ghez and G.S. Becker, Report No. 7217, Center for Mathematical Studies in Business and Economics, University of Chicago, April 1972.

Gorman, W.M., "Tastes, Habits, and Choices." *International Economic Review* 2 (June 1967): 218-22.

Gramlich, E. M. "State and Local Governments and Their Budget Constraint"(as in the MIT-FRB Model). *International Economic Review* 10 (June 1969): 163-81.

Griliches, Z., and W. Mason, "Education, Income, and Ability." *Journal of Political Economy Supplement* 80, 3 (1972).

_____. "Research Expenditures and Growth Accounting." Paper for International Economic Association Conference, 1971, at St. Anton, Austria.

Grossman, M. "The Concept of Health Capital and the Demand for Health." *Journal of Political Economy* 80 (March-April 1972): 223-55.

Haley, W. J., "Human Capital Accumulation over the Life Cycle", MS, Michigan State University, November 1971.

Hamberger, M.J. "Household Demand for Financial Assets." *Econometrica* 36 (January 1968): 97-118.

Hanoch, Giora. "An Economic Analysis of Earnings And Schooling." *Journal of Human Resources* 2 (Summer 1967). 310-29.

Hansen, Lee. "Proposals for Financing Higher Education and Their Implications with Respect to Equity." MS. University of Wisconsin.

————. "Total and Private Rates of Return to Investment in Schooling." *Journal of Political Economy* 71 (April 1963): 128-40.

Hansen, Lee, and B.A. Weisbrod. *Benefits, Costs, and Finance of Public Higher Education.* Chicago: Markham Publishing Co., 1969.

Harberger, A.C., ed. *The Demand for Durable Goods.* Chicago: University of Chicago Press, 1960.

Harris, S. E. *A Statistical Portrait of Higher Education.* Berkeley: Carnegie Commission on Higher Education, 1972.

Hartman, Robert W. *Credit for College: Public Policy for Student Loans.* New York: McGraw Hill, 1971.

————. "The Rationale for Federal Support of Higher Education." In *Does College Matter?* Edited by L.C. Solomon and P.J. Taubman, pp. 271-92. New York: Academic Press, 1973.

————. "Higher Education Subsidies: An Analysis of Selected Programs in Current Legislation." In *The Economics of Federal Subsidy Programs,* A Compendium of Papers, Joint Economic Committee, Part 4, 92nd Cong., 2d sess., 1972b, pp. 465-96.

Hause, J.C., "The Role of Ability and Schooling in Determining the Lifetime Earnings Profile." *Journal of Political Economy Supplement* 80, 3, (1972): S108-S138.

Hess, Alan C. "Household Demand for Durable Goods: The Influence of Rates of Return and Wealth." The Review of Economics and Statistics 55 (February 1973): 9-15.

Hicks, J. R. *Value and Capital.* Oxford: The Clarendon Press, 1936.

Hines, F.K., L. Tweeten, and J.M. Redfern. "Social and Private Rates of Return to Investment in Schooling by Race, Sex, Groups, and Regions." *Journal of Human Resources* 5 (Summer 1970): 318-40.

Hirshleifer, J. "On the Theory of Optimal Investment Decision." *Journal of Political Economy* 66 (August 1958): 329-52.

Hoenack, Stephen A. *Private Demand for Higher Education in California.* Office of Analytical Studies. Berkeley: University of California, 1967.

Houthakker, H. S., and L. D. Taylor. *Consumer Demand in the United States: Analyses and Projections.* Cambridge: Harvard University Press, 1970.

James, H. T., J. Thomas, and H. Dyck. *Wealth, Expenditures, and Decision Making for Education.* U.S. Office of Education Cooperative Research Project 1241. Stanford: School of Education, Stanford University, 1963.

Jencks, Christopher. *Inequality.* New York: Basic Books, 1972.

Johns, R. L., I. J. Goffman, K. Alexander, and D. H. Stollar. *Economic Factors Affecting the Financing of Education,* Vol. 2. Gainesville: National Educational Finance Project, 1970.

Johnston, T. "Returns from Investment in Human Capital." *American Economic Review* 60 (September 1970): 546-60.

Jorgensen, Dale. "Econometric Studies of Investment Behavior: A Survey." *Journal of Economic Literature* 9 (December 1971): 1111-47.

Kaysen, Carl. "Some General Observations on the Pricing of Higher Education." *Review of Economics and Statistics Supplement* 42, 3, pt. 2 (August 1960): 56-57.

_____ . *The Higher Learning, the Universities, and the Public.* Princeton: Princeton University Press, 1969.

Keller, J. "Higher Education Objectives: Measures of Performance and Effectiveness." MS. Ford Foundation Grant 68-267, Office of the Vice-President for Planning and Analysis. Berkeley: University of California, 1970.

Keynes, J. M. *The General Theory of Employment, Interest, and Money.* New York: Harcourt, Brace & World, Inc., 1964.

Krueger, A. O. "Factor Endowments and Per Capita Income Differences Among Countries." *Economic Journal* 78 (September 1968): 641-59.

Kuznets, Simon. "Economic Growth and Income Inequality." *American Economic Review* 45 (March 1955): 1-28.

_____ . *Modern Economic Growth.* New Haven: Yale University Press, 1966.

Layard, P. R. G., and D. Verry. *Cost Functions for Teaching and Research in U.K. Universities.* MS. London: London School of Economics, September 1973.

Levy, F. K. "Sources of Economies of Scale in Universities." *The Economics and Financing of Higher Education,* pp. 295-304. U.S. Congress, Joint Economic Committee. Washington, D.C.: U.S. Government Printing Office, 1969.

Massachusetts Board of Higher Education, Metropolitan Planning Council, *Higher Education in the Boston Metropolitan Area,* Vol. 6. Board of Higher Education Series (1969).

McMahon, Walter W. "An Economic Analysis of Major Determinants of

Expenditures on Public Education." *Review of Economics and Statistics* (August 1970): 242-52.

————— . "Cyclical Growth of Public Expenditure." *Public Finance,* no. 1 (1971a): 75-105.

————— . "Dynamic Interdependence in Consumer Stocks, Tastes, and Choices. *Abstracts,* Allied Social Science Association Meetings, December 1971b, at New Orleans.

————— . "Policy Issues in the Economics of Higher Education and Related Research Opportunities in Britain and the United States." *Higher Education* 3 (May 1974).

McMahon, Walter W., and Alan P. Wagner, *A Study of the College Investment Decision, Project Report I.* Iowa City: The American College Testing Program, 1973.

Michael, Robert. "The Effect of Education on the Efficiency of Consumption." National Bureau of Economic Research, Occasional Paper No. 116. New York: Columbia University Press, 1972.

————— . "The Role of Education in Production Within the Household." Proposal for Research. Washington, D.C.: U.S. Office of Education, January 1972.

Miller, Leonard S. "The Demand for Higher Education in the United States"' MS. National Bureau of Economic Research Conference on Education as an Industry, June 1971, at Chicago.

Mundel, David S. "Federal Aid to Higher Education: An Analysis of Federal Subsidies to Undergraduate Education." U.S. Congress, Joint Economic Committee. MS. Cambridge: J. F. Kennedy School, December 1971.

Musgrave, Richard A. *Fiscal Systems.* New Haven: Yale University Press, 1969.

Musgrave, Richard A., and A. Peacock. *Classics in the Theory of Public Finance.* London: Macmillan, 1958.

Mushkin, Selma J. "Public Financing of Higher Education." In *Universal Higher Education,* edited by Logan Wilson and O. Mills, pp. 153-78. Washington, D.C.: American Council on Education, 1972.

Nadiri, M. Ishaq, and S. Roach. "A Disequilibrium Model of Household Behavior." MS. Department of Economics, New York University, October 1972.

O'Neill, June. *Resource Use in Higher Education.* Berkeley: Carnegie Commission on Higher Education, 1971.

Oniki, H., "On Deriving the Individual's Demand Function for Educational Investment." Harvard Institute of Economic Research, Discussion Paper No. 154. Cambridge, 1970.

Orwig, M. D., ed., *Financing Higher Education*. Iowa City: American College Testing Program, 1971.

Pechman, Joseph A. "Distribution of Federal and State Income Taxes by Income Class." *Journal of Finance* 27 (May 1972): 179-91.

Pollak, Robert A. "Habit Formation and Dynamic Demand Functions." *Journal of Political Economy* 78 (July-August 1970): 745-63.

Popp, Dean O. "Human Capital Formation by Expenditures on Education." *Quarterly Review of Economics and Business* 12 (1972): 19-38.

Radner, Roy, and L. Miller. *Econometric Studies of Financing*. Berkeley and State University of New York. Stonybrook, N.Y.: Carnegie Commission, 1971.

Reischauer, Robert D., and Robert W. Hartman. *Reforming School Finance*. Washington D.C.: The Brookings Institution, 1973.

Rivlin, Alice M. *Toward a Long Run Plan for Financial Support of Higher Education*. A Report to the President, Assistant Secretary for Planning and Evaluation. Washington D.C.: U.S. Department of Health, Education, and Welfare, 1969.

——— . *Systematic Thinking for Social Action*. Washington D.C.: The Brookings Instituion, 1971.

Rosen, Sherwin. "Knowledge, Obsolescence, and Income." MS. University of Rochester. November 1970.

Samuelson, Paul A. "Lifetime Portfolio Selection by Dynamic Stocastic Programming." *Review of Economics and Statistics* 51 (August 1969): 239-46.

——— . "Social Indifference Curves." *Quarterly Journal of Economics* 70 (February 1956), pp. 1-22. Reprinted in *The Collected Scientific Papers of Paul A. Samuelson*. Cambridge: The MIT Press, 1966, pp. 1073-94.

Schultz, T. Paul. "An Economic Model of Family Planning and Fertility." *Journal of Political Economy* 77 (March-April 1969): 153-80.

——— . "Secular Trends and Cyclical Behavior of Income Distribution in the United States 1944-65." In *Six Papers on The Size Distribution of Wealth and Income*, edited by L. Soltow. New York: National Bureau of Economic Research 1969.

——— . "The Distribution of Income: Case Study the Netherlands." Unpublished diss. Cambridge, Mass.: MIT, 1965.

Schultz, T. W. *Investment in Human Capital*. New York: Free Press, 1971.

—————— . "The Human Capital Approach to Education." *Economic Factors Affecting the Financing of Education*. Vol. 2, edited by R. L. Johns, I. J. Goffman, K. Alexander, and D. H. Stollar, pp.29-57 Gainesville, Fla.: National Educational Finance Project, 1970.

—————— . "Optimal Investment in College Instruction: Equity and Efficiency." *Journal of Political Economy Supplement* 80, no. 3, part 2, (1972a): S2-S33.

—————— . "Human Capital: Policy Issues and Research Opportunities." *Human Resources,* edited by G. S. Becker. pp. 1-84 National Bureau of Economic Research Colloquium. New York: National Bureau of Economic Research, 1972b.

—————— . "The High Value of Human Time: Population Equilibrium." *Journal of Political Economy Supplement* (1974). See also the eight other articles on the economic role of women in this supplement edited by Schultz and the articles on fertility and children in the preceding 1973 *Journal of Political Economy Supplement*.

—————— . "Resources for Higher Education: An Economist's View." *Journal of Political Economy* 76 (May-June 1968): 327-47.

—————— . *Education as Human Capital,* Vol. 35. New York: National Bureau of Economic Research, 1970.

Schultze, Charles L. *The Politics and Economics of Public Spending* Washington, D.C.: The Brookings Instituion, 1971.

Solomon, Lewis. "Proposal for a Study of the Social Benefits of Higher Education." Panel on the Benefits of Higher Education, Board of Human Resources. Washington, D.C.: National Research Council, 1972.

—————— . *Education and Savings Behavior*. New York: National Bureau of Economic Research, 1973.

Stigler, George. "The Economics of Information." *Journal of Political Economy* 69 (June 1961: 213-25.)

Verry, D.W. "Production Functions in Higher Education." MS. Higher Education Research Unit, London School of Economics, 1973.

—————— . "Regression Analysis of the Vice-Chancellor's Cost Data." MS. Higher Education Research Unit, London School of Economics, 1973.

Von Weizsäcker, C.C. "Notes on Endogenous Change of Tastes I." *Journal of Economic Theory* 3 (1972): 345-72.

Wackman, D.B., and S. Ward. "College Student Reactions to Variable Term Loan Plans." A Report to the Ford Foundation Division of Education and Research (October 1971).

Weisbrod, Burton A. *External Benefits of Public Education*. Research Report Series 105. Princeton: Industrial Relations Section, Department of Economics, Princeton University, 1964.

_____ . "Education and Investment in Human Capital." *Journal of Political Economy Supplement* 70 (October 1962): 106-23.

Weisbrod, Burton A., and P. Karpoff. "Monetary Returns to College Education, Student Ability and College Quality." *Review of Economics and Statistics* 50 (November 1968): 491-502.

Welch, Finis. "Black-White Differences in Returns to Schooling." *The American Economic Review*, 63, no. 5, (December 1973): 893-907.

_____ . "Education in Production." *Journal of Political Economy* 78 (January-February 1970): 35-59.

_____ . "Information as a Factor of Production." MS. New York: National Bureau of Economic Research, 1971.

_____ . "Measurement of the Quality of Schooling." *American Economic Review* 56 (Papers and Proceedings, May, 1966): 358-92.

West, E.D., R.L. Farrell, and M.F. Blakeslee. "Trends in College Costs." *College and University Journal* 3, no. 3 (1964): 38.

Western Interstate Commission for Higher Education. *Outputs of Higher Education, Their Identification, Measurement and Evaluation*. Boulder, Colo. July 1970.

Wilson, Logan, and O. Mills, eds. *Universal Higher Education*. Washington, D.C.: American Council on Education, 1972.

II. Government Documents and Related Data Sources

Federal Reserve Board of Governors, *Federal Reserve Bulletin*, March, annually. (Washington, D.C.: Federal Reserve System, 1974).

National Commission on the Financing of Postsecondary Education, *Financing Postsecondary Education in the United States* (Washington, D.C.: U.S. Government Printing Office, December 1973).

National Education Association, *Estimates of School Statistics, Research Report*, 1967-68 through 1972-73 issues. (Washington D.C.: Research Division, National Education Association, 1972).

National Science Foundation, *Federal Funds for Research Development and Other Scientific Activities, Fiscal Years 1971, 1972, 1973*, (Washington D.C.: U.S. Government Printing Office, 1973).

U.S. Bureau of the Census (S.E.S.A.), *Current Population Reports, Series P-20*, Nos. 6, 15, 99, 121, 138, 158, 169, 182, 194, 207, and 229 (Washington D.C.: U.S. Government Printing Office, 1972).

U.S. Bureau of the Census (S.E.S.A.), *Current Population Reports Series P-25,* Nos. 311, 314, 385, 416, 441, and 448 (Washington D.C.: U.S. Government Printing Office, 1972).

————— , *Historical Statistics of the United States, Colonial Times to 1957* (Washington D.C.: U.S. Government Printing Office, 1967 and 1973).

————— , *Present Value of Estimated Lifetime Earnings,* Technical Paper No. 16 (Washington D.C.: U.S. Government Printing Office, 1967).

————— , *Statistical Abstract of the United States,* annual issues 1929 to 1973 (Washington D.C.: U.S. Government Printing Office, 1973).

U.S. Bureau of Labor Statistics, *Consumer Expenditures Survey of 1960-61, and Consumer Expenditures Survey of 1972* (Washington D.C.: Bureau of Labor Statistics, 1973).

U.S. Congress, Joint Economic Committee, *The Economics and Financing of Higher Education,* a Compendium of Papers (Washington D.C.: U.S. Government Printing Office, 1969).

————— , *Planning, Programming and Budgeting System,* a Compendium of Papers (Washington D.C.: U.S. Government Printing Office, 1970).

U.S. Congress, *Education Amendments of 1972,* 92d Cong. 2d sess., Conference Report, HR92-1085 (Washington D.C.: U.S. Government Printing Office, 1972).

U.S. Department of Commerce, Office of Economic Analysis, *National Income and Product,* Accounts of the United States 1929-1965, 1966 Supplement of the *Survey of Current Business,* and subsequent 1967-1973 July "National Income Issues" (Washington D.C.: U.S. Government Printing Office, 1973).

U.S. Executive Office of the President, *The Budget of the United States Government, Fiscal 1975* (Washington D.C.: U.S. Government Printing Office, 1974).

————— , *Special Analyses of the Budget,* Fiscal 1975 (Washington, D.C.: U.S. Government Printing Office, 1974).

————— , *The Economic Report of the President and Annual Report of the Council of Economic Advisors* (Washington D.C.: U.S. Government Printing Office, February 1974 and earlier issues).

U.S. Office of Education, *Biennial Survey of Education in the United States 1927-8 (to 1957-8),* Chap. 4 (Washington D.C.: U.S. Government Printing Office, 1962).

_____ , *Financial Statistics of Institutions of Higher Education: Current Funds Revenues and Expenditures, 1960-1* (to 1969-70), National Center for Educational Statistics (Washington D.C.: U.S. Government Printing Office, 1973).

_____ , *Financial Statistics of Higher Education: Property,* National Center for Educational Statistics (Washington D.C.: U.S. Government Printing Office, 1965-66).

_____ , *Higher Eudcation Finances, Selected Trend and Summary Data,* National Center for Educational Statistics (Washington D.C.: U.S. Government Printing Office, 1968).

_____ , *Opening Fall Enrollments in Higher Educational Institutions,* various issues, National Center for Education Statistics (Washington, D.C.: U.S. Government Printing Office, 1973).

_____ , *Projections of Educational Statistics to 1981-2 (and 80-1),* National Center for Educational Statistics (Washington, D.C.: U.S. Government Printing Office, 1973).

U.S. Office of Education, *Statistics of State School Systems,* various issues, National Center for Educational Statistics (Washington D.C.: U.S. Government Printing Office, 1973).

Index

Index

About the Author

Walter W. McMahon is professor of economics at the University of Illinois at Urbana-Champaign. His research on "Why Families Invest in Higher Education" is supported by a research grant from the National Institute of Education, U.S. Department of Health, Education, and Welfare. Dr. McMahon received the Ph.D. from the University of Iowa in 1957. While this manuscript was being completed he was a guest scholar at The Brookings Institution, Washington, D.C. and at the Higher Education Research Unit, London School of Economics, Universtiy of London. Dr. McMahon has done research on the economics of primary and secondary education, public expenditure analysis, policy issues in higher education, household saving and investment decisions, and related topics; his articles have appeared in numerous professional journals.